AF478048

SIDESHOW.

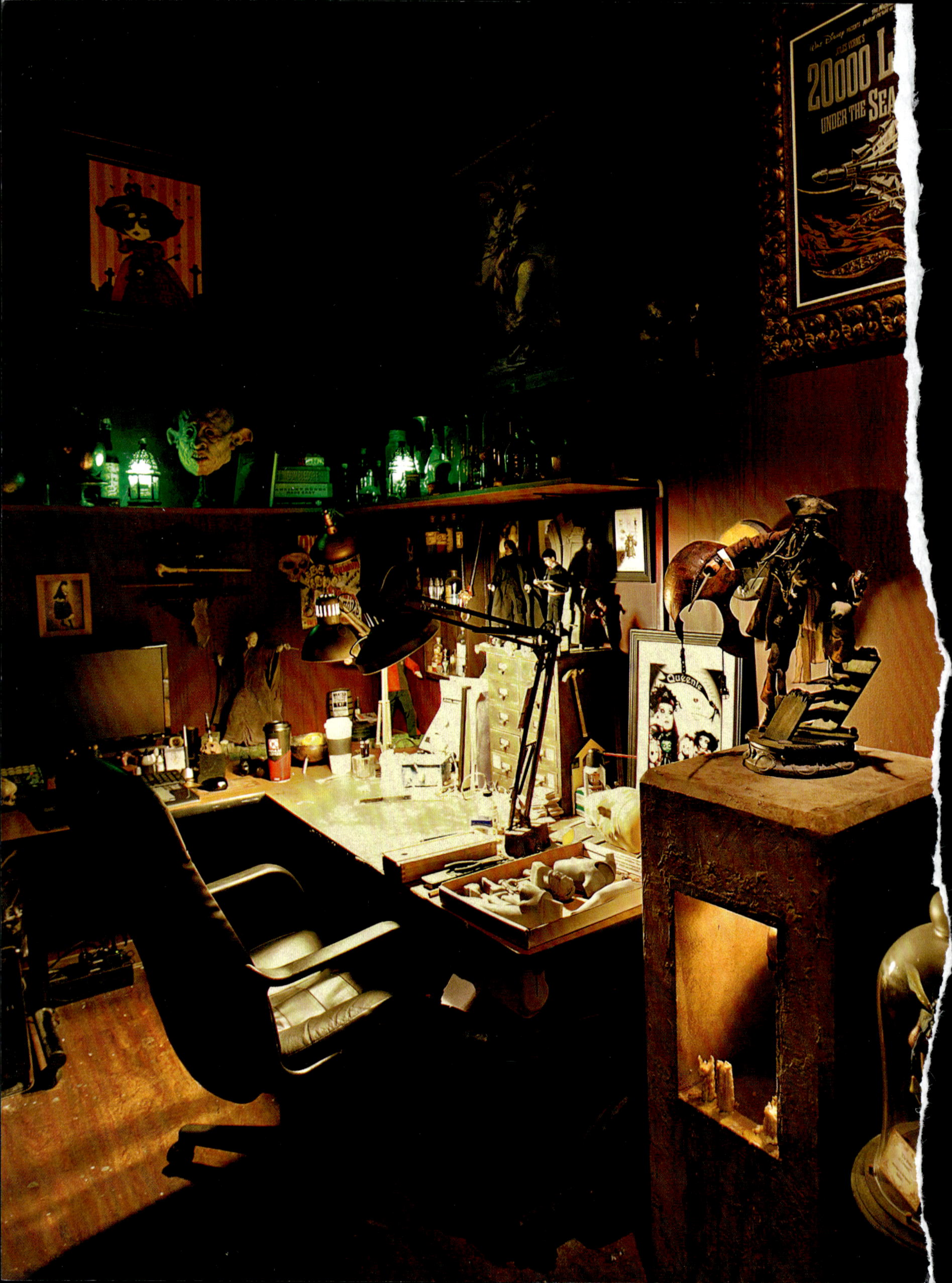
20000 L
UNDER THE SEA
Queenie

INSIDE THE

SIDESHOW STUDIO

A MODERN RENAISSANCE ENVIRONMENT

INSIGHT EDITIONS

San Rafael, California

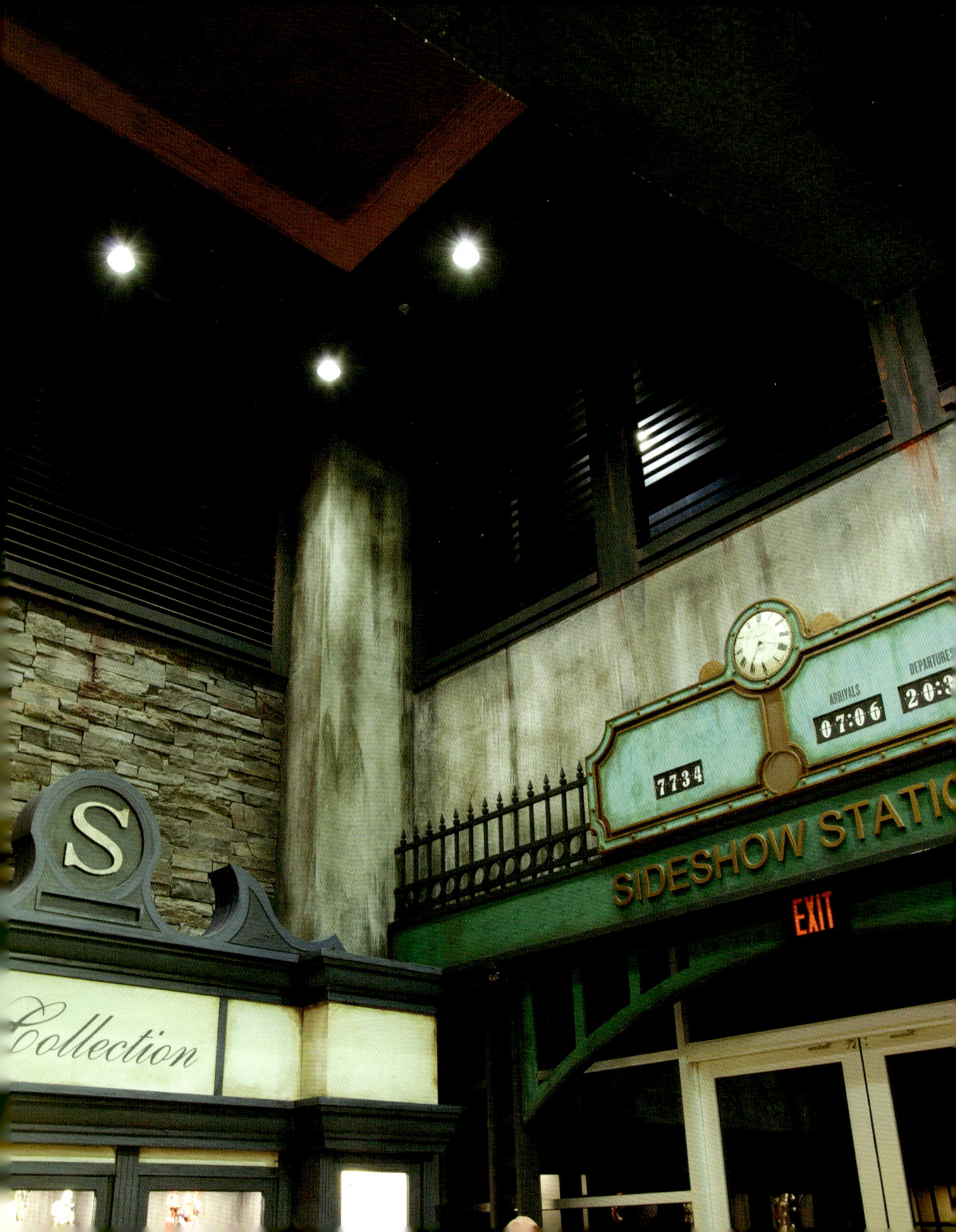

S
Collection
ARRIVALS
07:06
DEPARTURES
20:3
7734
SIDESHOW STATION
EXIT

CONTENTS

INTRODUCTION

WELCOME TO THE INNER WORLD OF SIDESHOW COLLECTIBLES . . . or perhaps I should say "worlds," for there are a variety of environments and experiences to behold in each section of this unique and amazing company.

Through the years I have witnessed Sideshow grow from an ambitious handful of talented visionaries making the world's coolest toys to a landmark company of over one hundred employees that includes what are perhaps the world's finest legion of devoted creators and craftspeople contained in one building.

The tour I recently took of their current facilities—a tour reflected in the following pages—was mind-expanding and revelatory.

The personal creativity of Sideshow's family of employees is reflected in their workspace environments. Employees are encouraged to indulge their fantasies and customize their work areas to reflect their own personal quirks and passions, creating mini-worlds in Sideshow's overall world of collector candy for the eye and touch.

Fantastic film sets, elements of Rick Baker's creature shop, and bold Disneyland-ish theme park-ery abound at Sideshow, with secret visual tricks and metaphors for those in the know that are nevertheless intriguing and entertaining for those who are not. A rainbow of creepy and stirring colors and tantalizing textures reflects the exotic beauty of what Sideshow does better than anyone else on the planet.

Bones, body parts, and apothecary jars with forbidden contents are the decorative norm here. Scary fairies, ghouls, vampires, beasties, superheroes, and villains all bump shoulders within these confines. Victorian steampunk and Jules Verne-ian technology collide with and are embraced and enhanced by the latest high-tech advances in their fields.

And the place is huge; Sideshow's vast warehouse is quite reminiscent of the final scene in *Raiders of the Lost Ark*.

I am especially impressed that, despite a plethora of worldly temptations, Sideshow has not fallen prey to what I call "Skunkworks Syndrome," in which the product of a team of brilliant creators gets taken over and diluted by the money people. I thought that Skunkworks Syndrome was inevitable until I saw Sideshow Collectibles in its current incarnation. High-pitched creativity and going the extra mile in terms of quality are still "Alive! ALIVE!" (as Dr. Frankenstein would shout) at Sideshow—and it's been operating that way now for over twenty years.

Sideshow has beaten The System.

There are important lessons to be learned here. Sideshow somehow found a way to successfully mix and balance fun and groundbreaking creativity with a good, strong business sense, allowing Sideshow's radically masterful creators to thrive and flourish.

Part of what feeds and grows Sideshow is a policy similar to Google's "20%" edict, in which employees are encouraged to pursue and develop their own personal projects as part of their work time. Google employees are encouraged to devote 20 percent of their time to work not associated with their current job tasks. Google has found that about 90 percent of all their company's new products originated as 20 percent projects.

The culmination of this vision is perhaps most deeply reflected in Sideshow's own intellectual property, Court of the Dead. Freed from the accepted (and expected) shackles of licensing approvals and restraints, Court of the Dead will lure and engulf Sideshow fans, leading them into a deeper, richer world than this genre has ever witnessed, a carefully constructed and devised domain with limitless potential.

The old saying "Good, better, best—never let them rest, until good is better and better best" seems to be the Sideshow company mantra, as the company's worker bees constantly search for and innovate ways to improve the already remarkable products they create in their creative hive and make them ever cooler.

Have I sipped the Sideshow Kool-Aid? Indeed I have. Now I want the rest of the pitcher (or picture), as well as a lifetime supply.

Thirsty for a secret taste of what helps drive these artisans to create the best of what the collectibles world has to offer?

Turn the page and take your own sip.

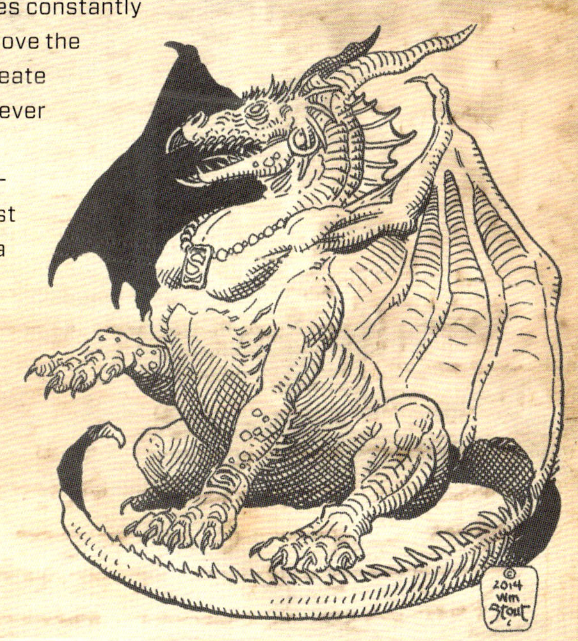

—Bill Stout
Pasadena, CA

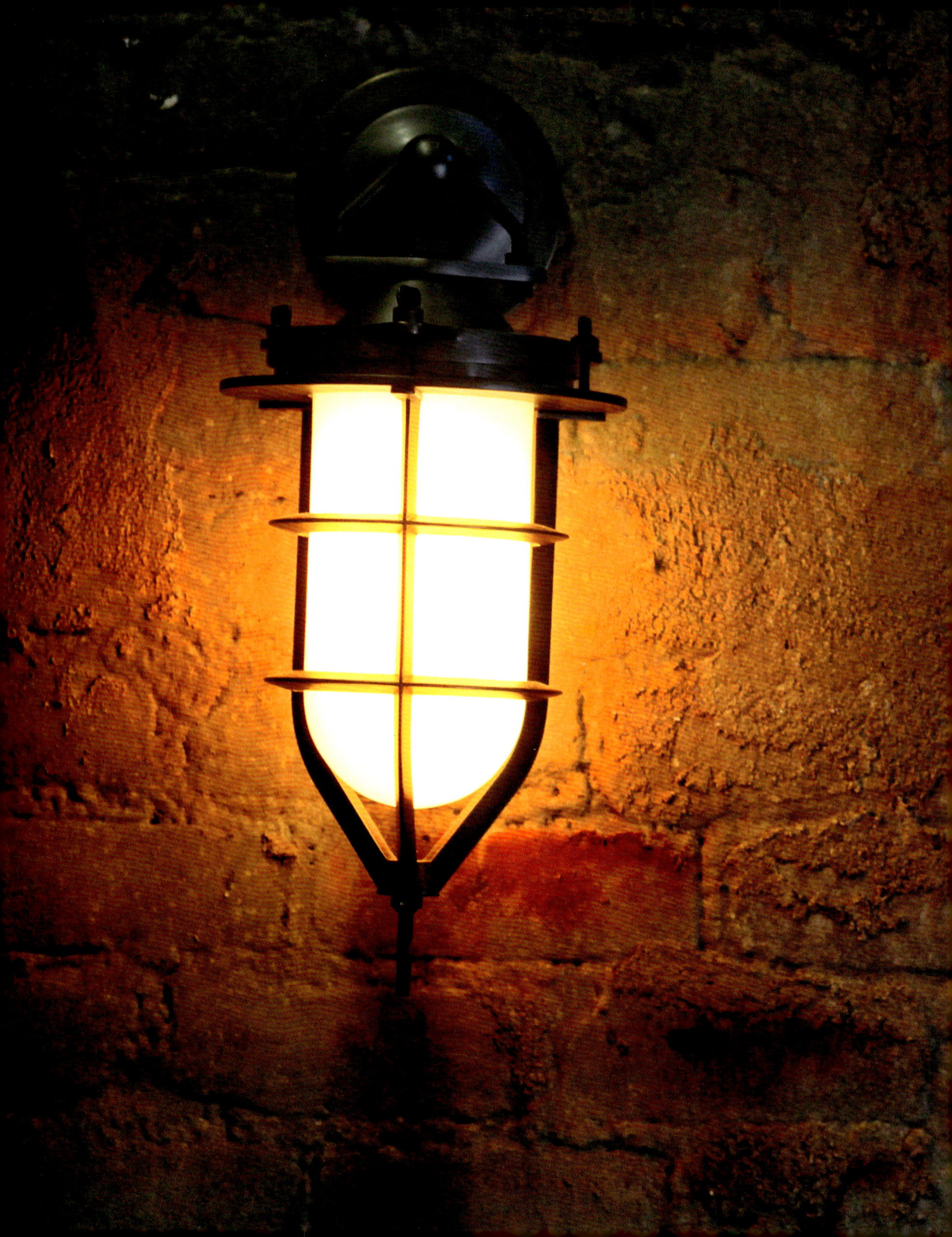

Welcome

It's a pleasure to open our doors and let you, the Sideshow Collectibles fan, get to know the different rooms and colorful hallways of our studio. We find great inspiration in our eclectic environment, in which our team of talented artists, sculptors, model makers, painters, and costumers works and creates every day. We invite you to explore these main hubs of our creative process. This is, after all, the birthplace of many of our spectacular original designs and the lovingly crafted likenesses of characters from the world of popular culture. We hope you enjoy this freewheeling tour of our modern-day renaissance art studio, which is fueled by passion, creativity, and the sheer magic of imagination. Buckle up for a fun ride.

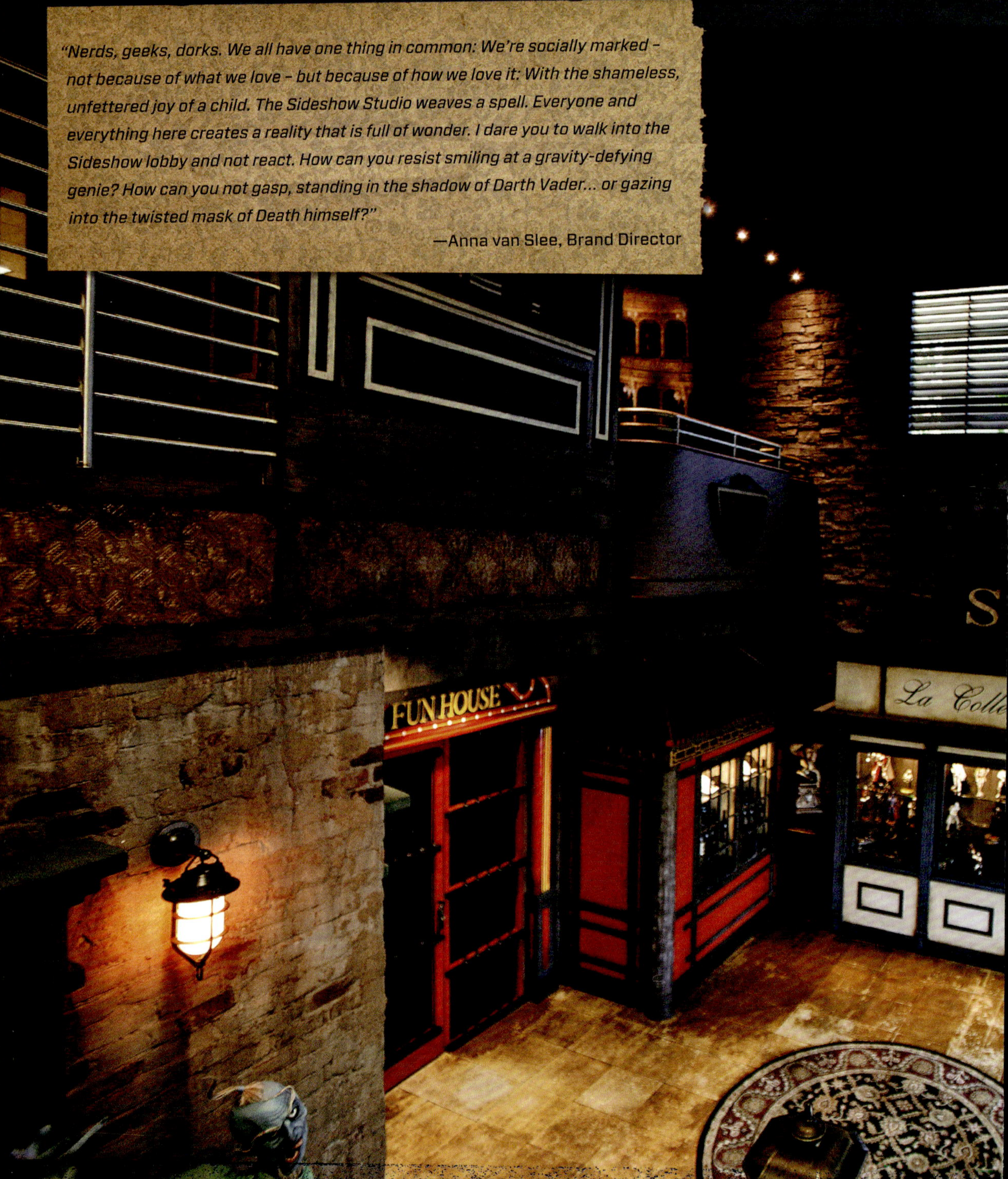

"Nerds, geeks, dorks. We all have one thing in common: We're socially marked – not because of what we love – but because of how we love it: With the shameless, unfettered joy of a child. The Sideshow Studio weaves a spell. Everyone and everything here creates a reality that is full of wonder. I dare you to walk into the Sideshow lobby and not react. How can you resist smiling at a gravity-defying genie? How can you not gasp, standing in the shadow of Darth Vader... or gazing into the twisted mask of Death himself?"

—Anna van Slee, Brand Director

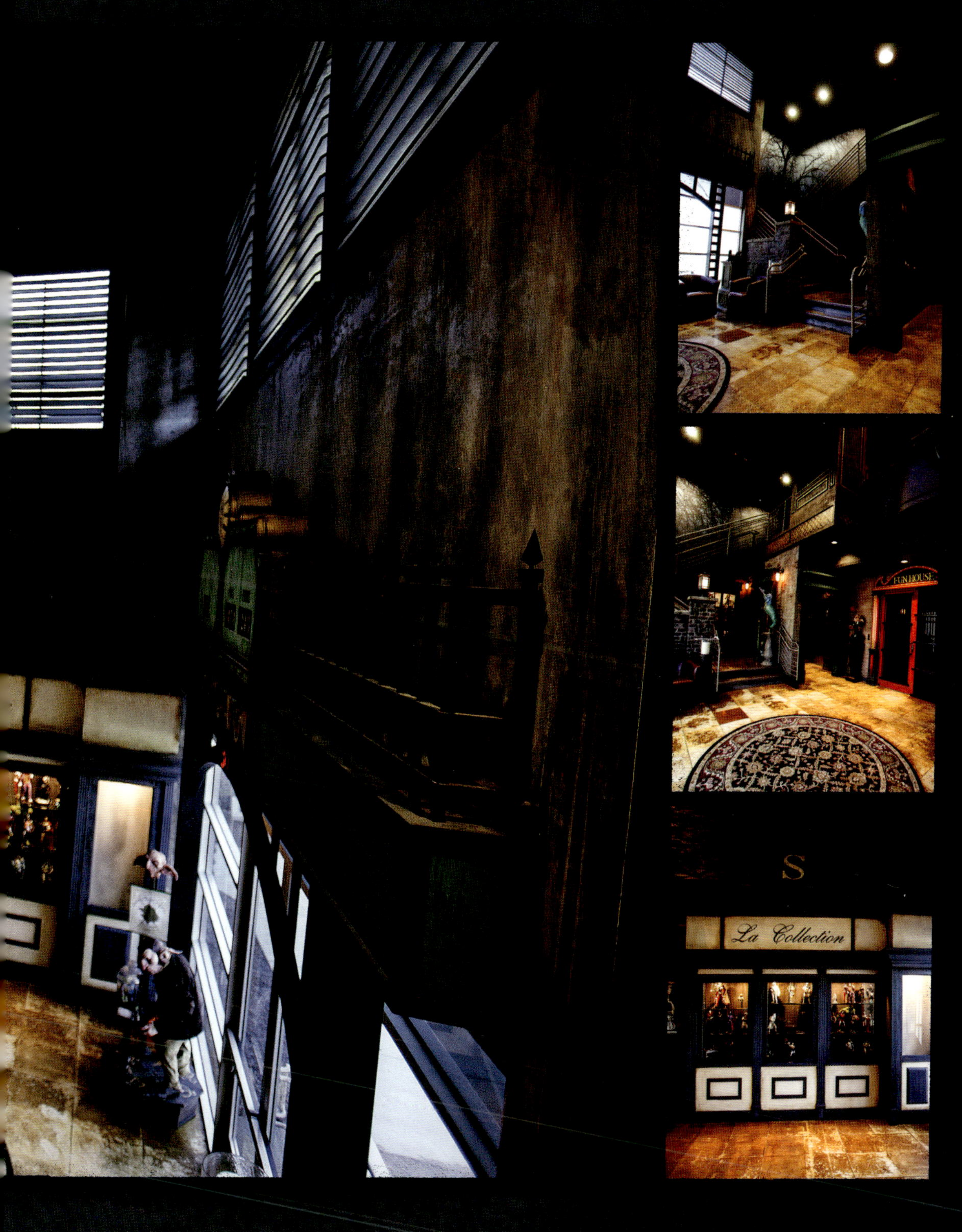
FUN HOUSE
S
La Collection

7734
SIDESHOW

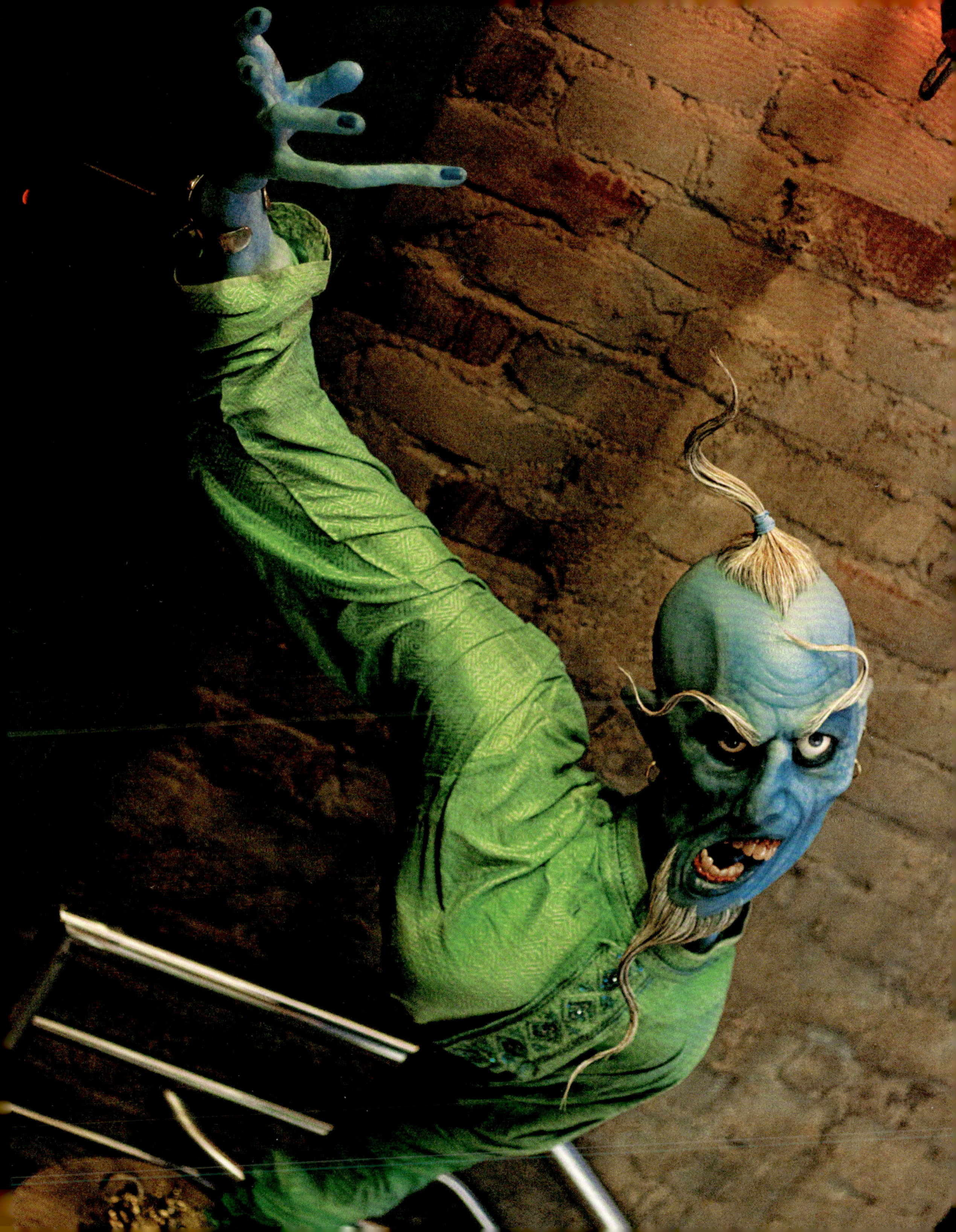

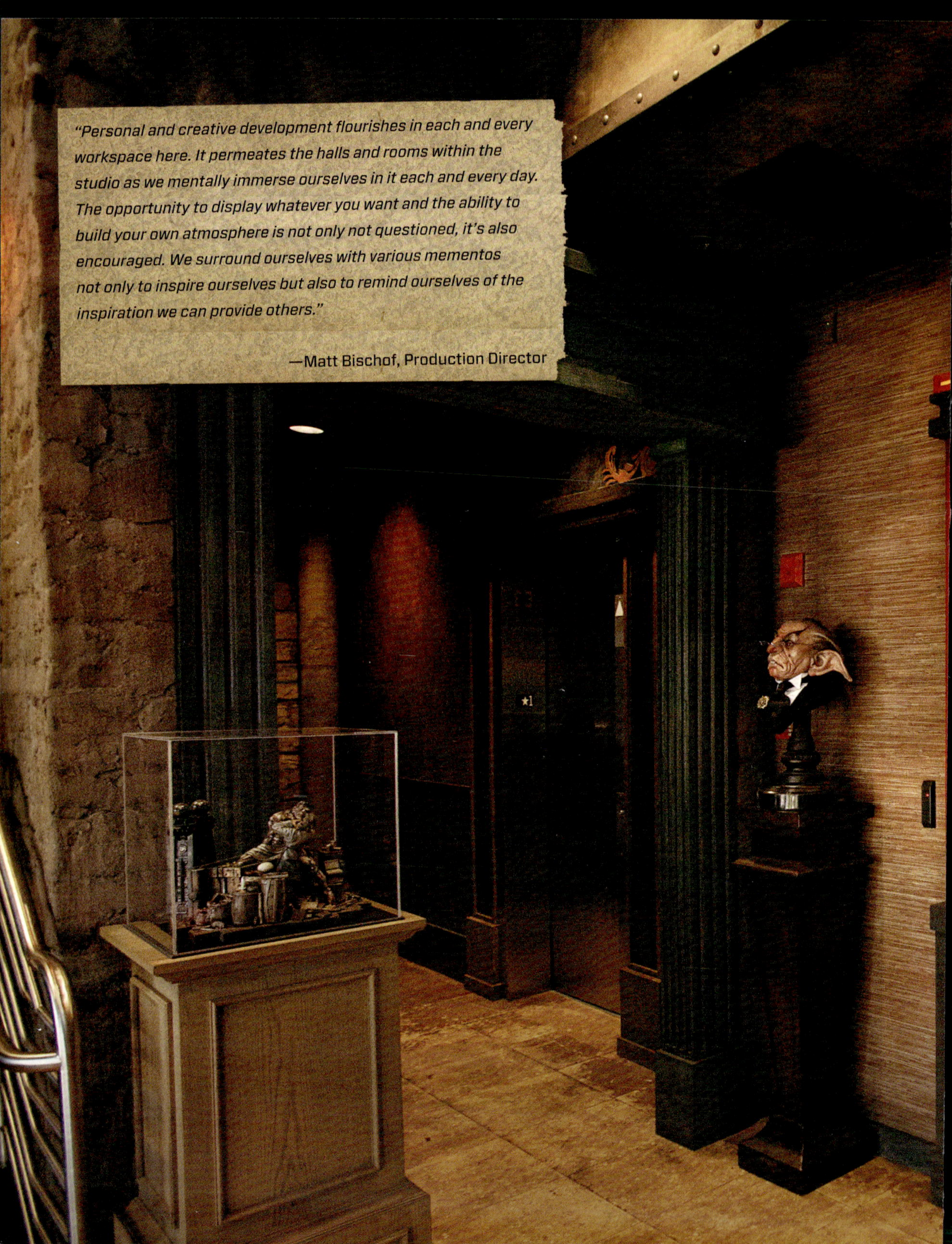

"Personal and creative development flourishes in each and every workspace here. It permeates the halls and rooms within the studio as we mentally immerse ourselves in it each and every day. The opportunity to display whatever you want and the ability to build your own atmosphere is not only not questioned, it's also encouraged. We surround ourselves with various mementos not only to inspire ourselves but also to remind ourselves of the inspiration we can provide others."

—Matt Bischof, Production Director

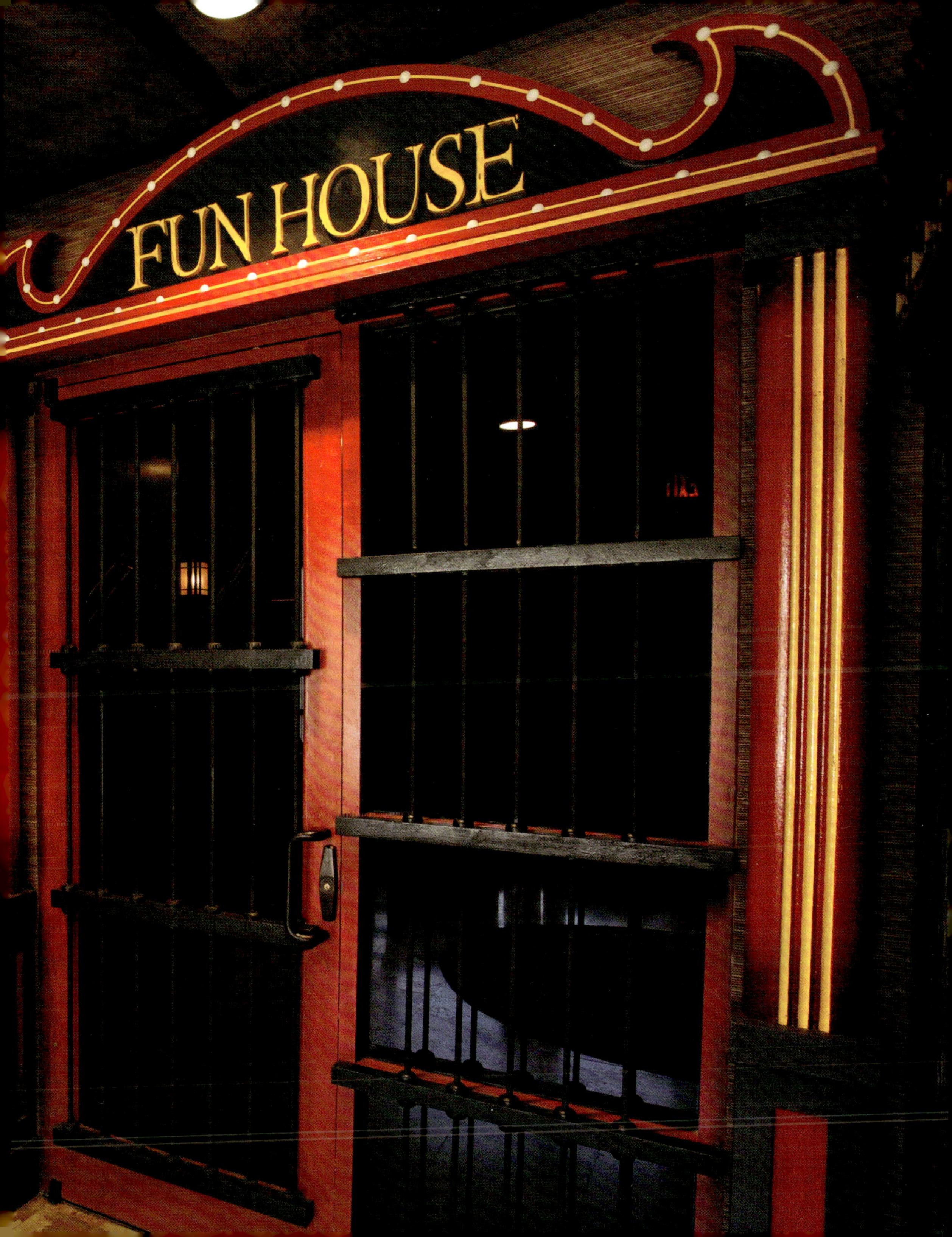
FUN HOUSE

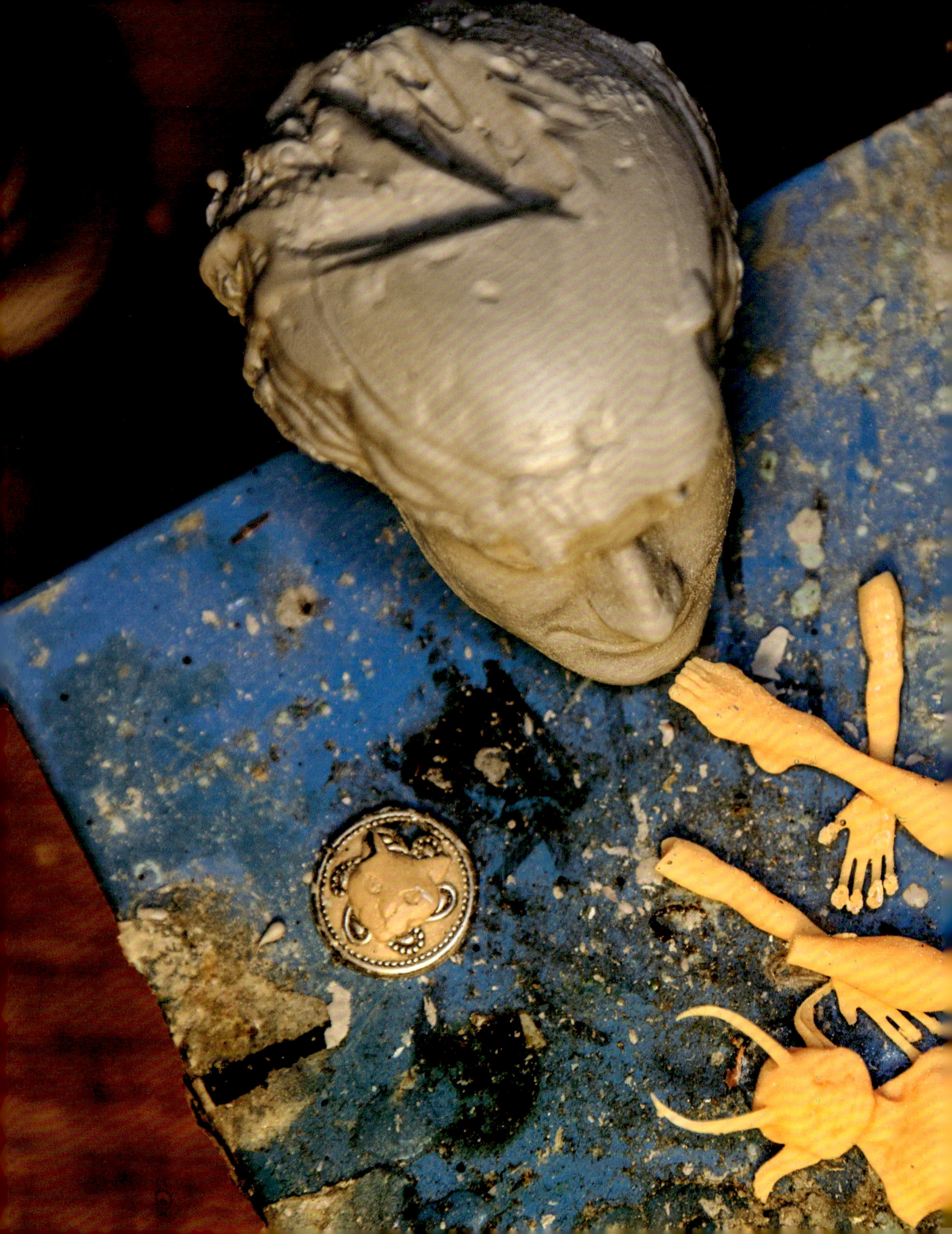

Waxworks

The "Waxworks" is the 3-D arm of the Design department; it takes the assets that have been generated and translates them into a real-world sculpture, using anything from clay and wax to ZBrush and Maya. Our team of sculptors, both in house and all over the world, is the one that brings to life the characters you know and love. We had the opportunity to create a studio at Sideshow that reflected our personalities. It's equal parts Hogwarts, Disney's Haunted Mansion, and Victorian spiritual parlor. It's both warm and homey as well as dark and ethereal.

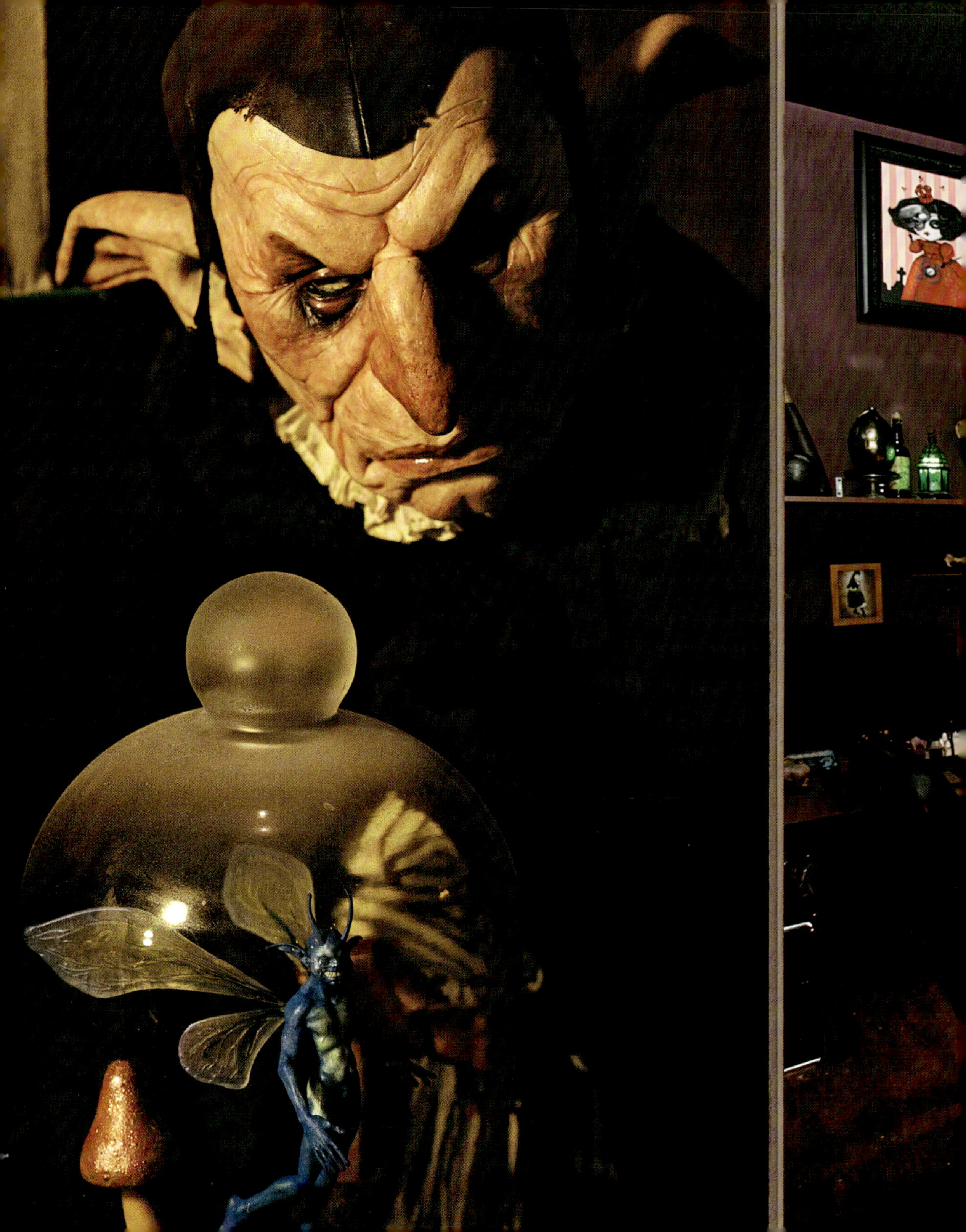

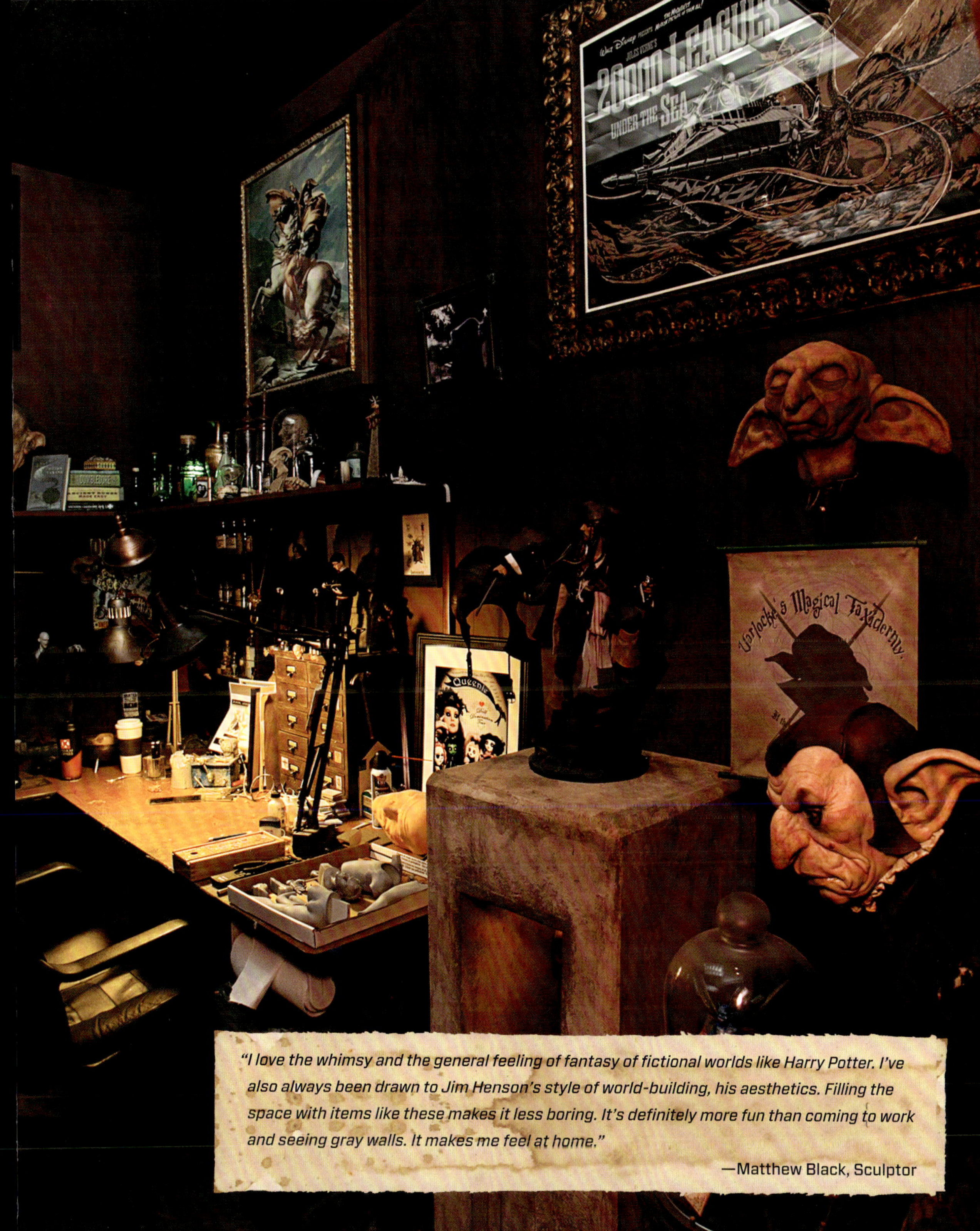

"I love the whimsy and the general feeling of fantasy of fictional worlds like Harry Potter. I've also always been drawn to Jim Henson's style of world-building, his aesthetics. Filling the space with items like these makes it less boring. It's definitely more fun than coming to work and seeing gray walls. It makes me feel at home."

—Matthew Black, Sculptor

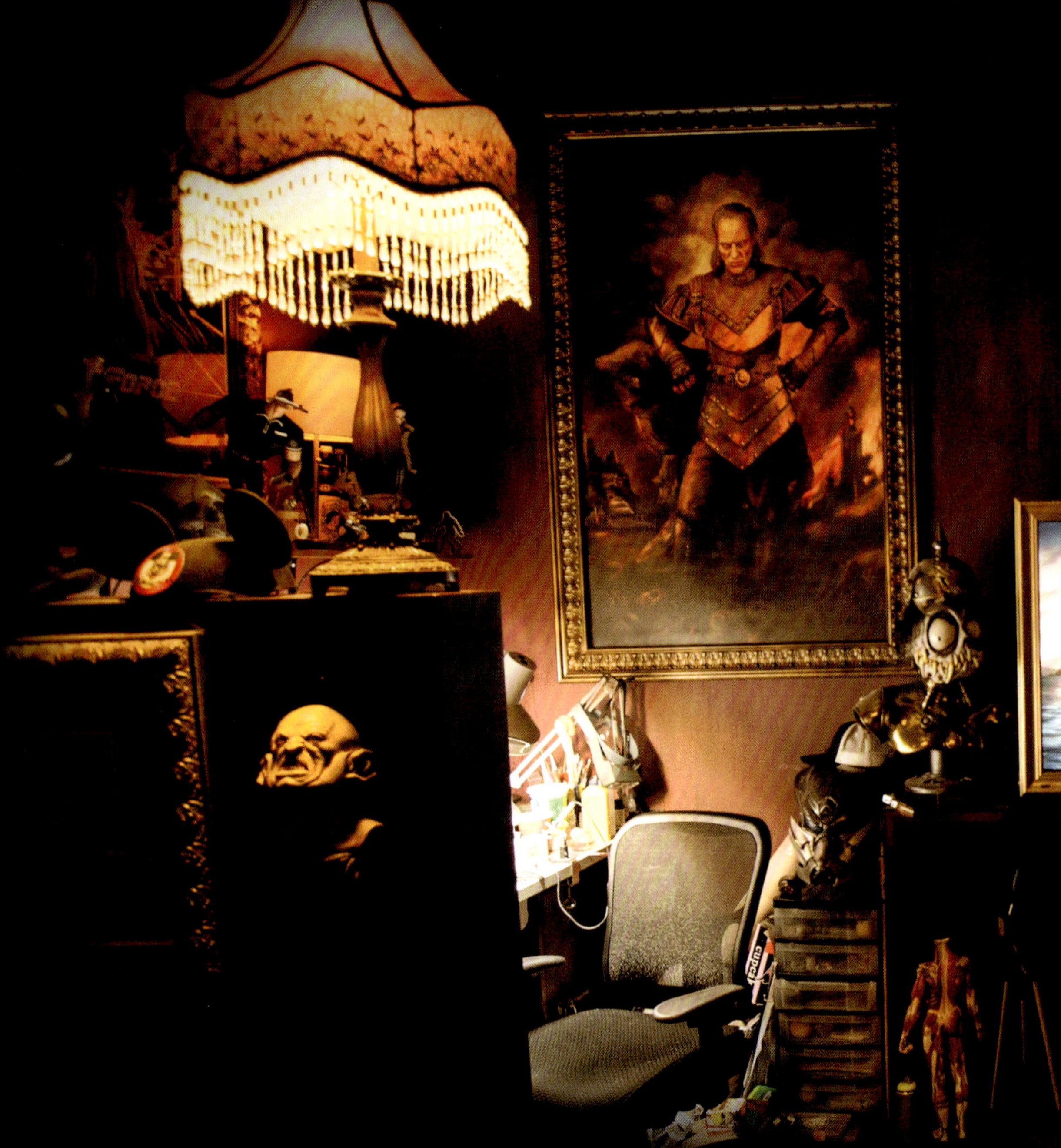

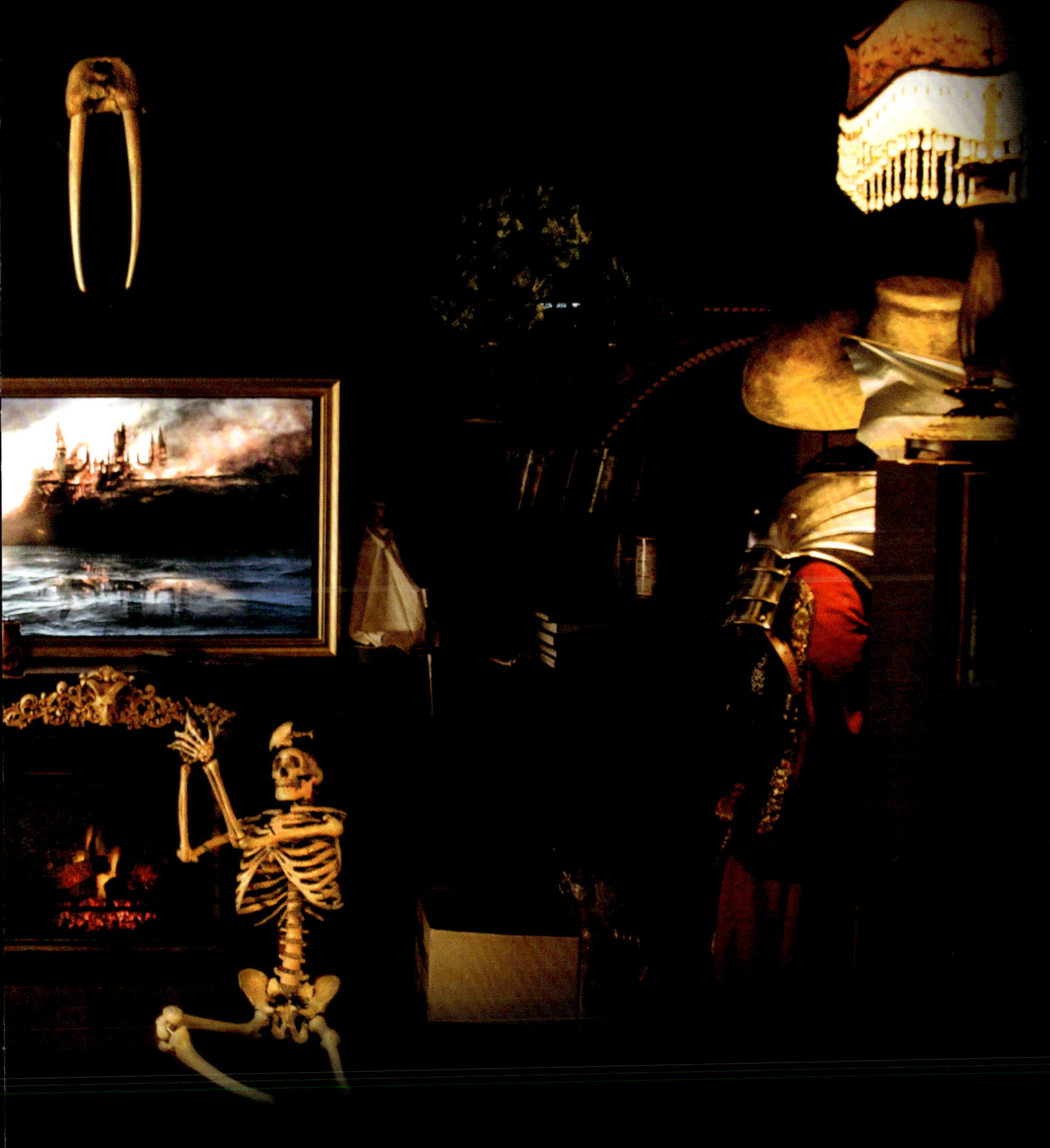

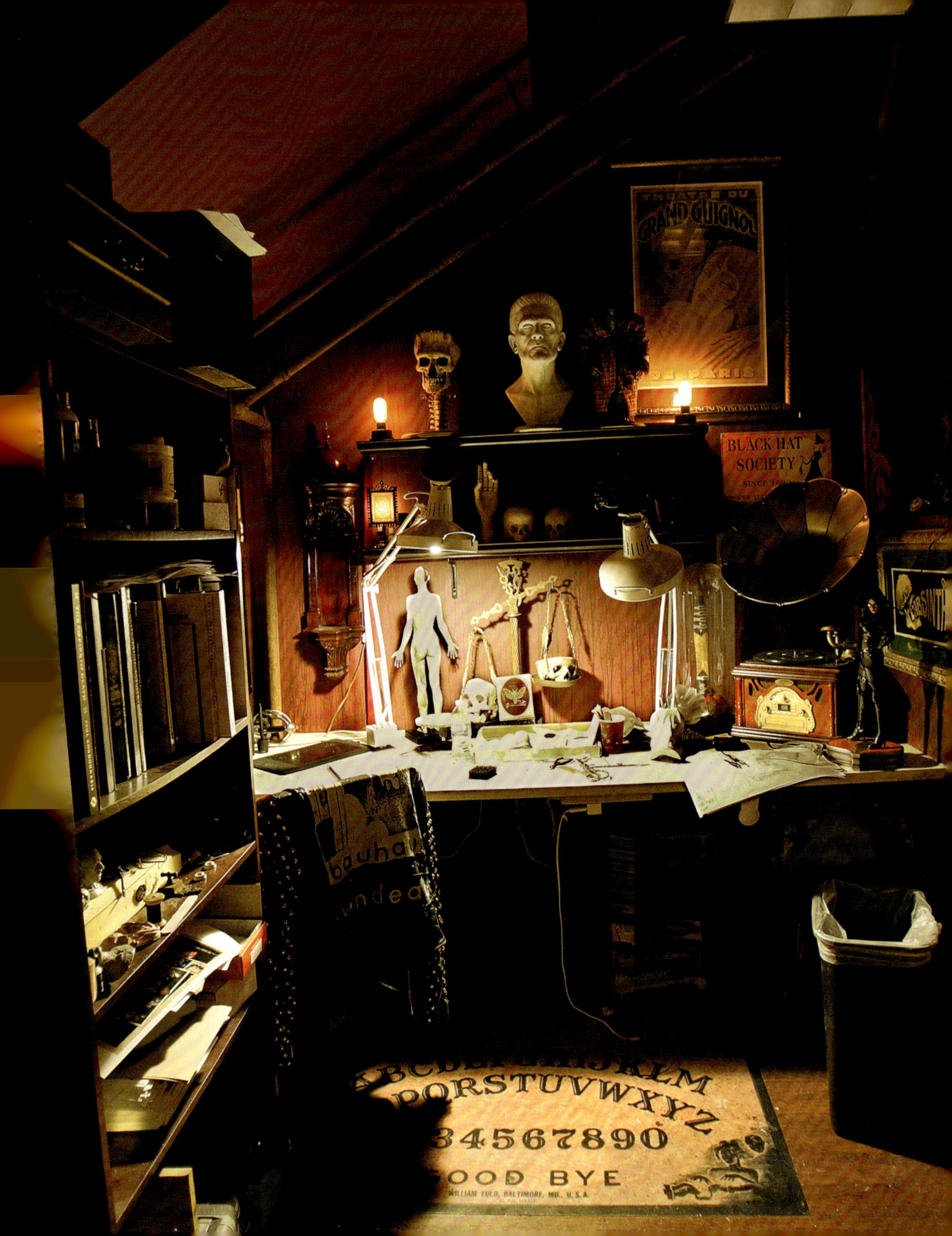
THEATRE DU
GRAND GUIGNOL
DE PARIS
BLACK HAT SOCIETY
SINCE
bauhaus
undead
ABCDEFGHIJKLM
NOPQRSTUVWXYZ
1234567890
GOOD BYE
WILLIAM FULD, BALTIMORE, MD., U.S.A.

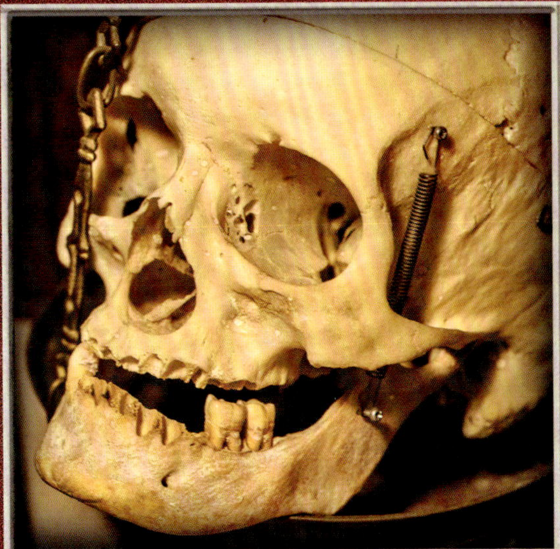

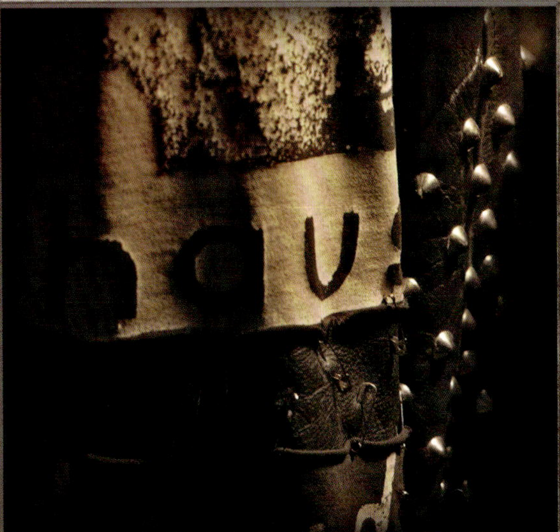

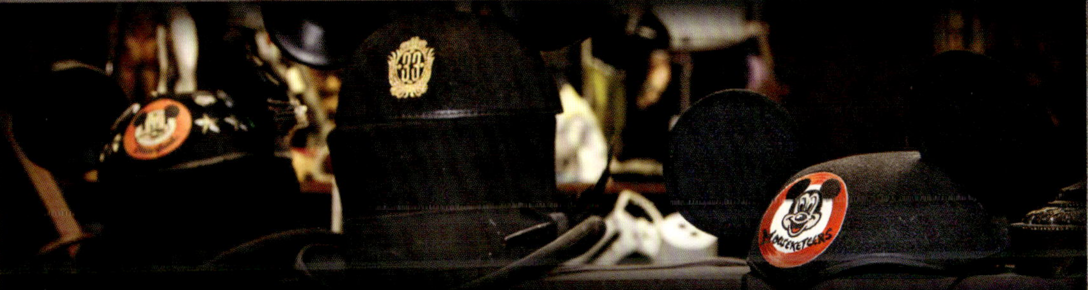

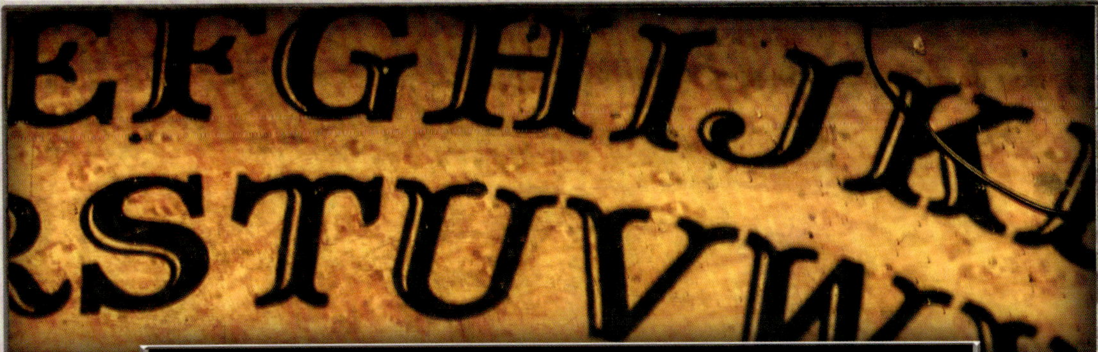

> "I always end up working with a bunch of projects at once, because of the nature of my work. I'll often have seven, eight, nine, ten random things on my desk—bits and pieces of projects that either are problematic or need a little bit of TLC before they can move on. It'll often be a combination of random Darth Vader parts or Adam West Batman parts. It's very functional chaos."
>
> —Walter O'Neal, Art Director

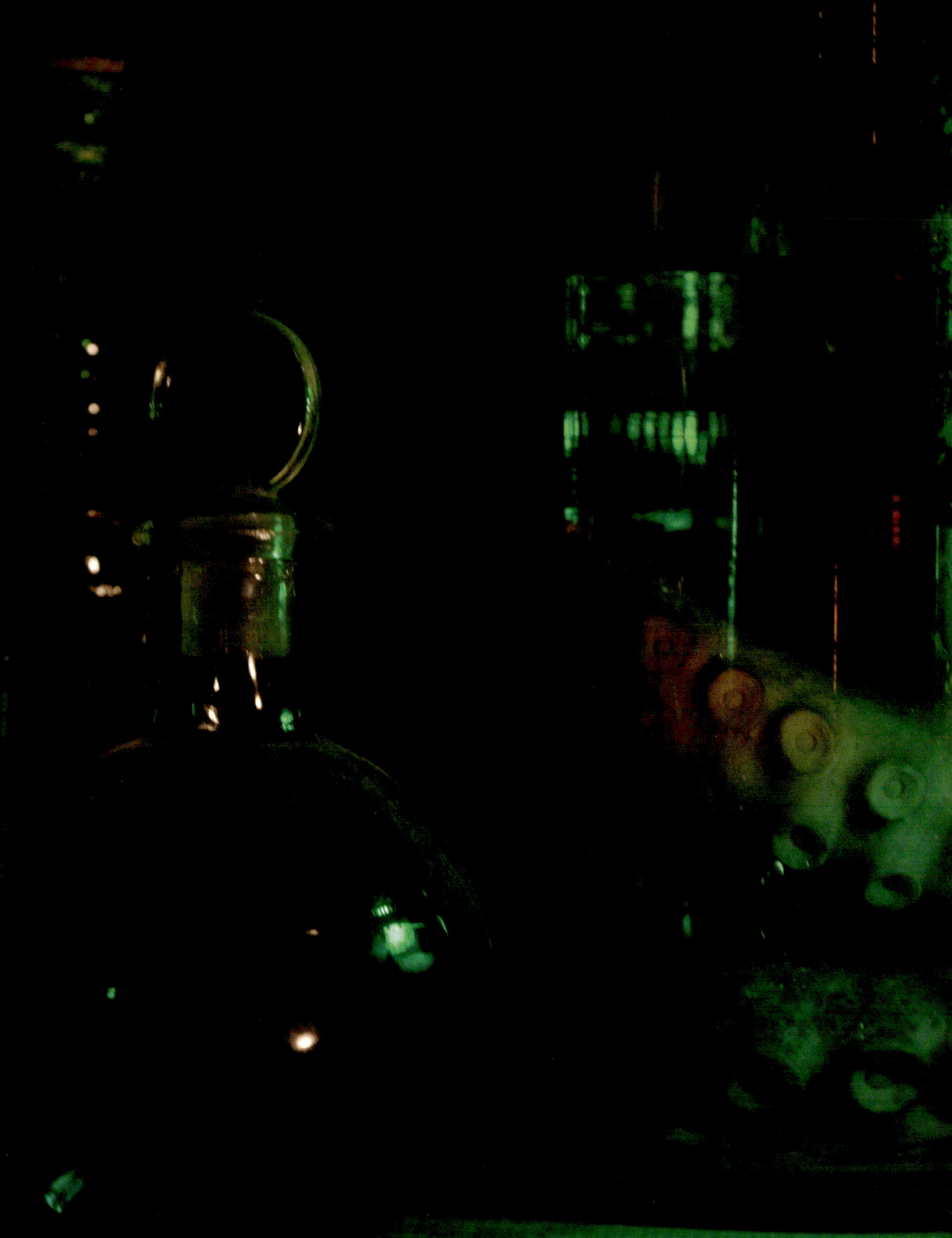

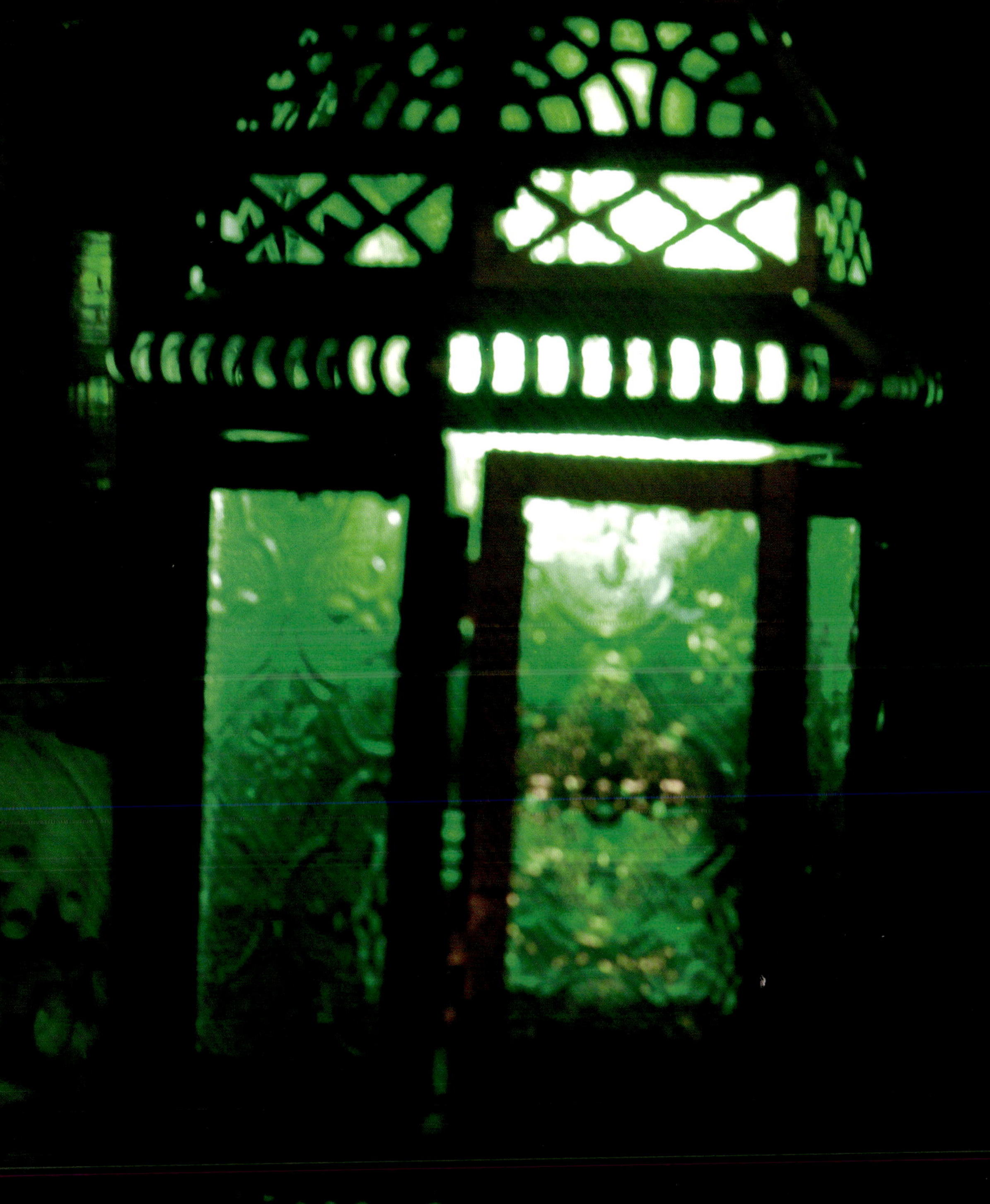

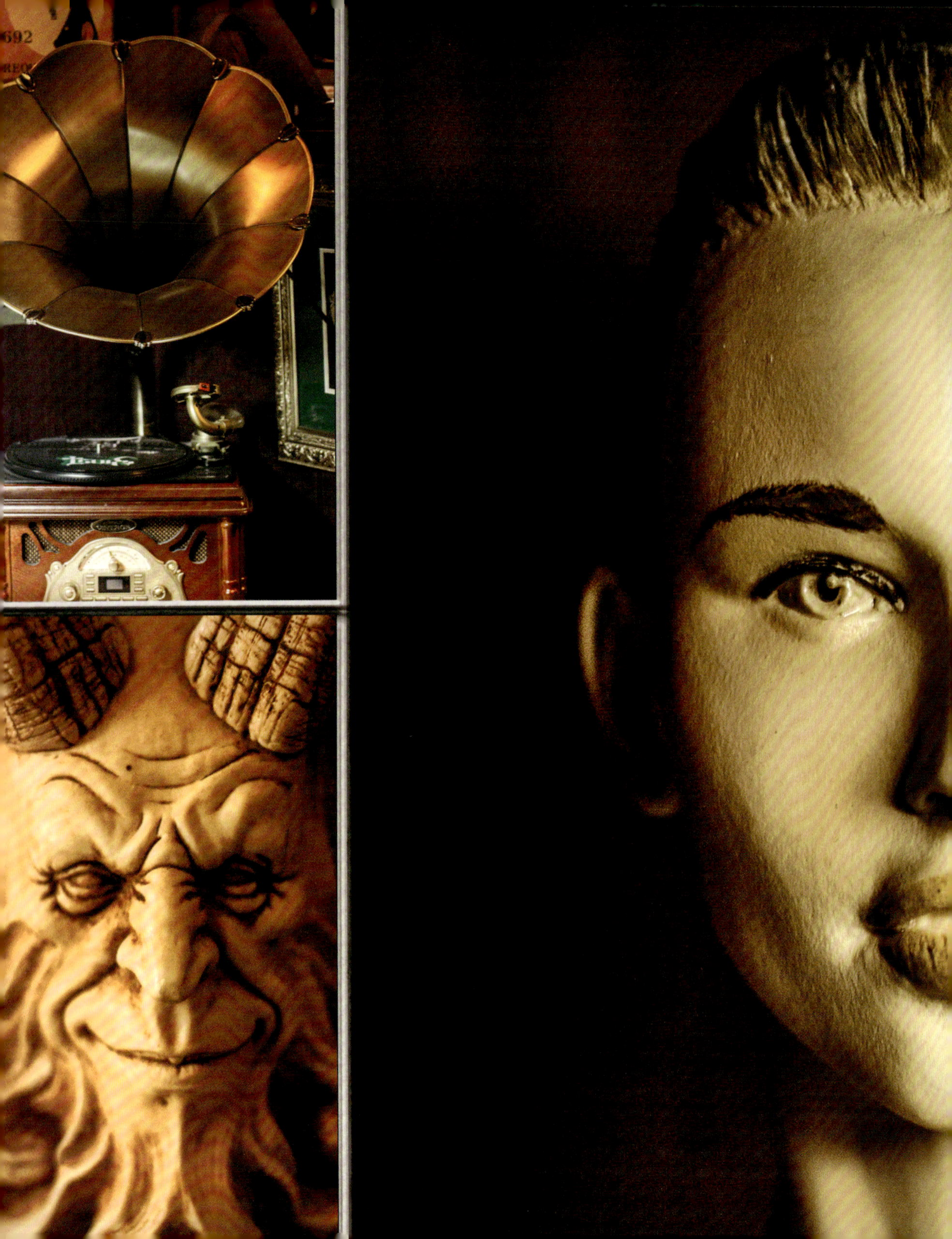

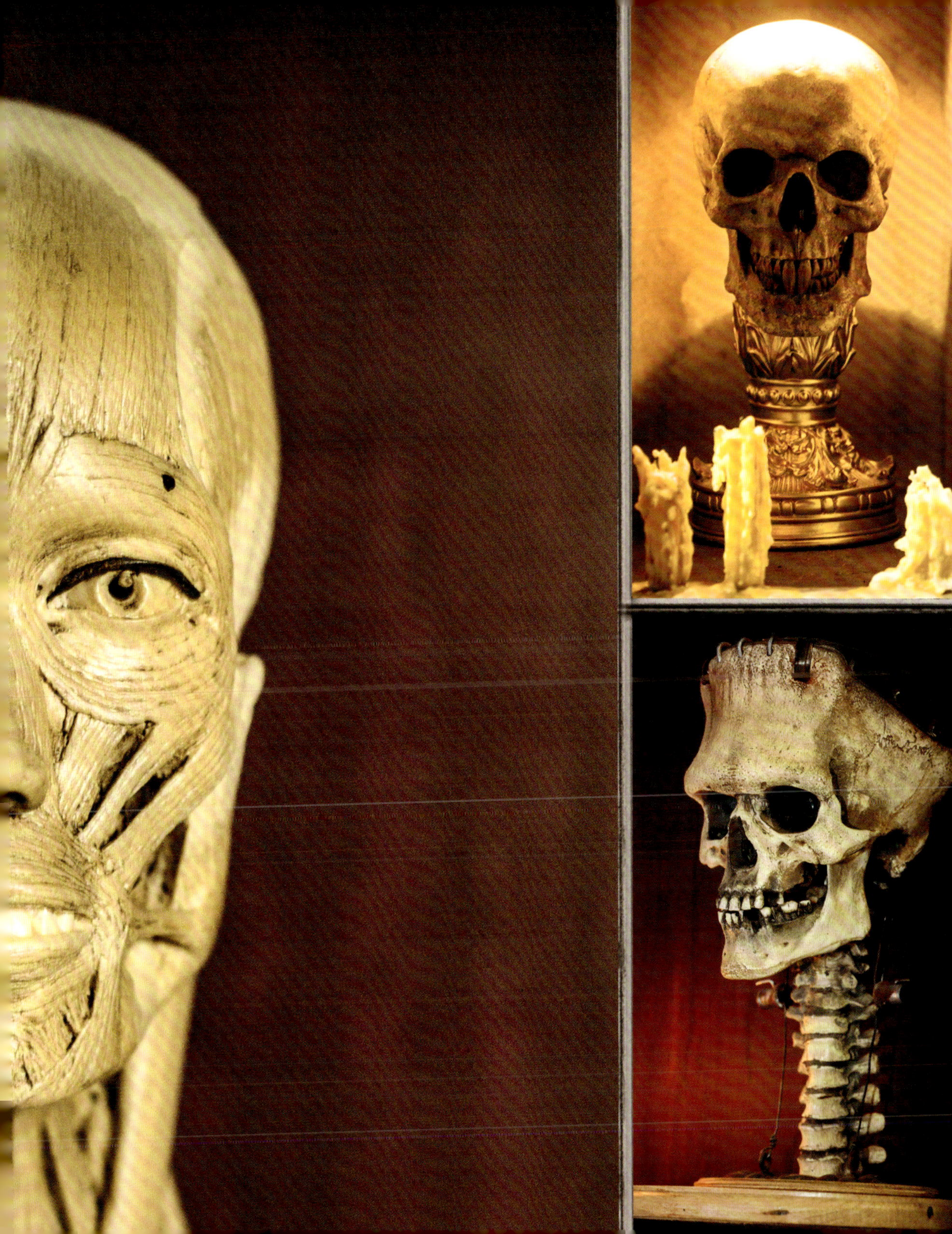

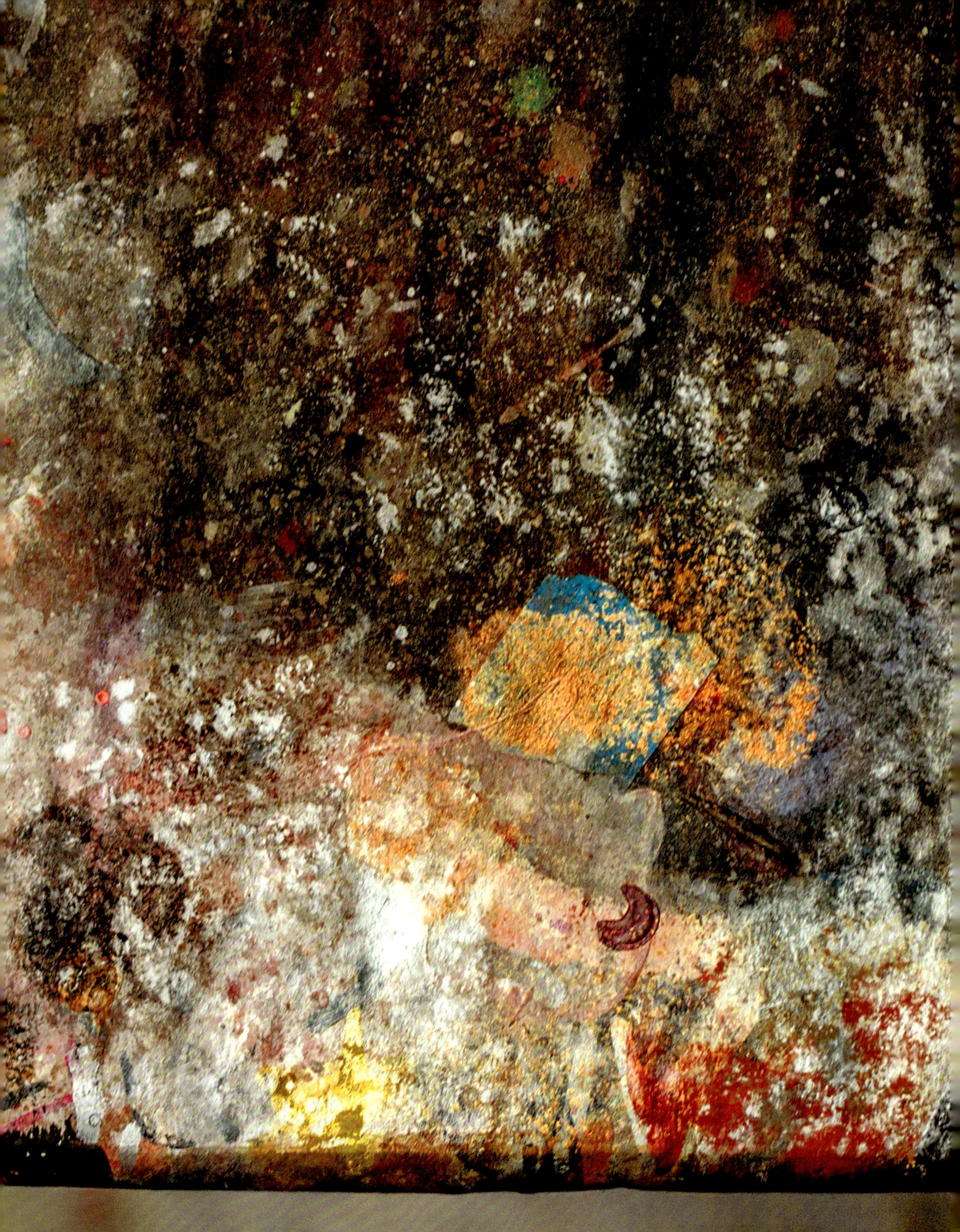

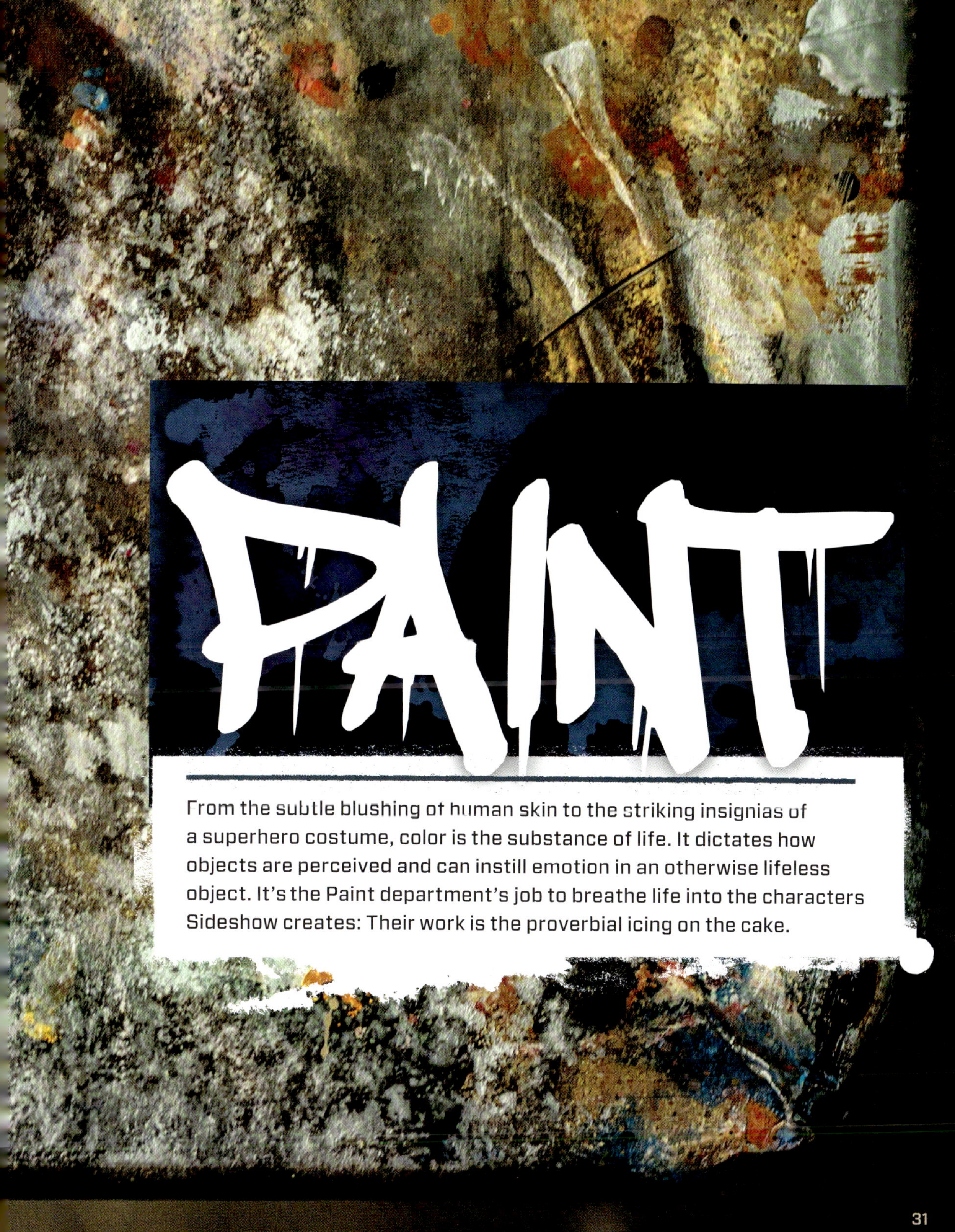

PAINT

From the subtle blushing of human skin to the striking insignias of
a superhero costume, color is the substance of life. It dictates how
objects are perceived and can instill emotion in an otherwise lifeless
object. It's the Paint department's job to breathe life into the characters
Sideshow creates: Their work is the proverbial icing on the cake.

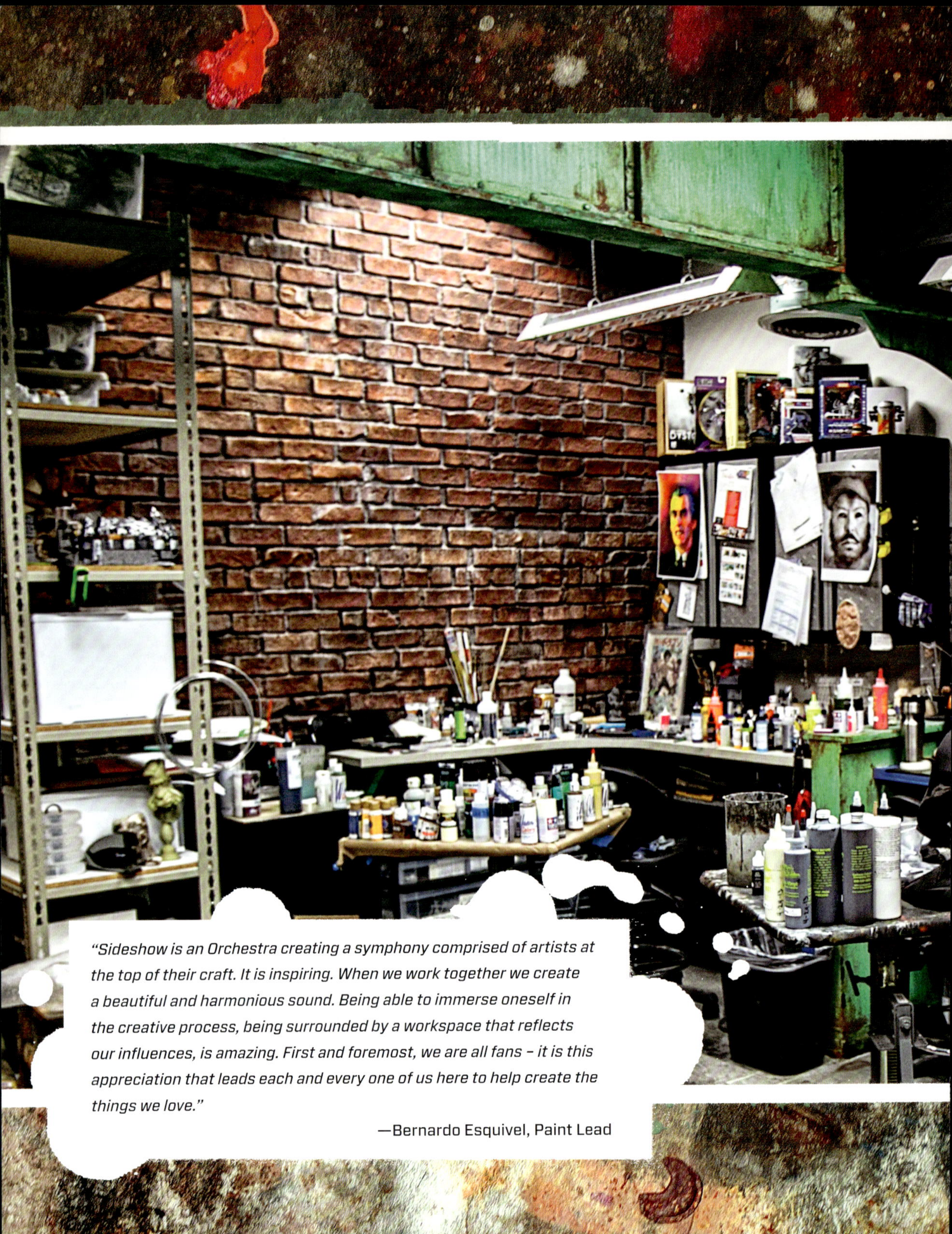

"Sideshow is an Orchestra creating a symphony comprised of artists at the top of their craft. It is inspiring. When we work together we create a beautiful and harmonious sound. Being able to immerse oneself in the creative process, being surrounded by a workspace that reflects our influences, is amazing. First and foremost, we are all fans – it is this appreciation that leads each and every one of us here to help create the things we love."

—Bernardo Esquivel, Paint Lead

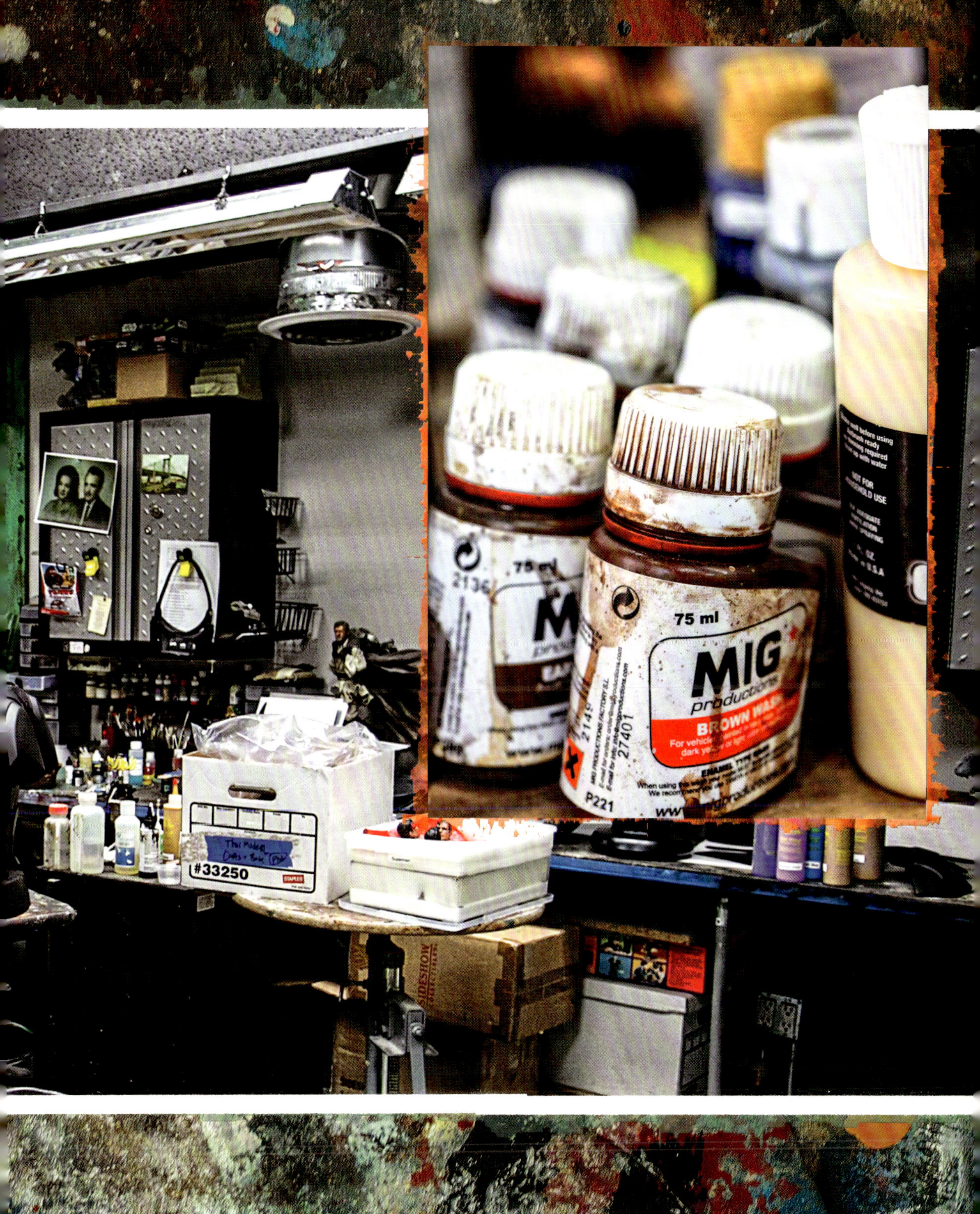
75 ml
MIG
productions
BROWN WASH
For vehicles covered in dark
dark yellow or light color...
ENAMEL TYPE...
27401
P221
2141

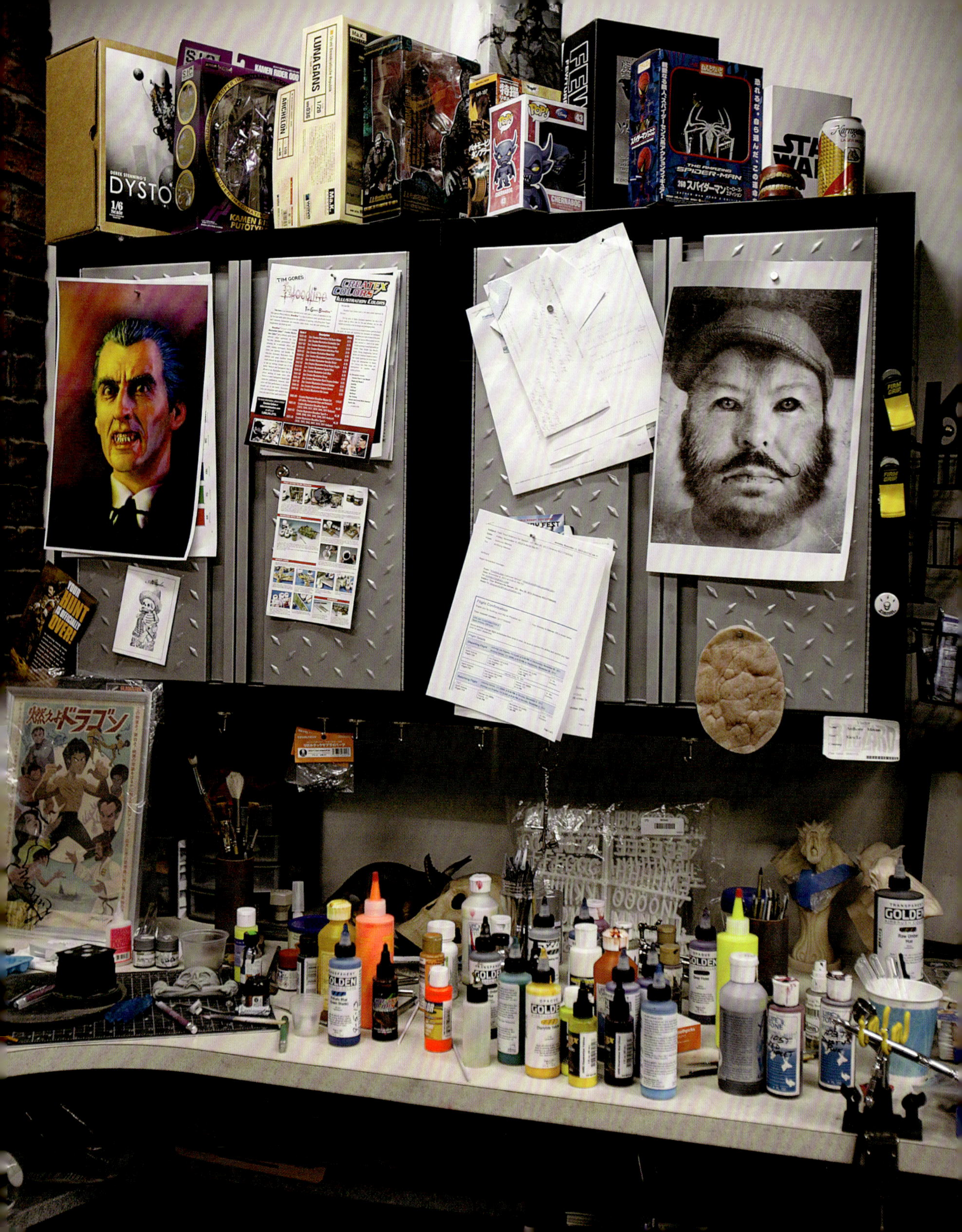

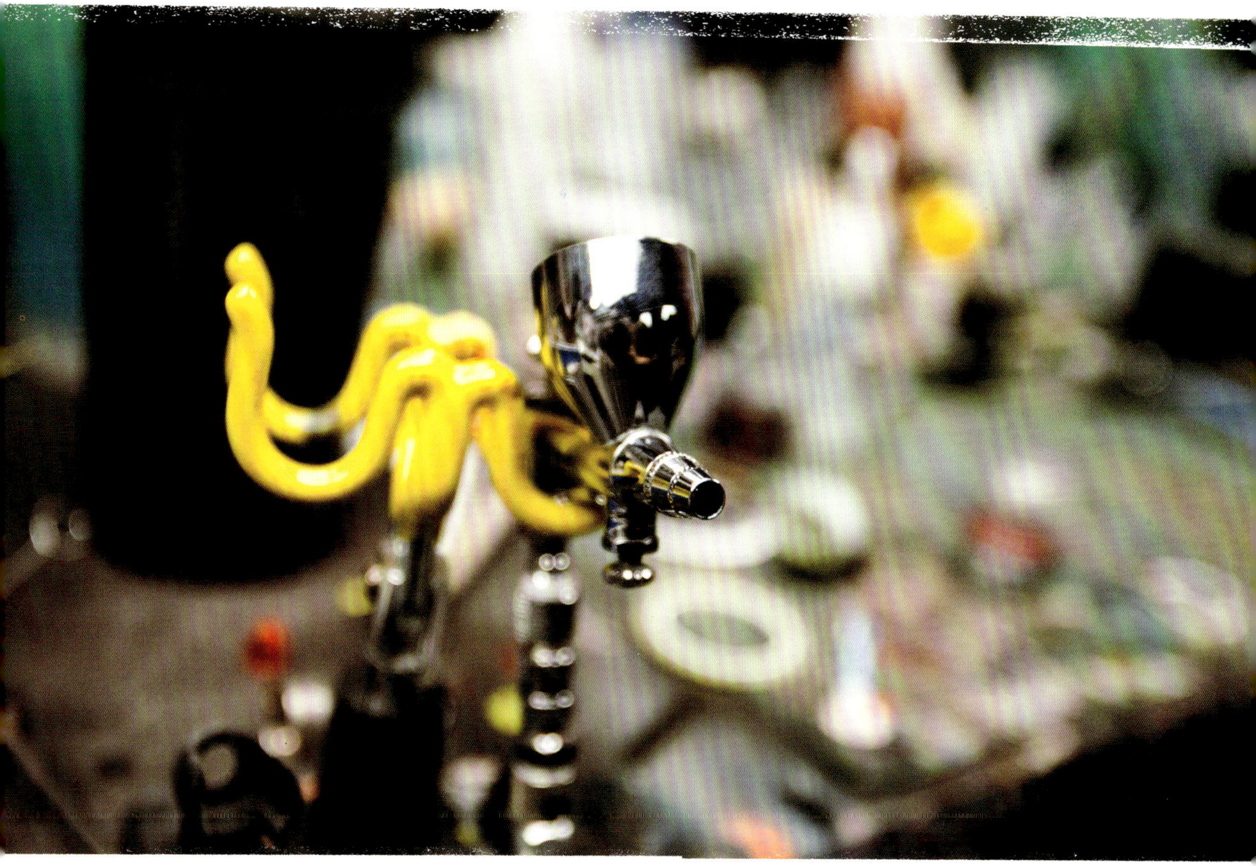

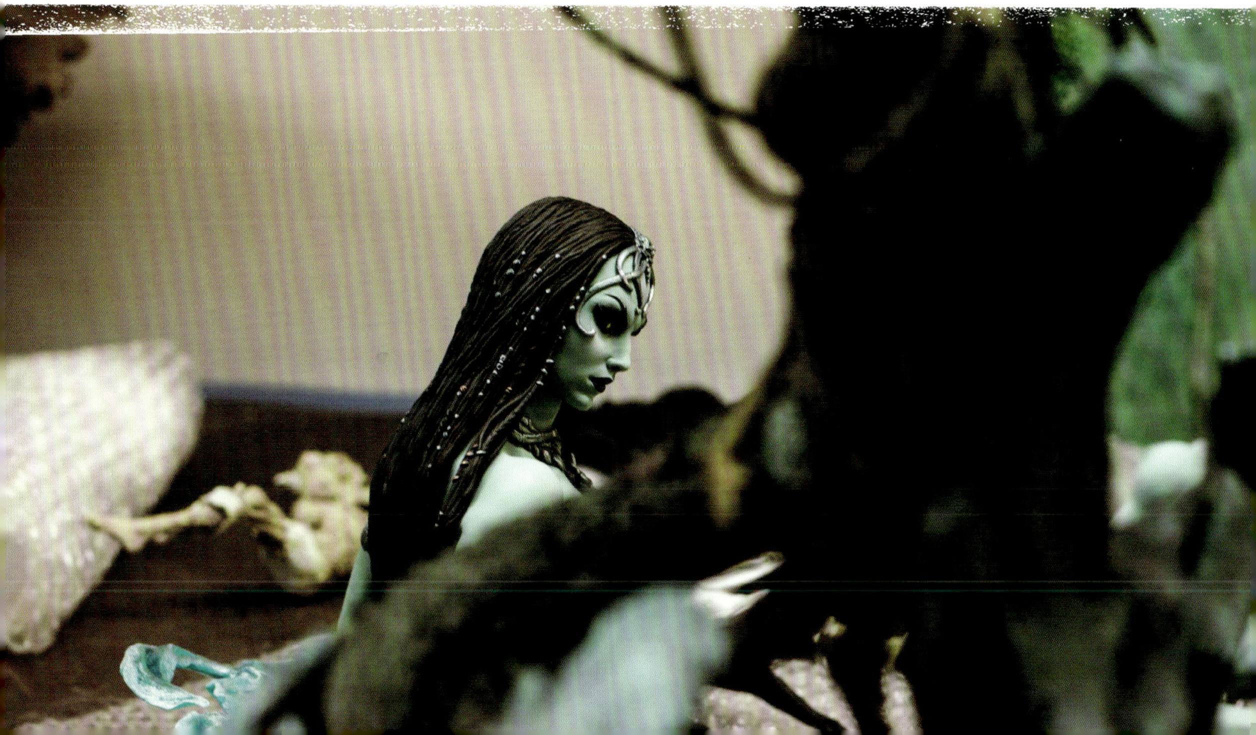

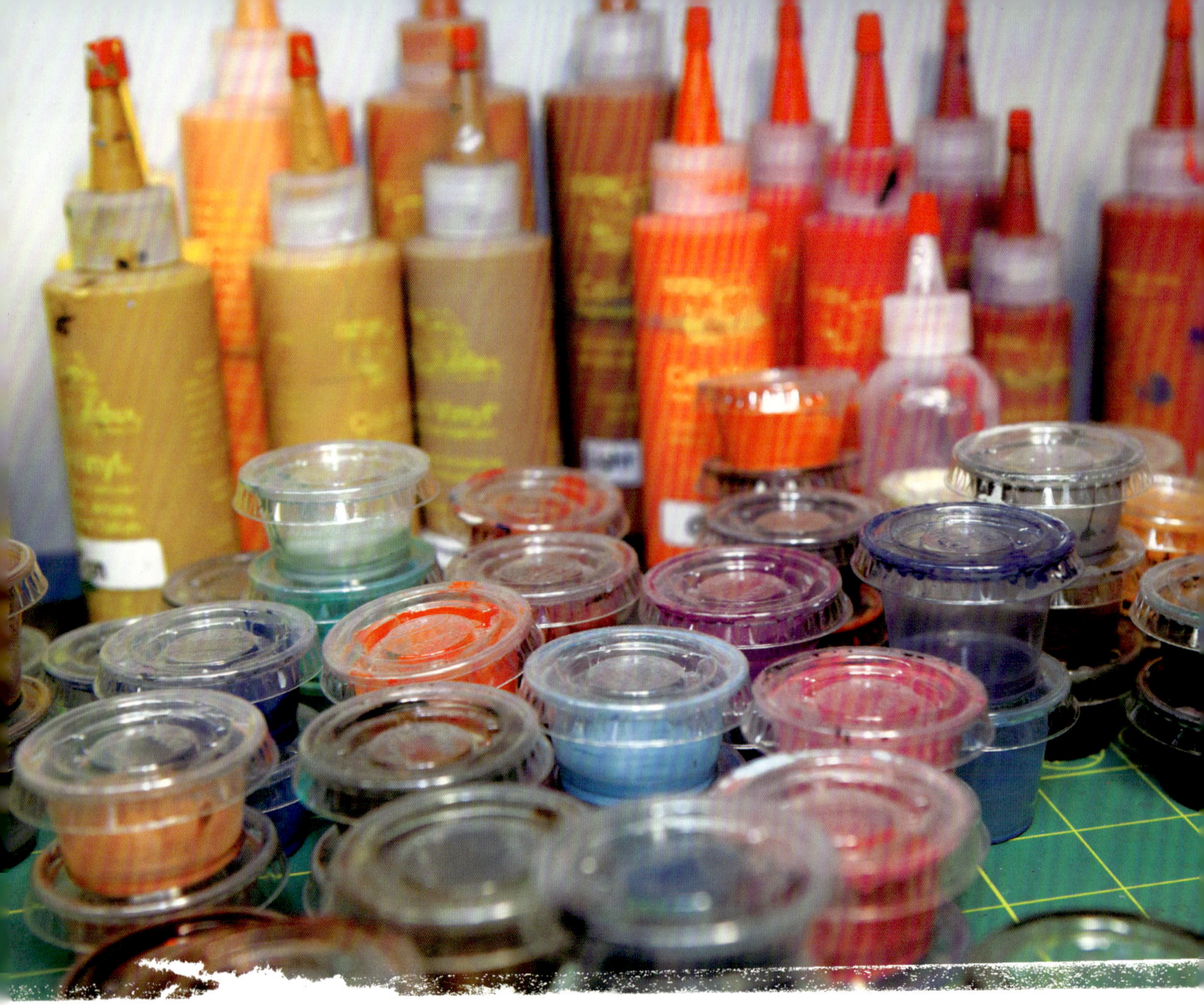

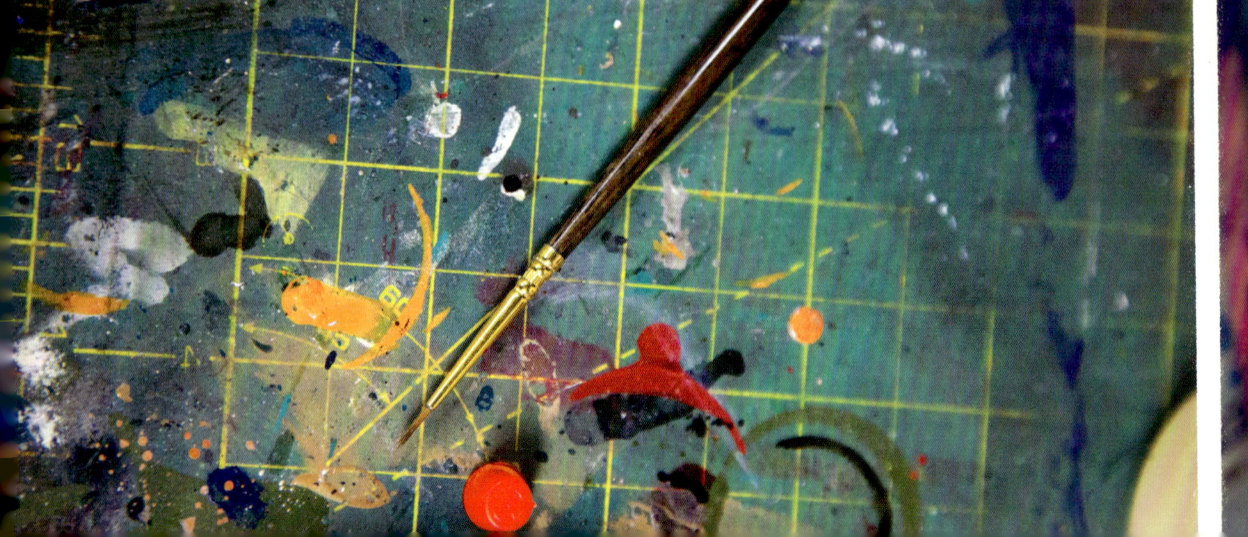

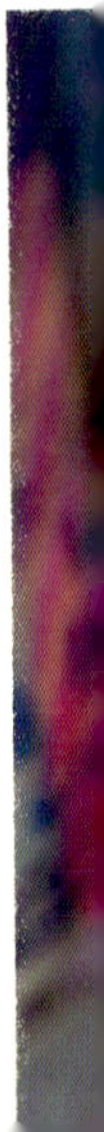

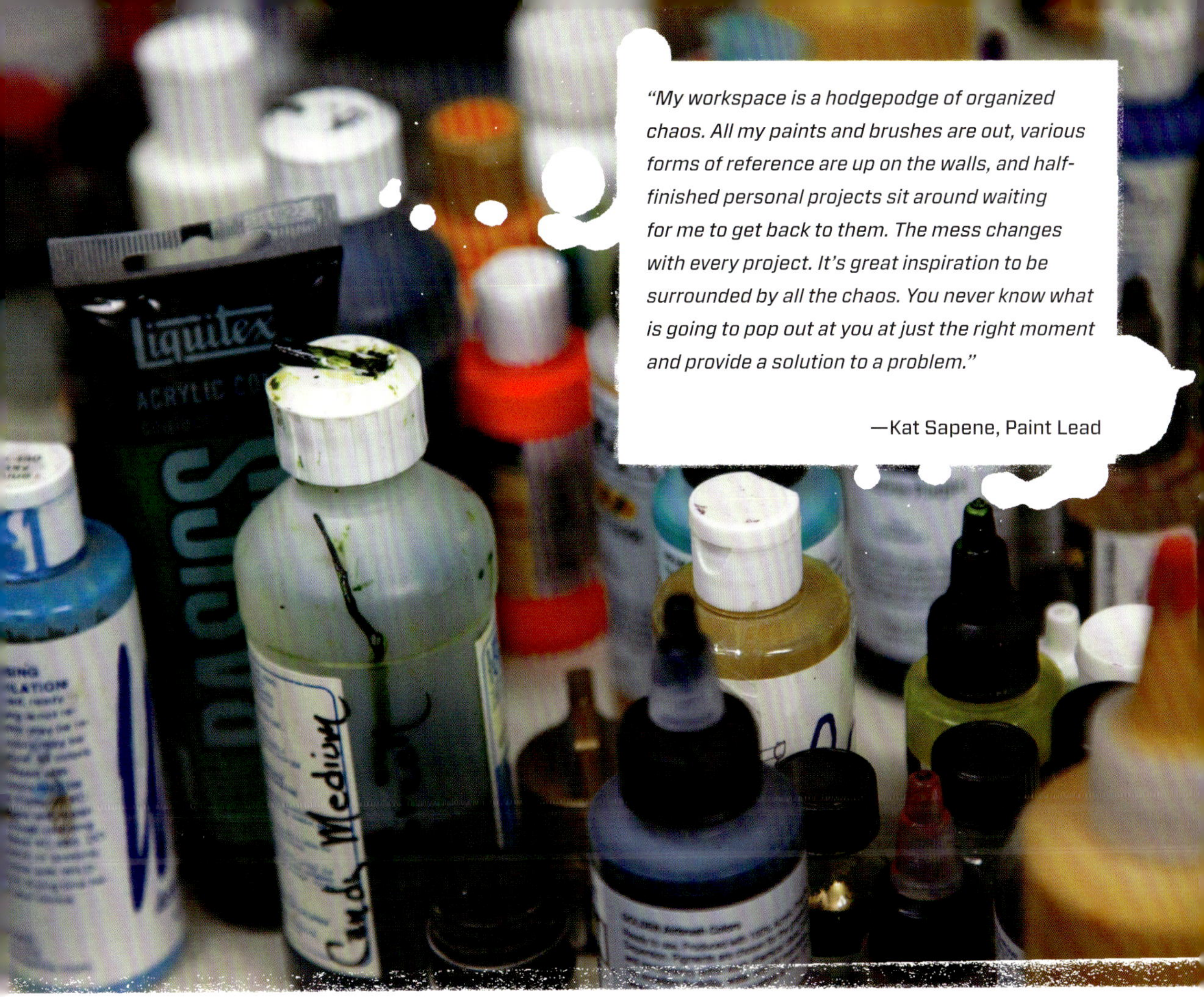

"My workspace is a hodgepodge of organized chaos. All my paints and brushes are out, various forms of reference are up on the walls, and half-finished personal projects sit around waiting for me to get back to them. The mess changes with every project. It's great inspiration to be surrounded by all the chaos. You never know what is going to pop out at you at just the right moment and provide a solution to a problem."

—Kat Sapene, Paint Lead

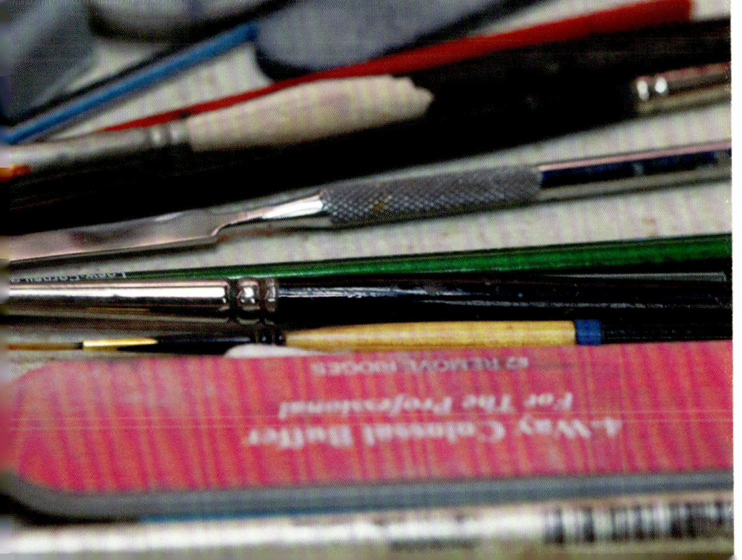

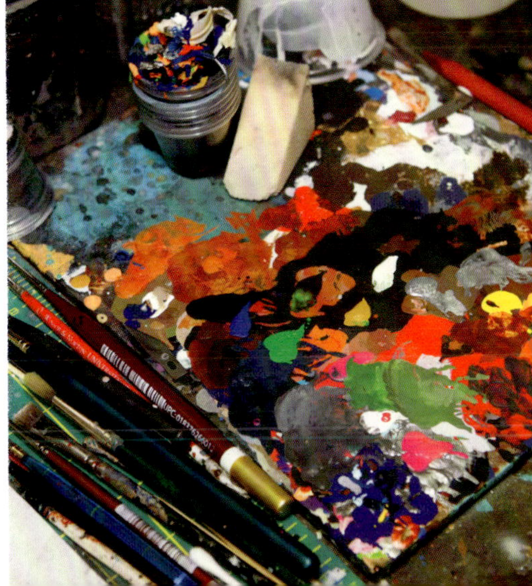

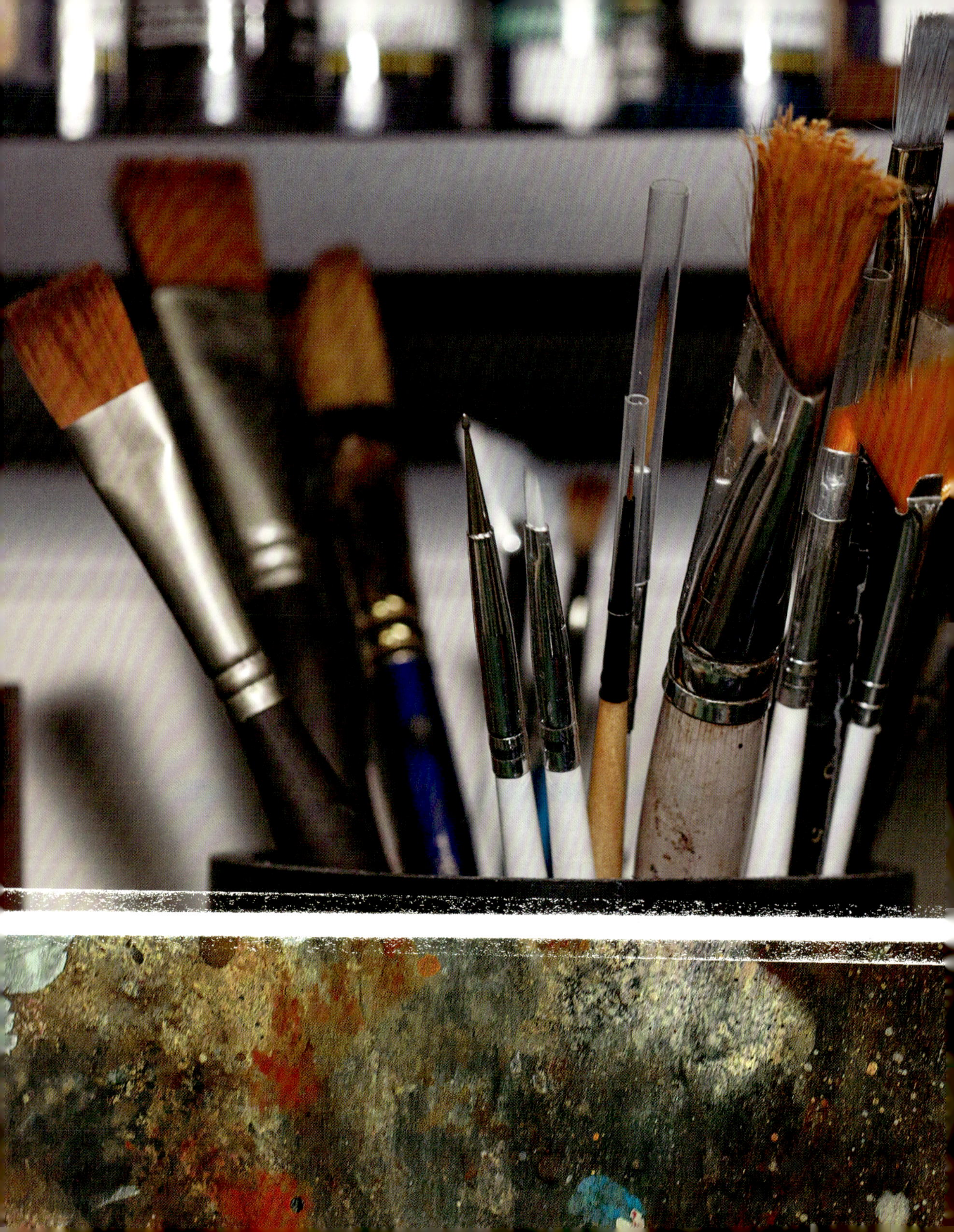

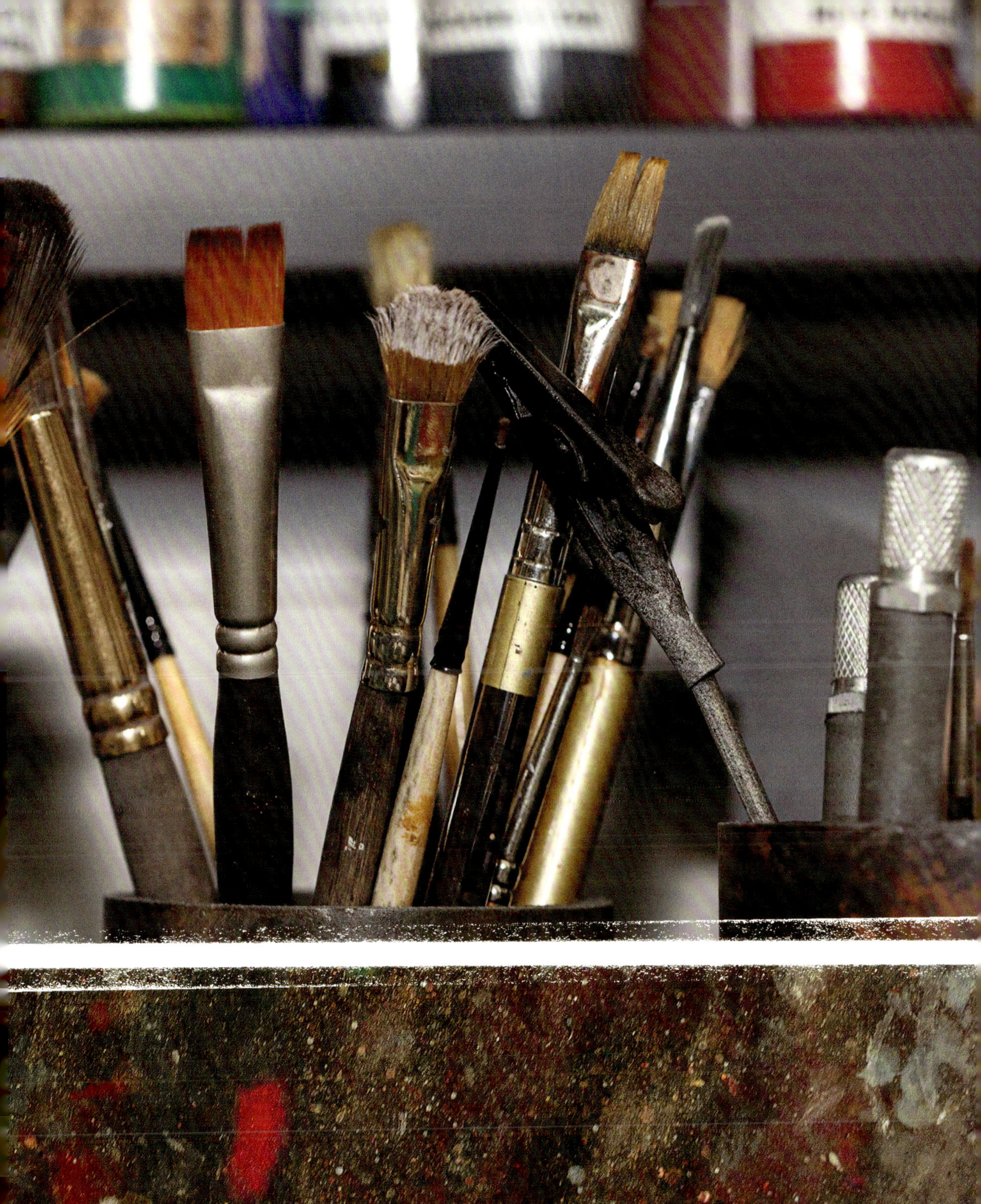

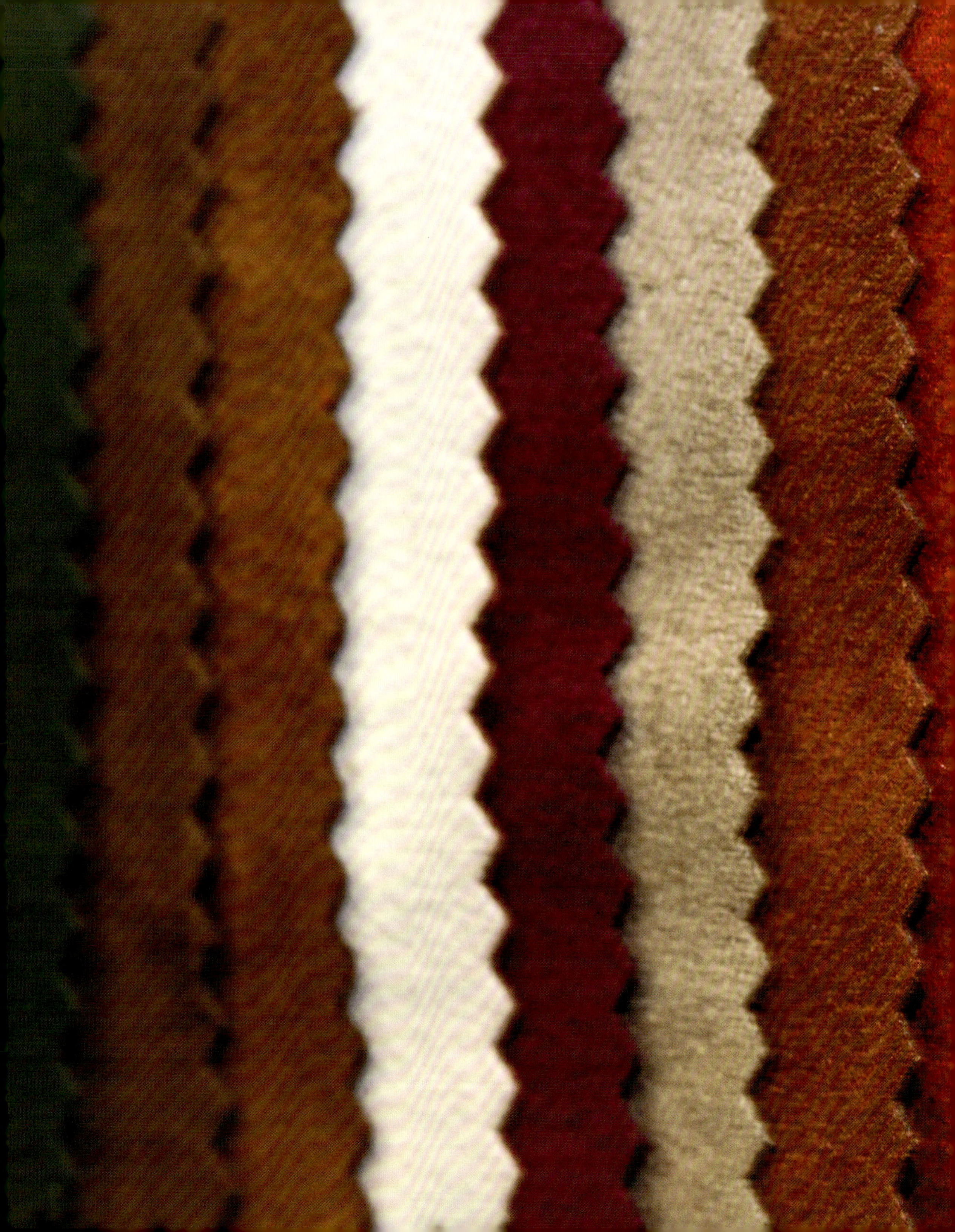

cut & sew &

Cut & Sew is all about adding the special touches to the process, taking it a step further with authentic costume fabrication, fabric accessories, leather work, chain, and a multitude of other eye-catching details. Prototypes are carefully dressed and prepared for their big debut to the collecting public. While no two characters are alike, the goal is always to give each individual piece a life and personality of its own. Whether the figure is fully dressed in multilayered, complex robes or in a posable cape to convey action, each costume provides a unique opportunity for the medium to shine. It falls to us to represent the character's essence with actual fabrics and carefully patterned garments, ranging from 12" figures all the way to life-size statues. The department contains a vast collection of fabrics of all types and colors, various threads, samples and swatches, dyes, patterns, some nifty sewing machines, and enough random crafting supplies to create just about anything our imaginations can muster. Sure, it's a little messy around here . . . but isn't that how you know we're working?

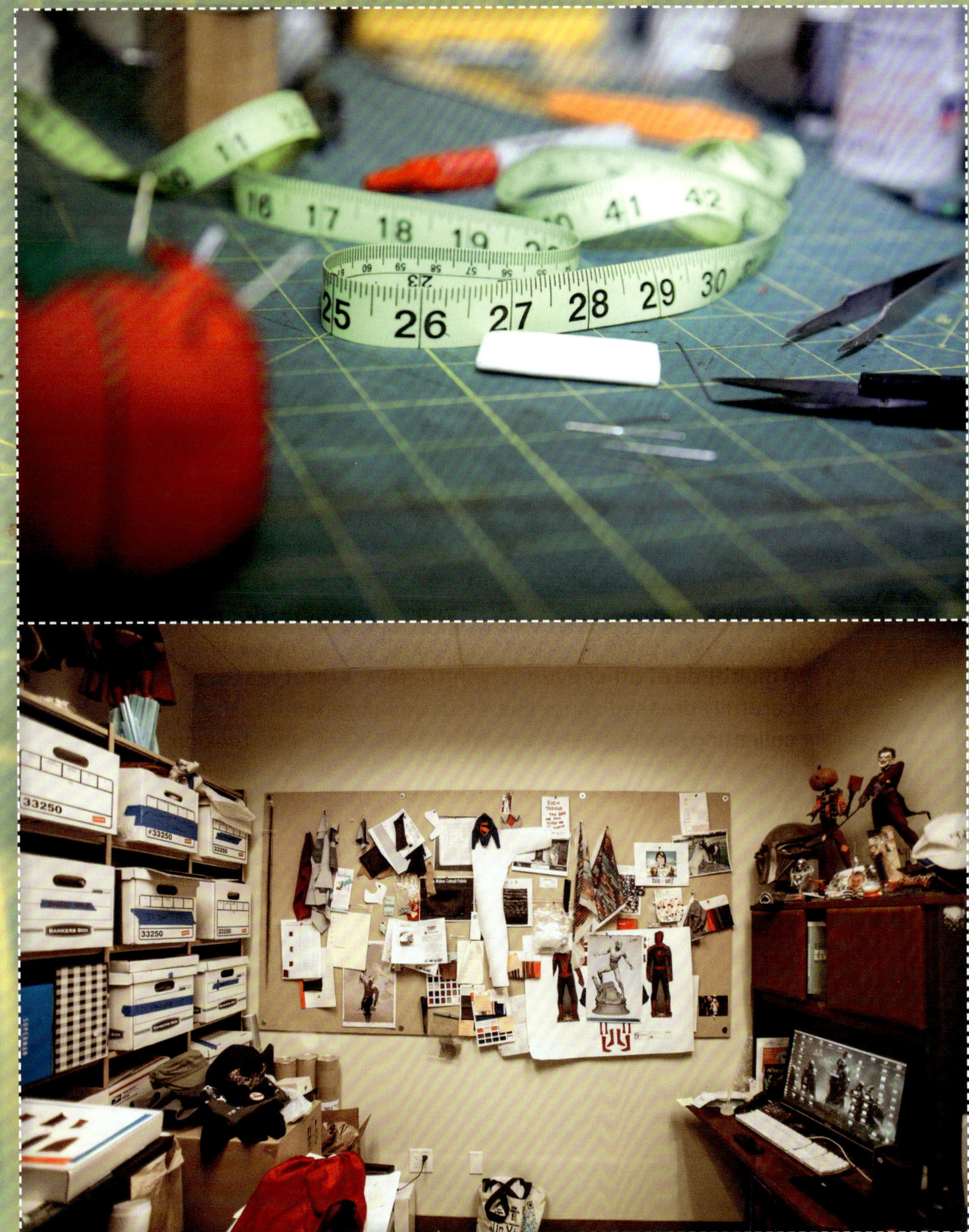

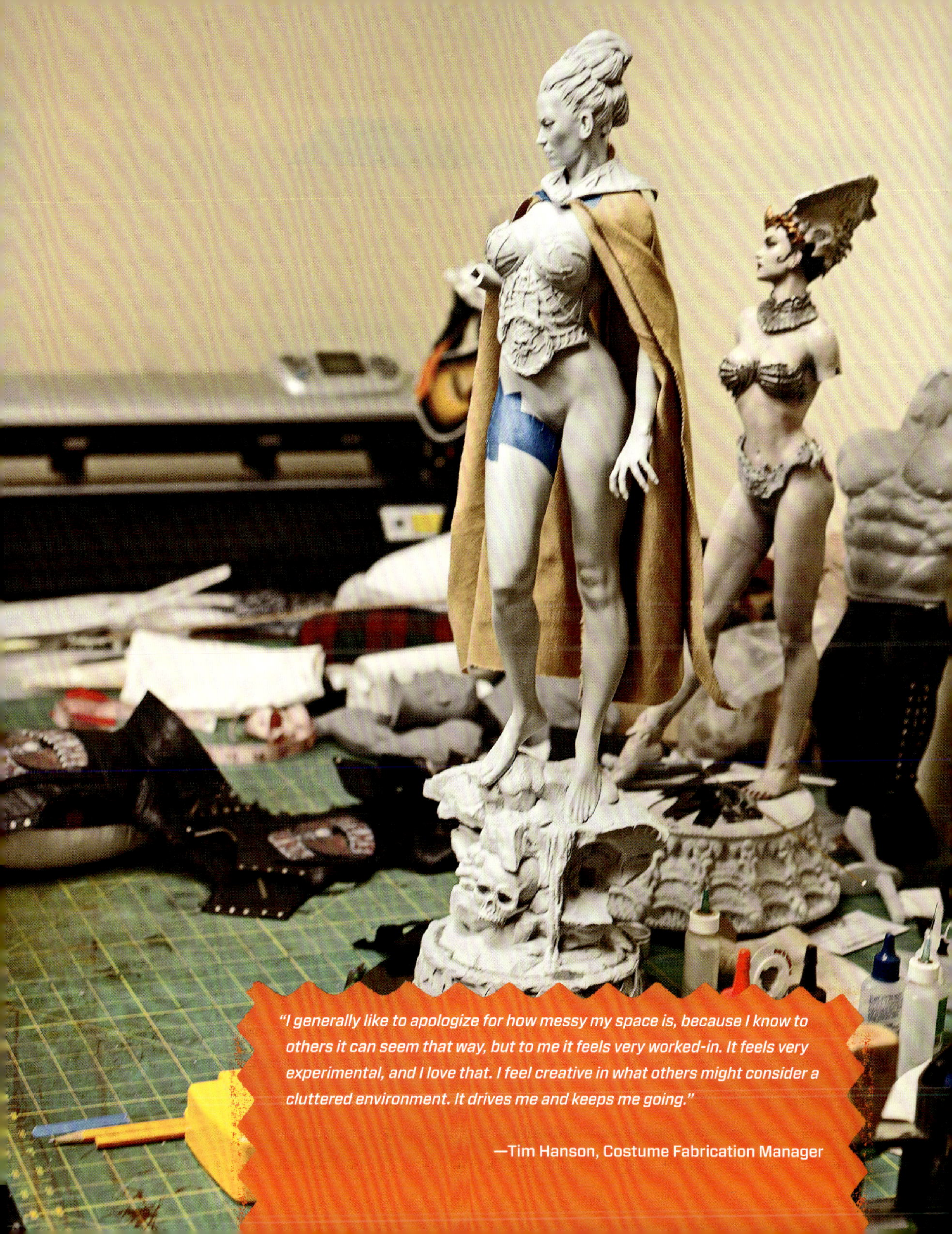

"I generally like to apologize for how messy my space is, because I know to others it can seem that way, but to me it feels very worked-in. It feels very experimental, and I love that. I feel creative in what others might consider a cluttered environment. It drives me and keeps me going."

—Tim Hanson, Costume Fabrication Manager

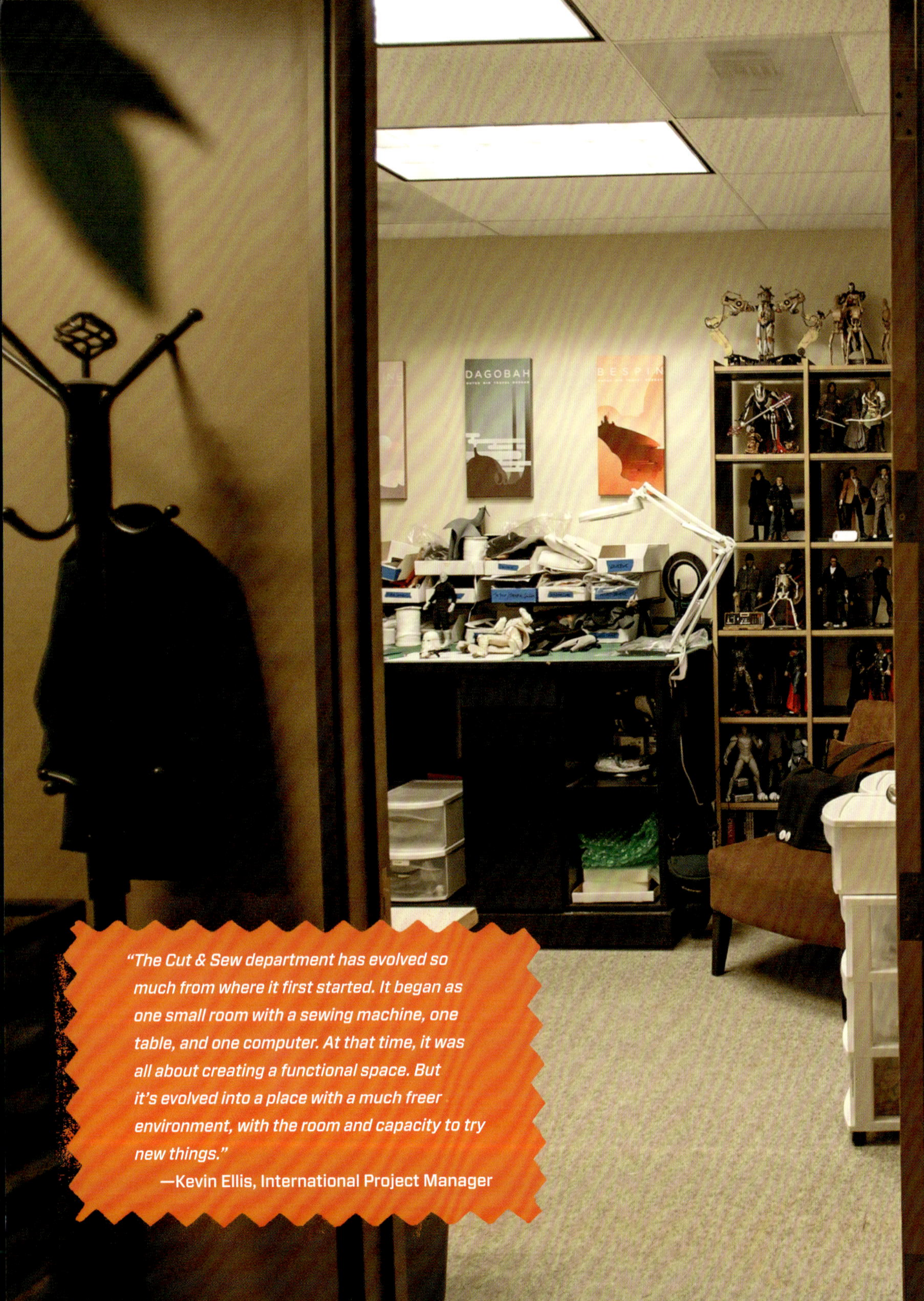

"The Cut & Sew department has evolved so much from where it first started. It began as one small room with a sewing machine, one table, and one computer. At that time, it was all about creating a functional space. But it's evolved into a place with a much freer environment, with the room and capacity to try new things."

—Kevin Ellis, International Project Manager

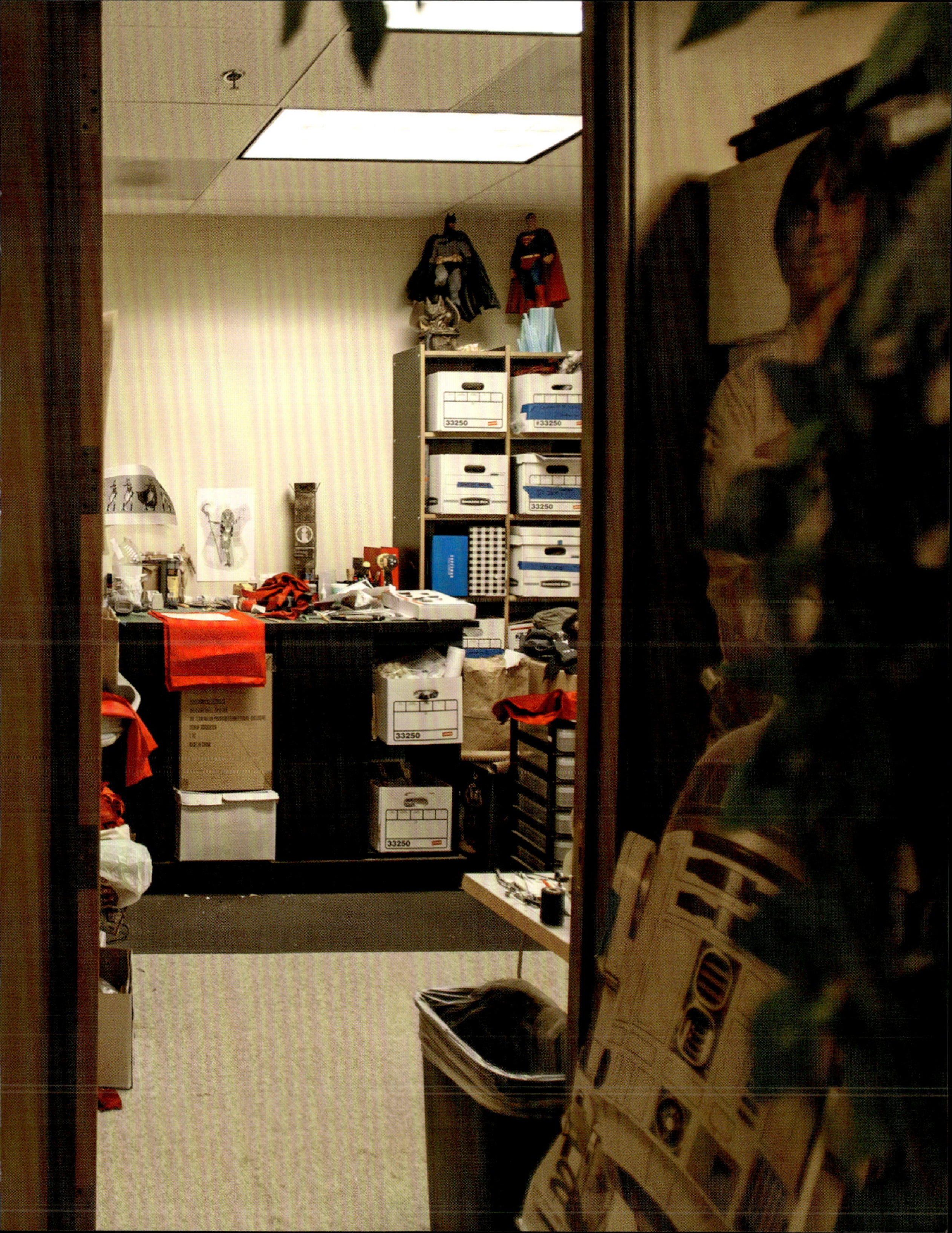

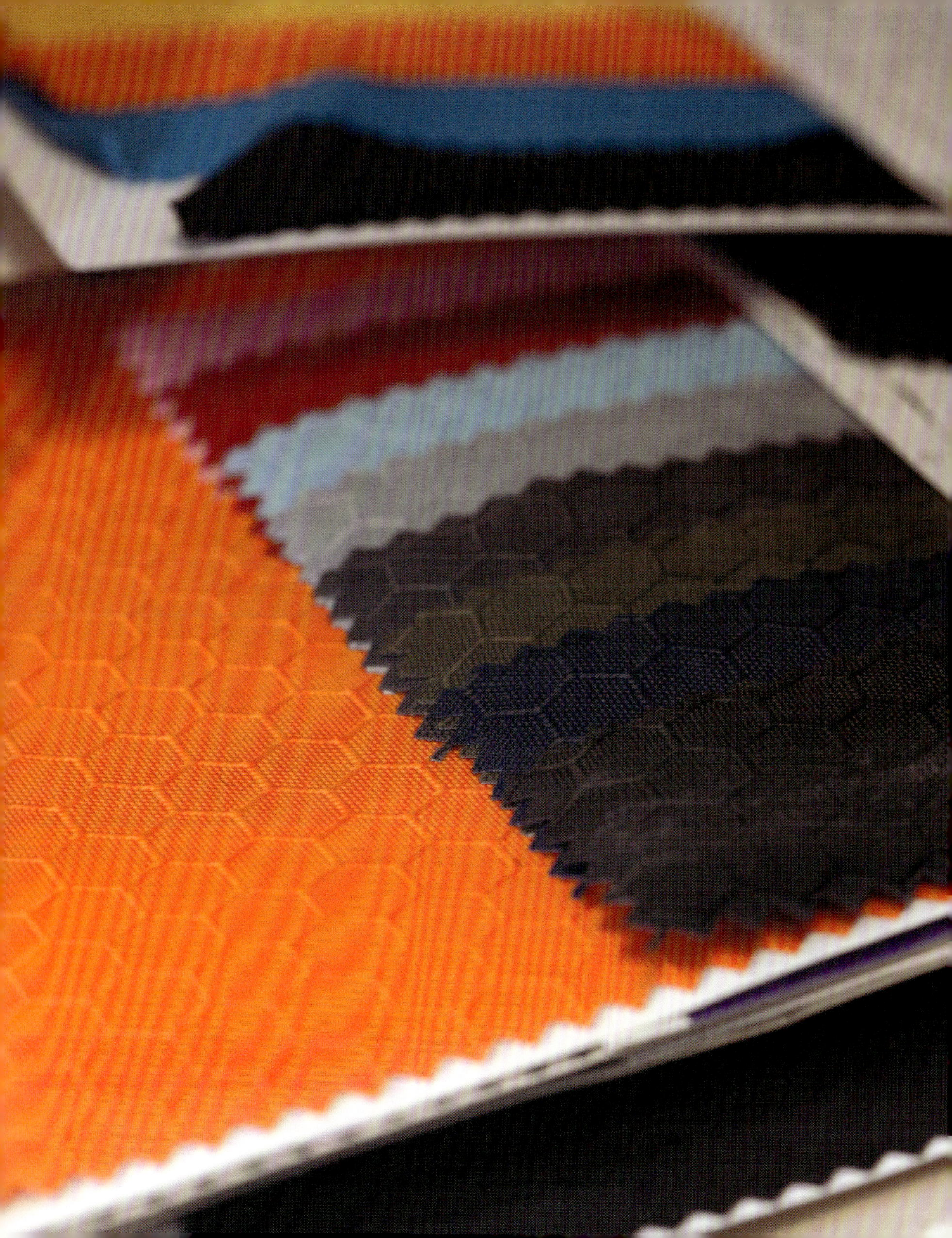

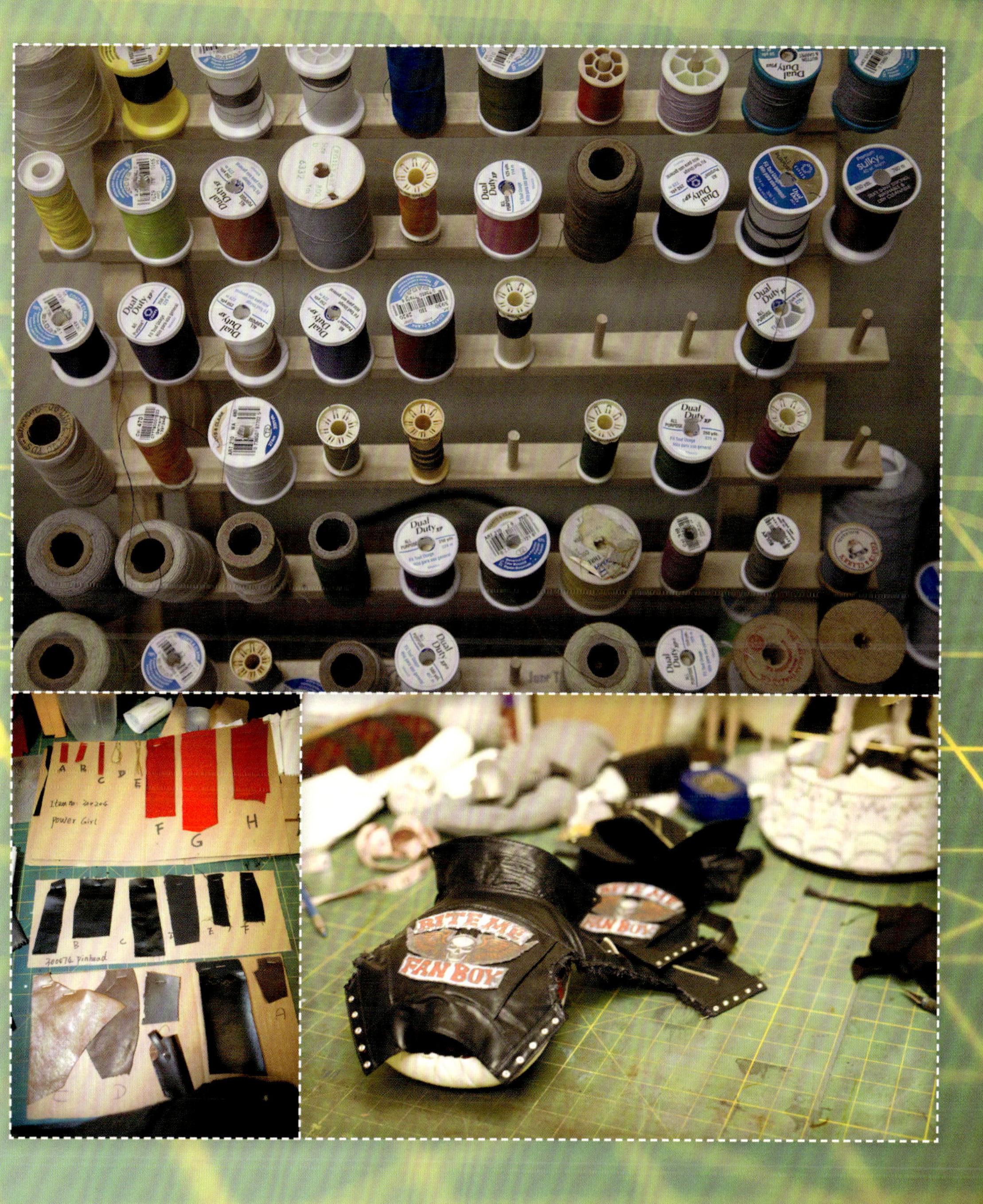
BITE ME
FAN BOY

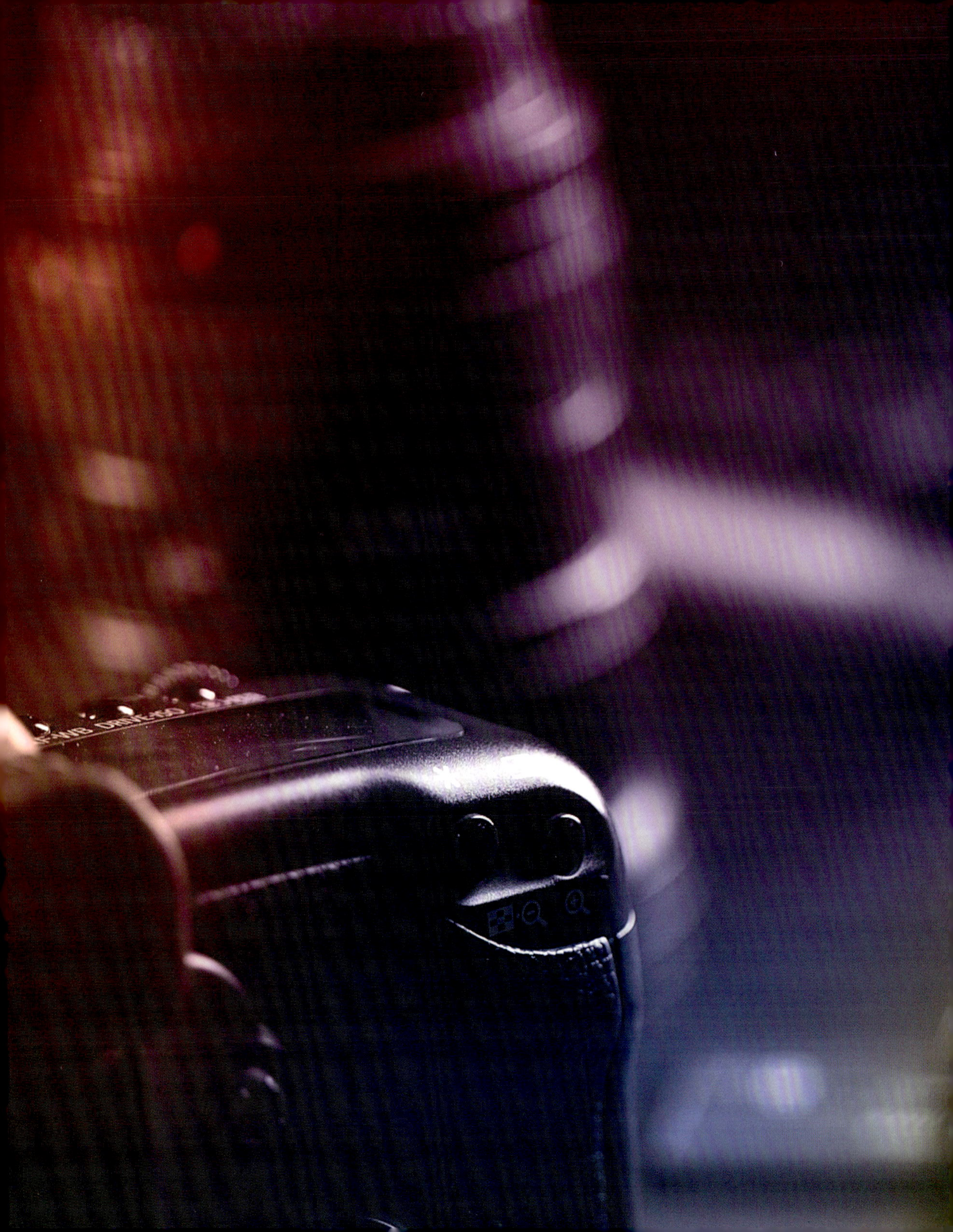

SHOOTING GALLERY

The team that generates all the photographic imagery for Sideshow—everything from press and print to the web—captures the best possible 2-D representations of our 3-D objects. The Photography department pays homage to all of the creative work that has preceded its shoots. These iconic photos are the easiest way for a true fan to own all the powerful representations of their beloved figures.

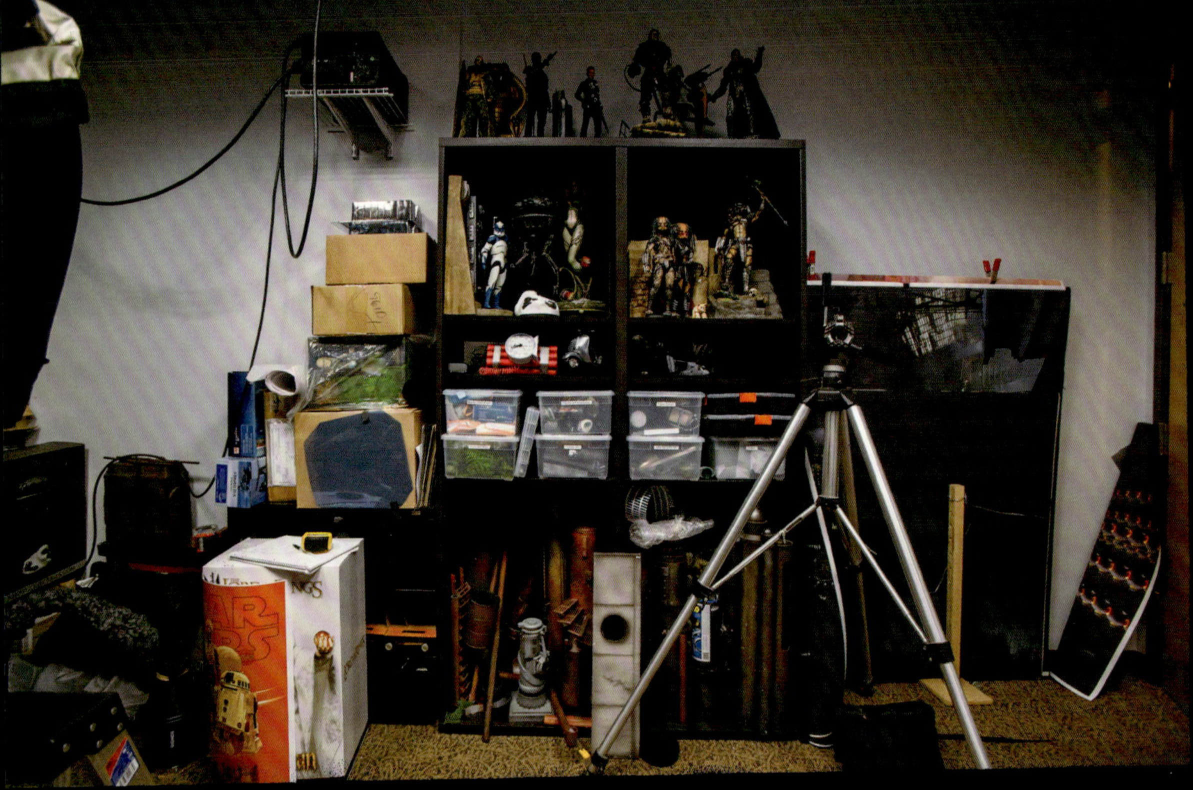

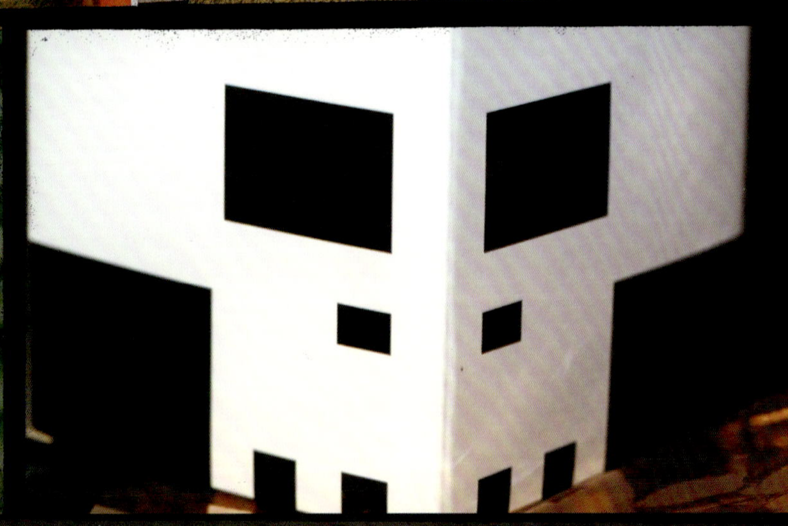

> "We have the freedom to customize our workspace according to our interests and inspirations. Whether it's a wall of cat pictures, a shelf littered with morbid curiosities, or a collection whimsical childhood toys, I think it's essential to have an environment that brings you joy. It not only fuels creativity, there's also just something magical about looking at other people's workspaces and peeling back the layers of their personalities."
>
> —Jeannette Villarreal Hamilton, Sr. Photographer/Manager

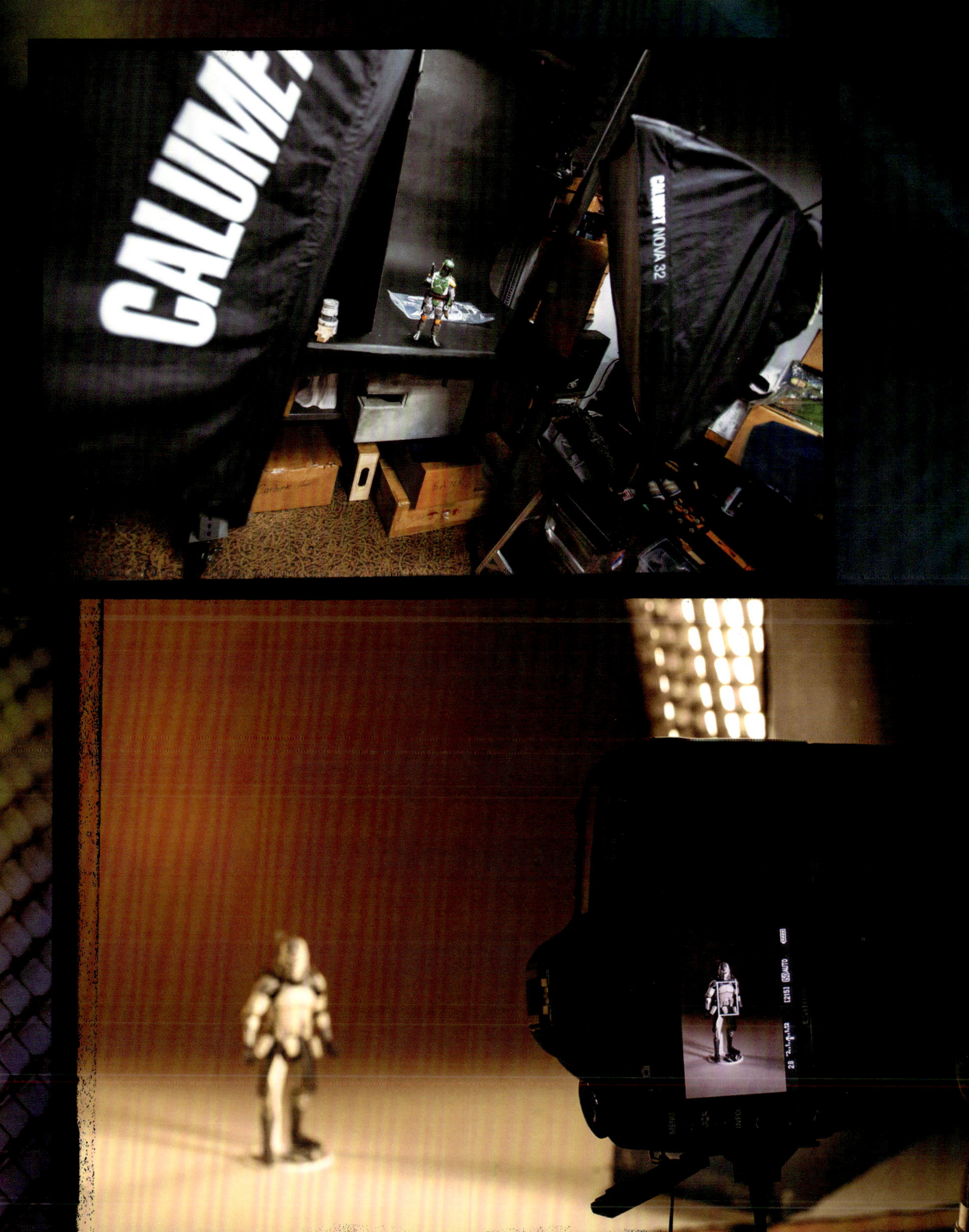

CALUMET
CALUMET NOVA 32

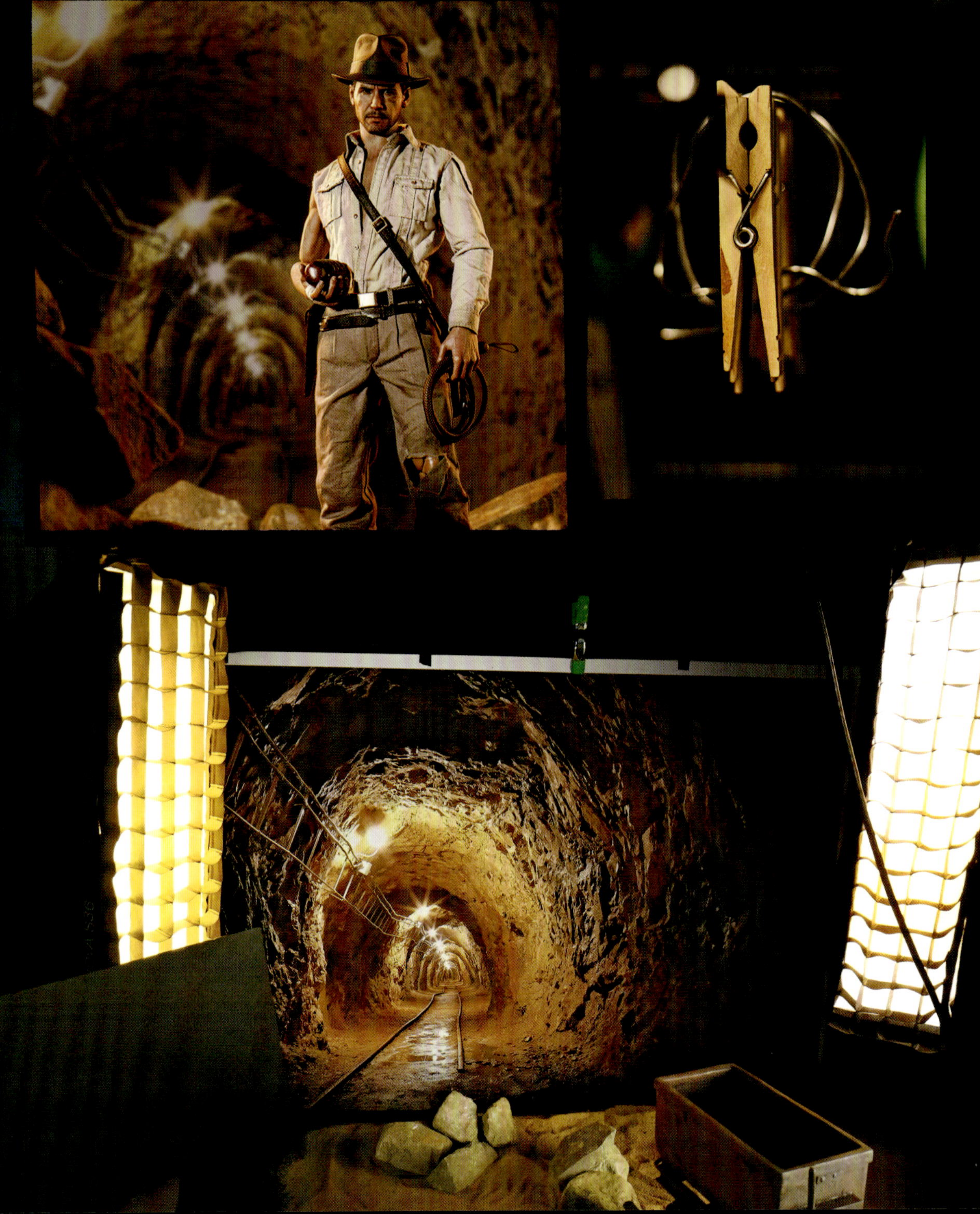

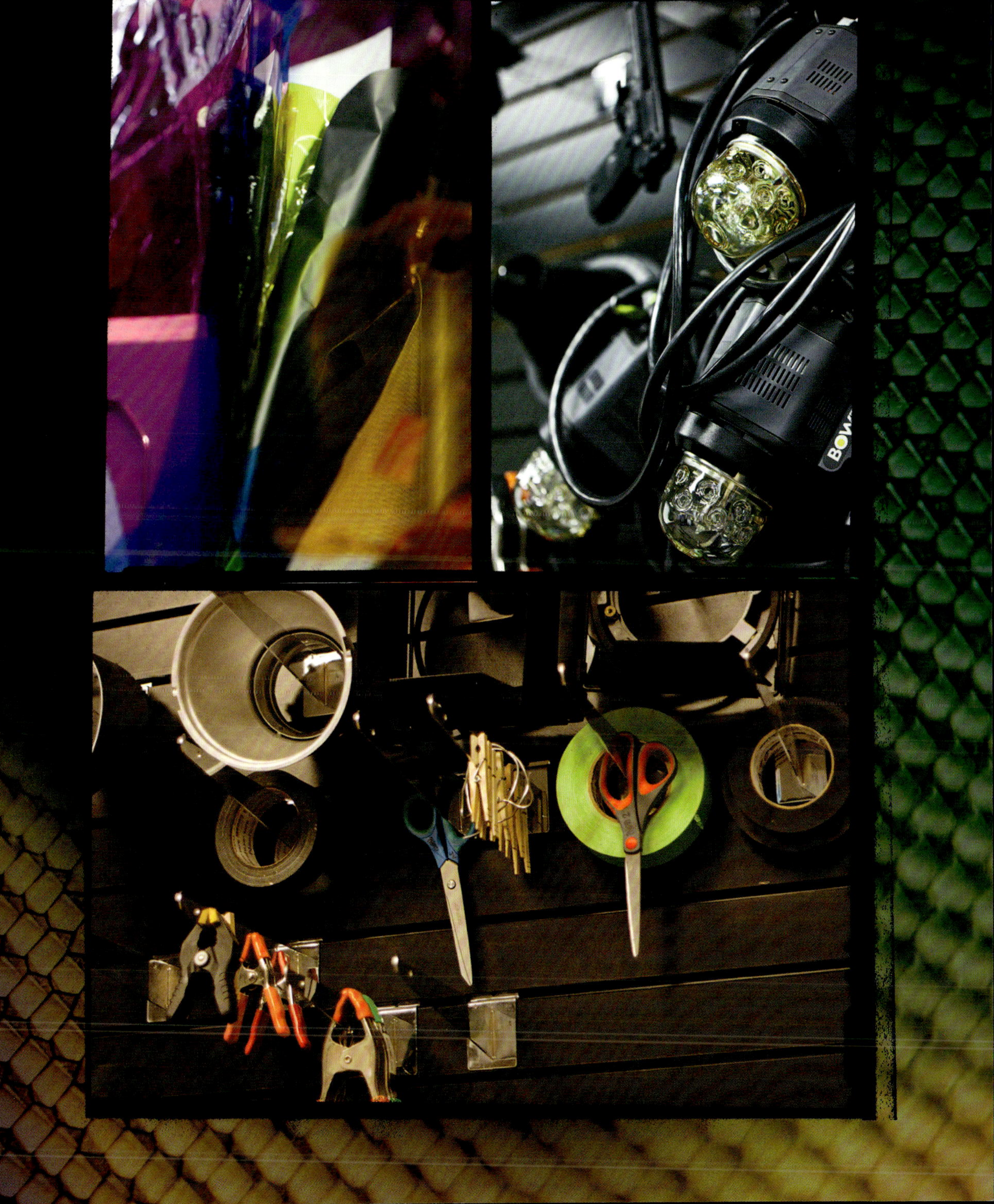

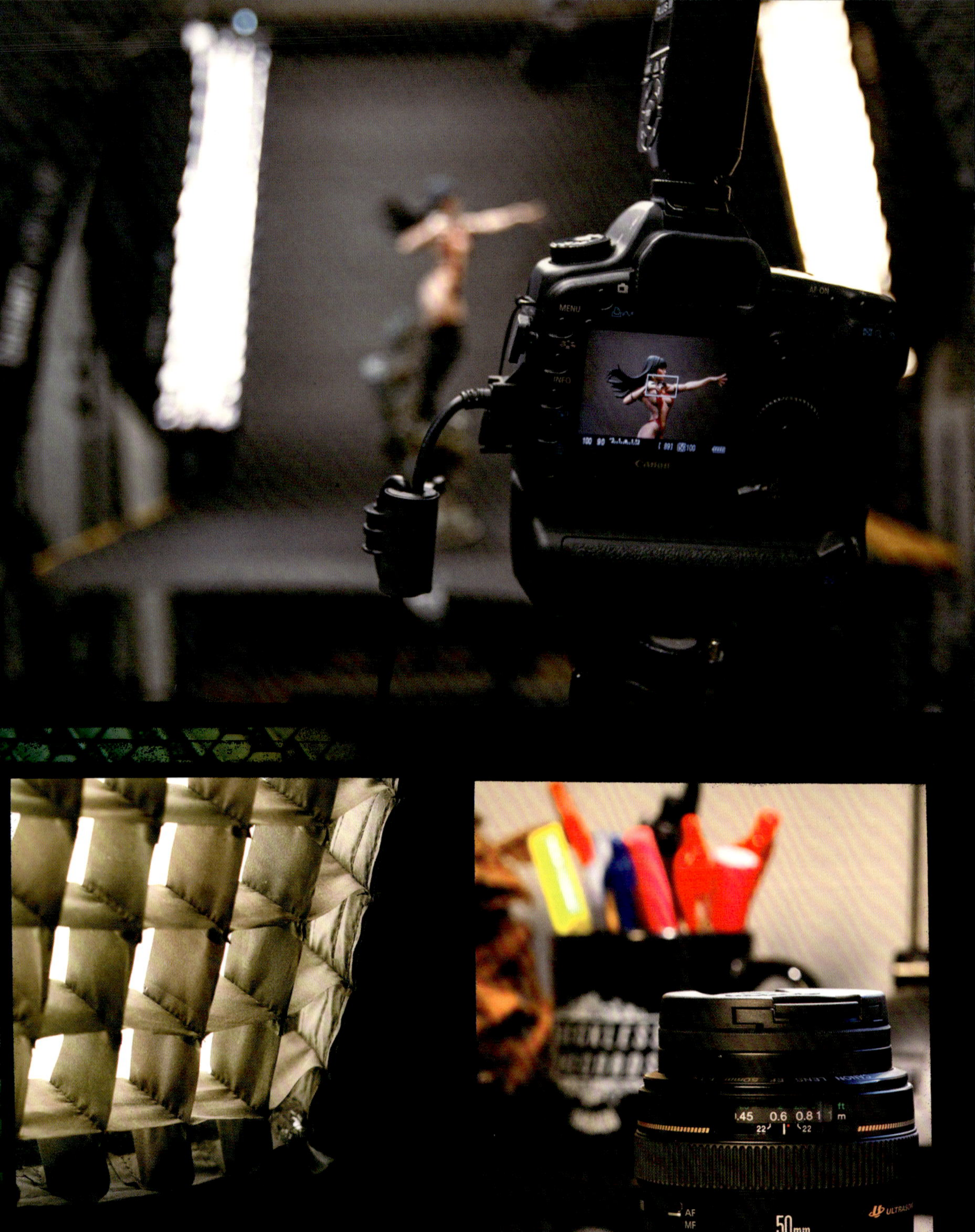

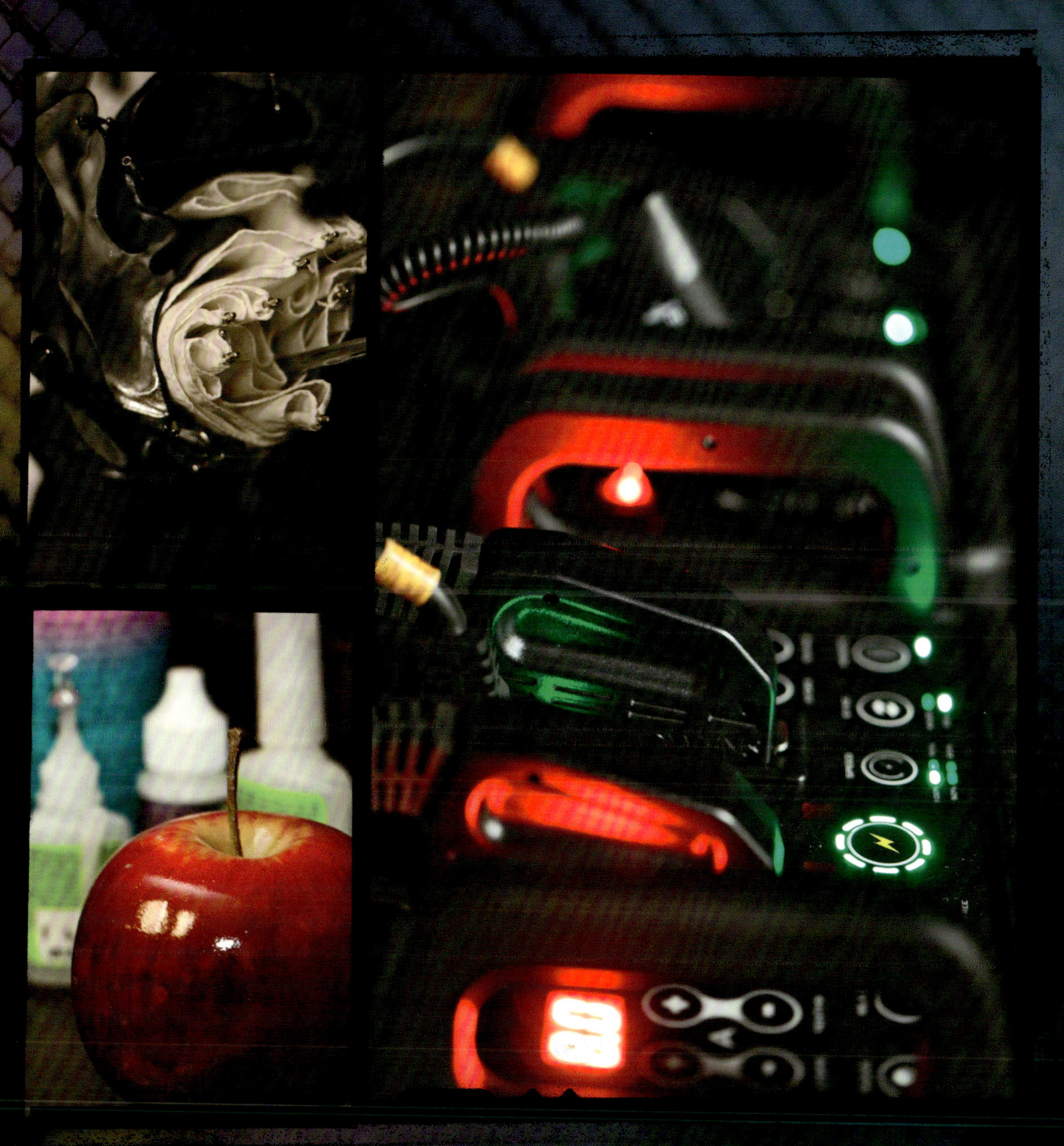

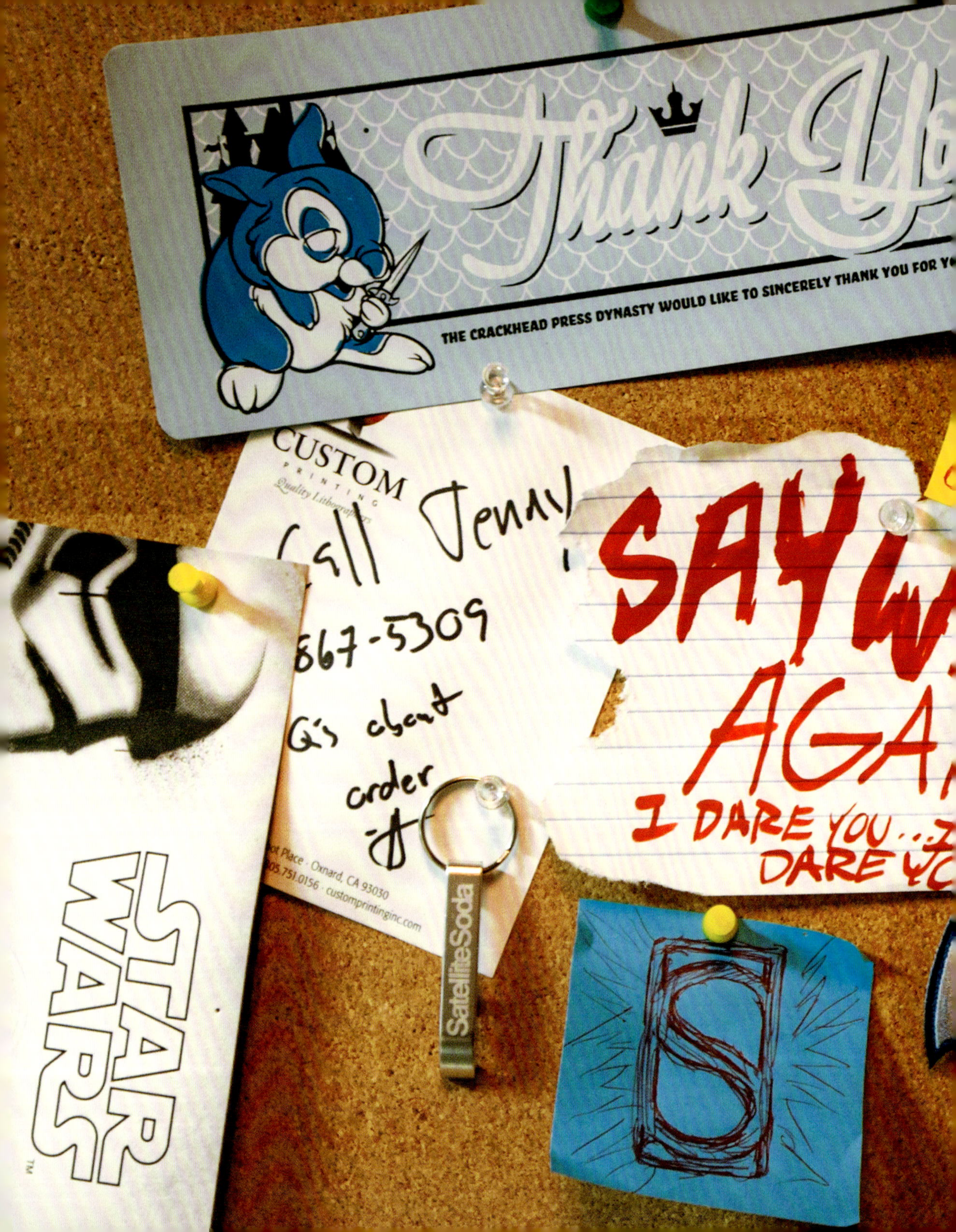

Thank Yo
THE CRACKHEAD PRESS DYNASTY WOULD LIKE TO SINCERELY THANK YOU FOR YO
CUSTOM
PRINTING
Quality Lithographers
Call Jenny
867-5309
Q's about
order
ot Place · Oxnard, CA 93030
05.751.0156 · customprintinginc.com
Satellite Soda
SAY W
AGA
I DARE YOU...I
DARE YO
STAR WARS
TM

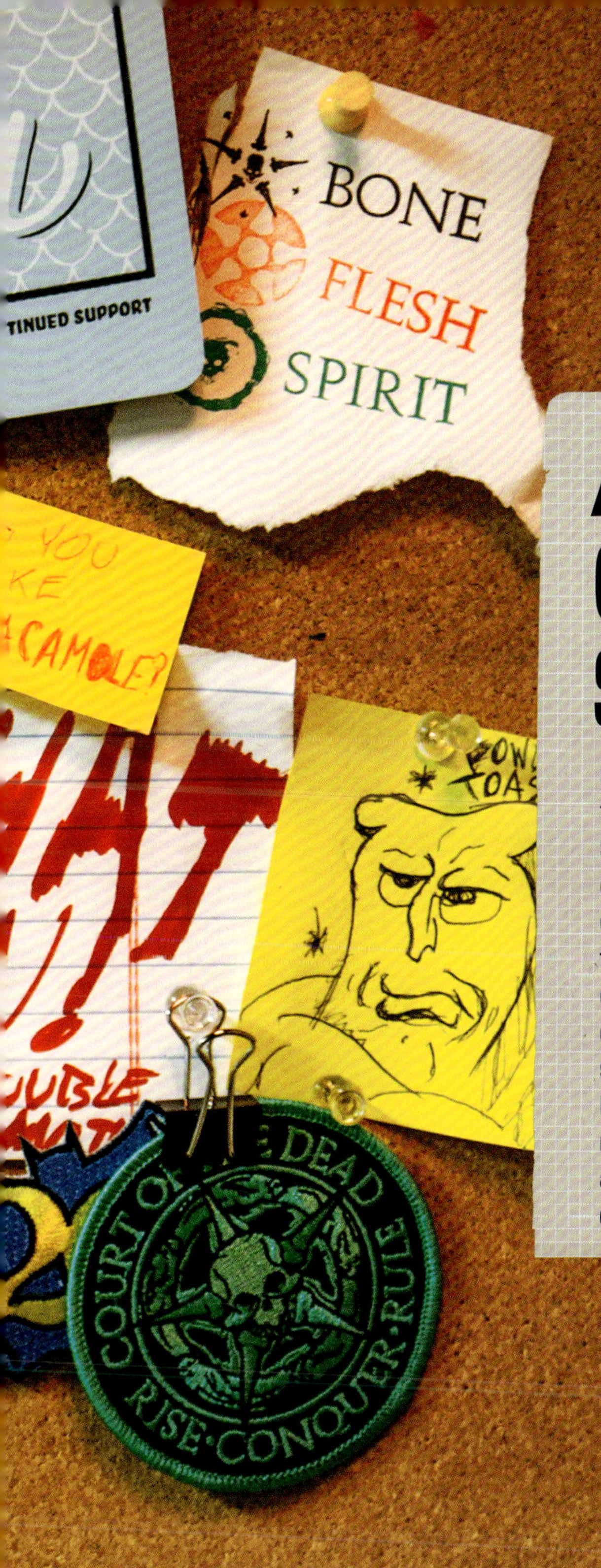

ADMIN & CUSTOMER SERVICE

Sideshow's Administration department is the central nervous system of the company. Shipping and processing schedules are calculated by our farmer's almanac. Our customer service team of scientists and theorists is on the front line ready to assist collectors with all their needs. Marketing campaigns are decided upon by playing high-stakes games of rock-paper-scissors. Our IT team never has fewer than ten hamsters running to ensure our servers stay powered, and our accounting team makes sure that all our overseas manufacturers are paid on time.

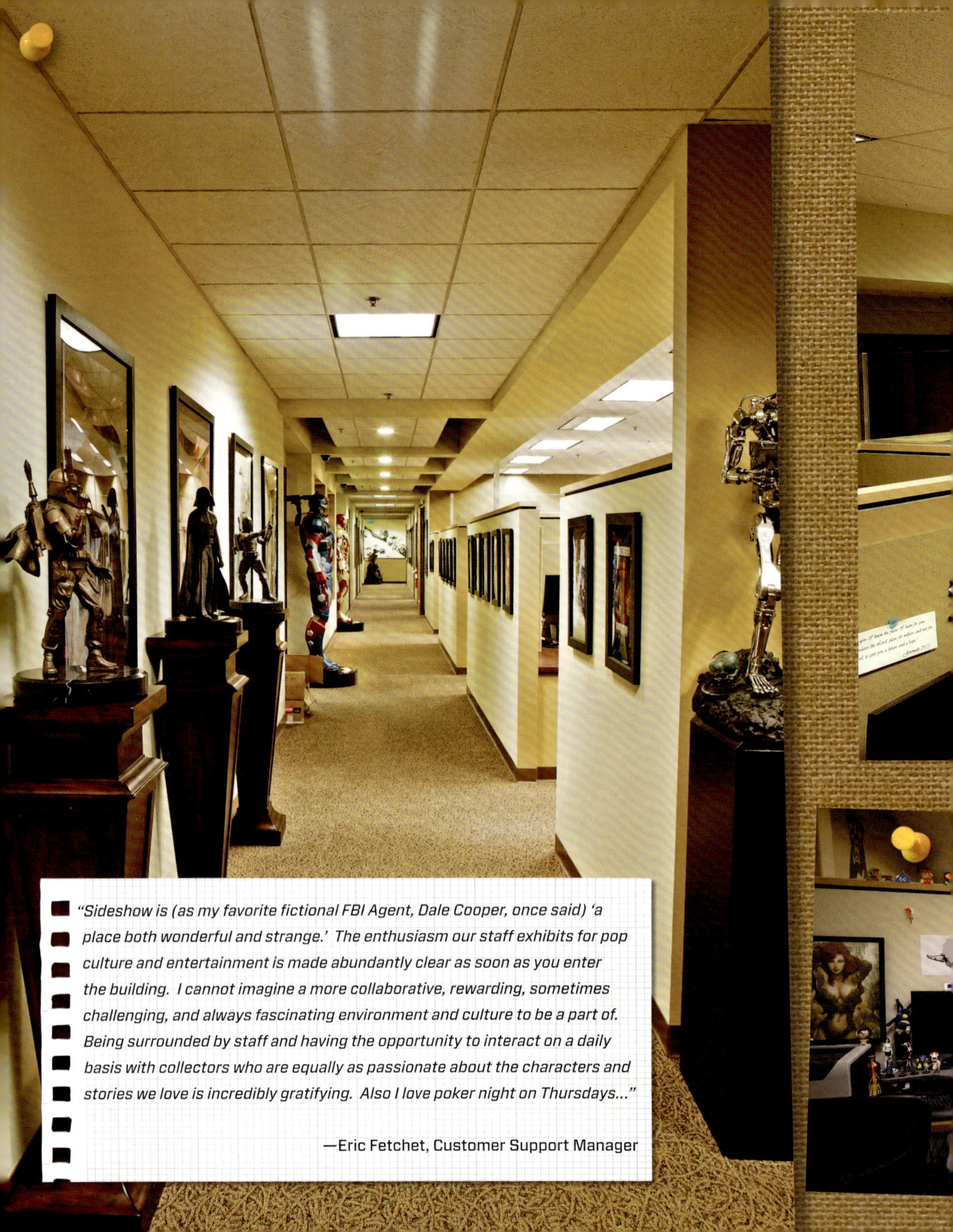

"Sideshow is (as my favorite fictional FBI Agent, Dale Cooper, once said) 'a place both wonderful and strange.' The enthusiasm our staff exhibits for pop culture and entertainment is made abundantly clear as soon as you enter the building. I cannot imagine a more collaborative, rewarding, sometimes challenging, and always fascinating environment and culture to be a part of. Being surrounded by staff and having the opportunity to interact on a daily basis with collectors who are equally as passionate about the characters and stories we love is incredibly gratifying. Also I love poker night on Thursdays..."

—Eric Fetchet, Customer Support Manager

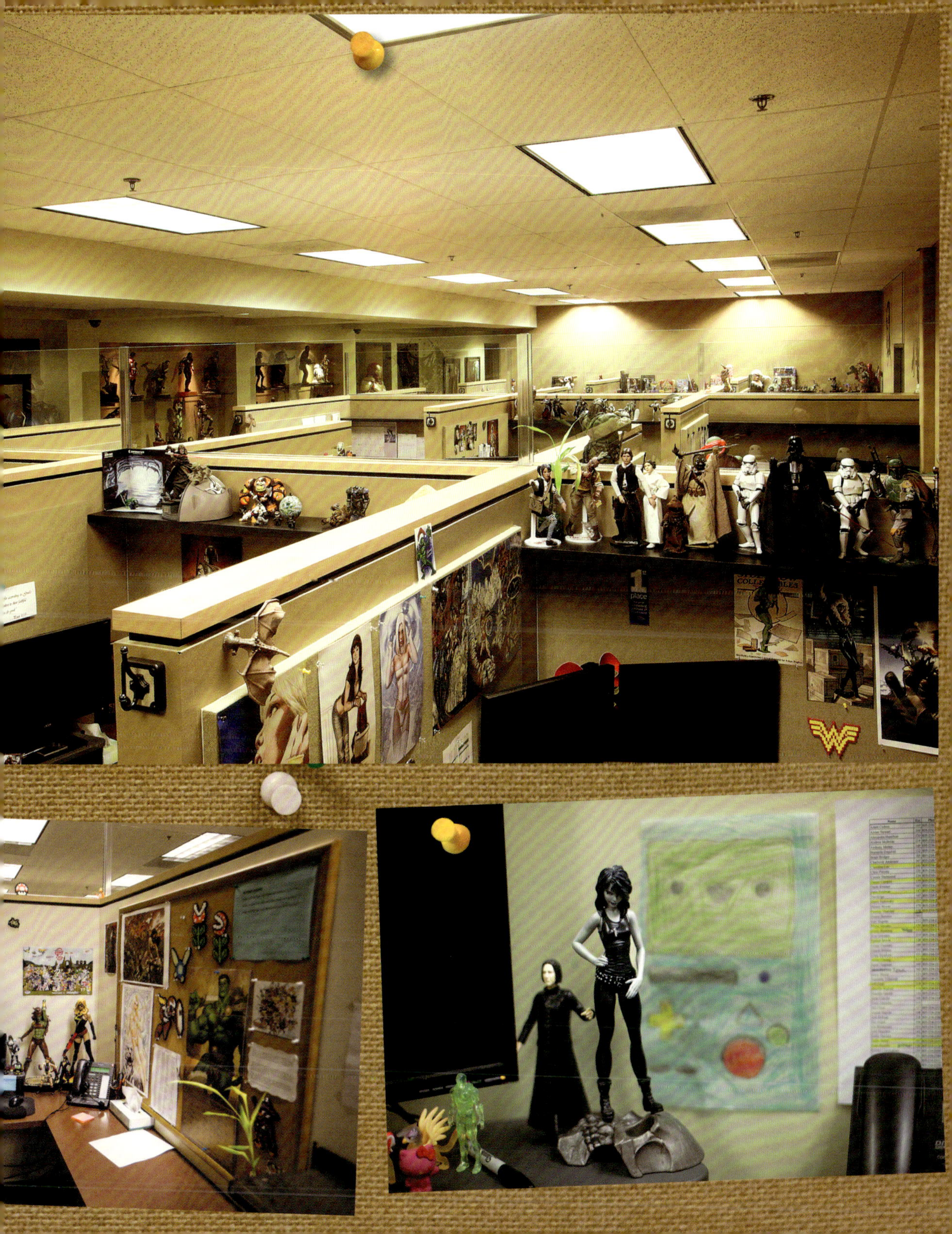

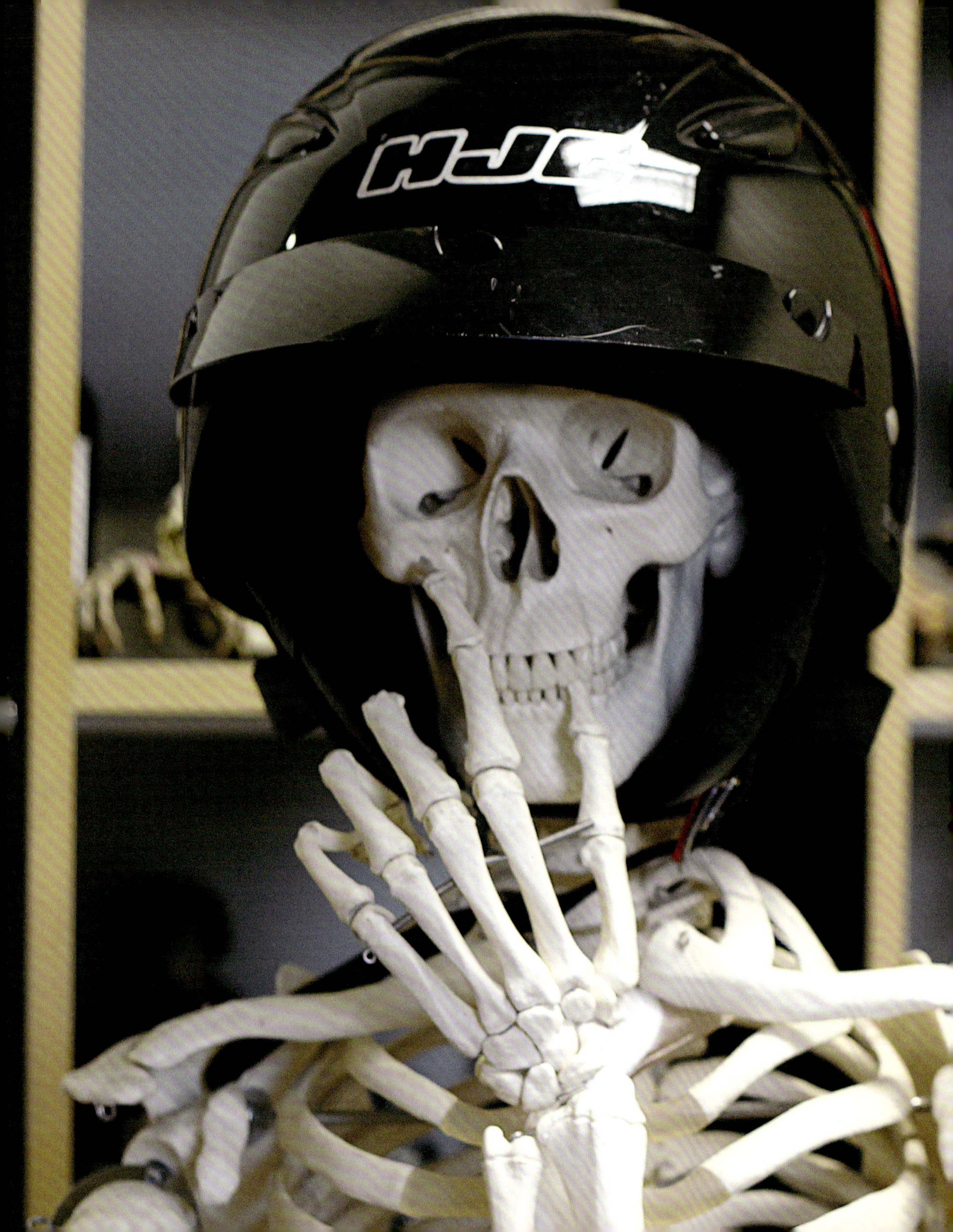

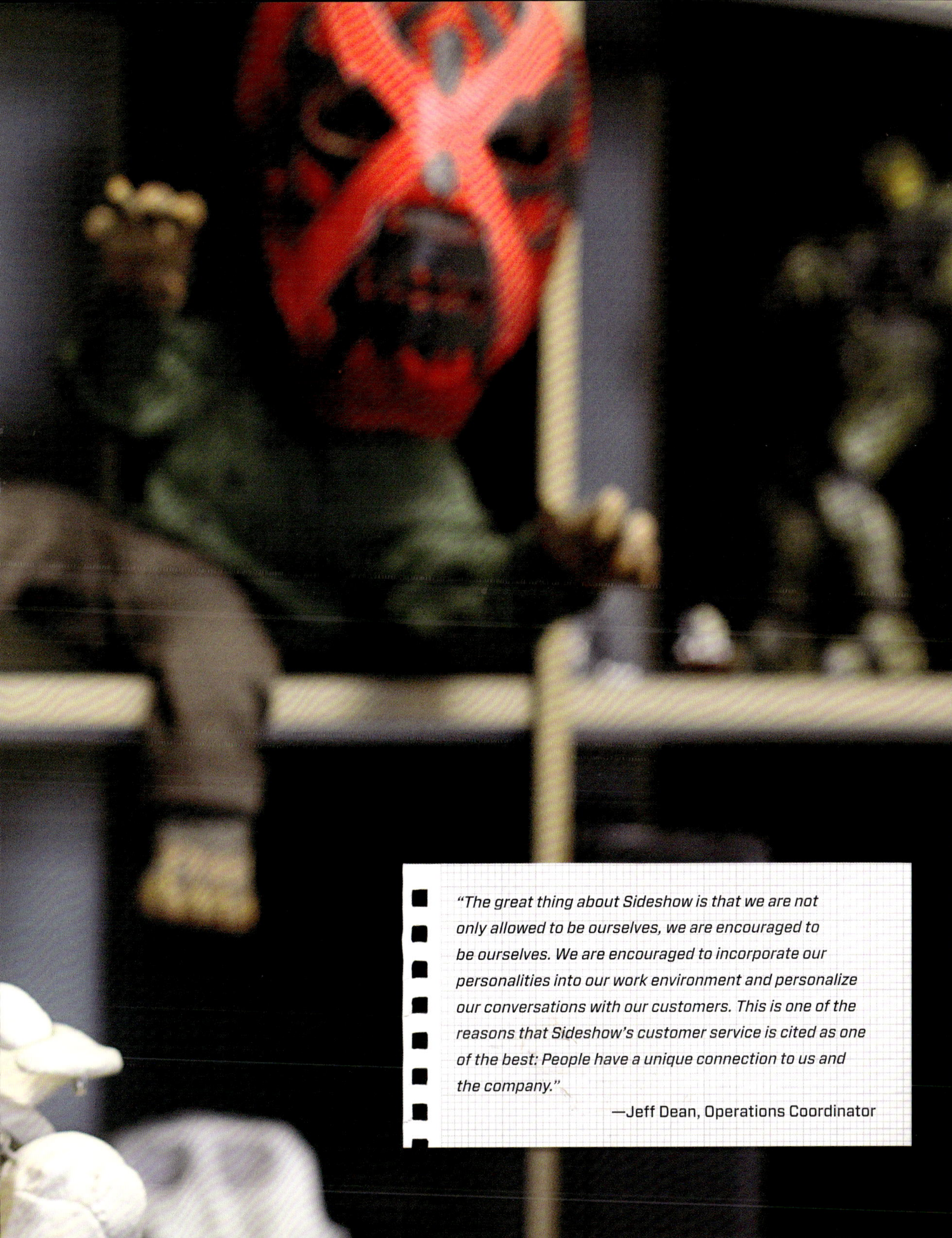

"The great thing about Sideshow is that we are not only allowed to be ourselves, we are encouraged to be ourselves. We are encouraged to incorporate our personalities into our work environment and personalize our conversations with our customers. This is one of the reasons that Sideshow's customer service is cited as one of the best: People have a unique connection to us and the company."

—Jeff Dean, Operations Coordinator

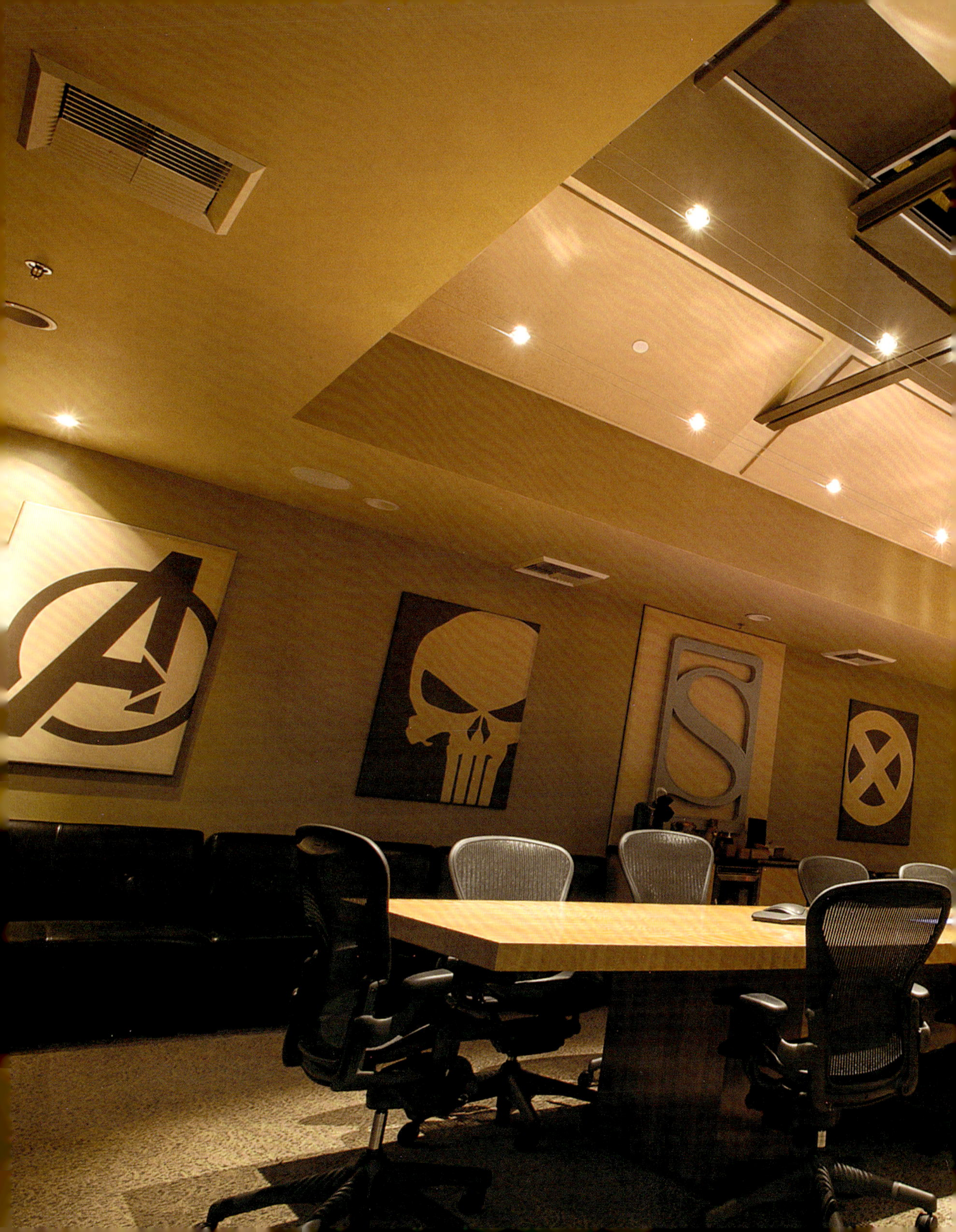

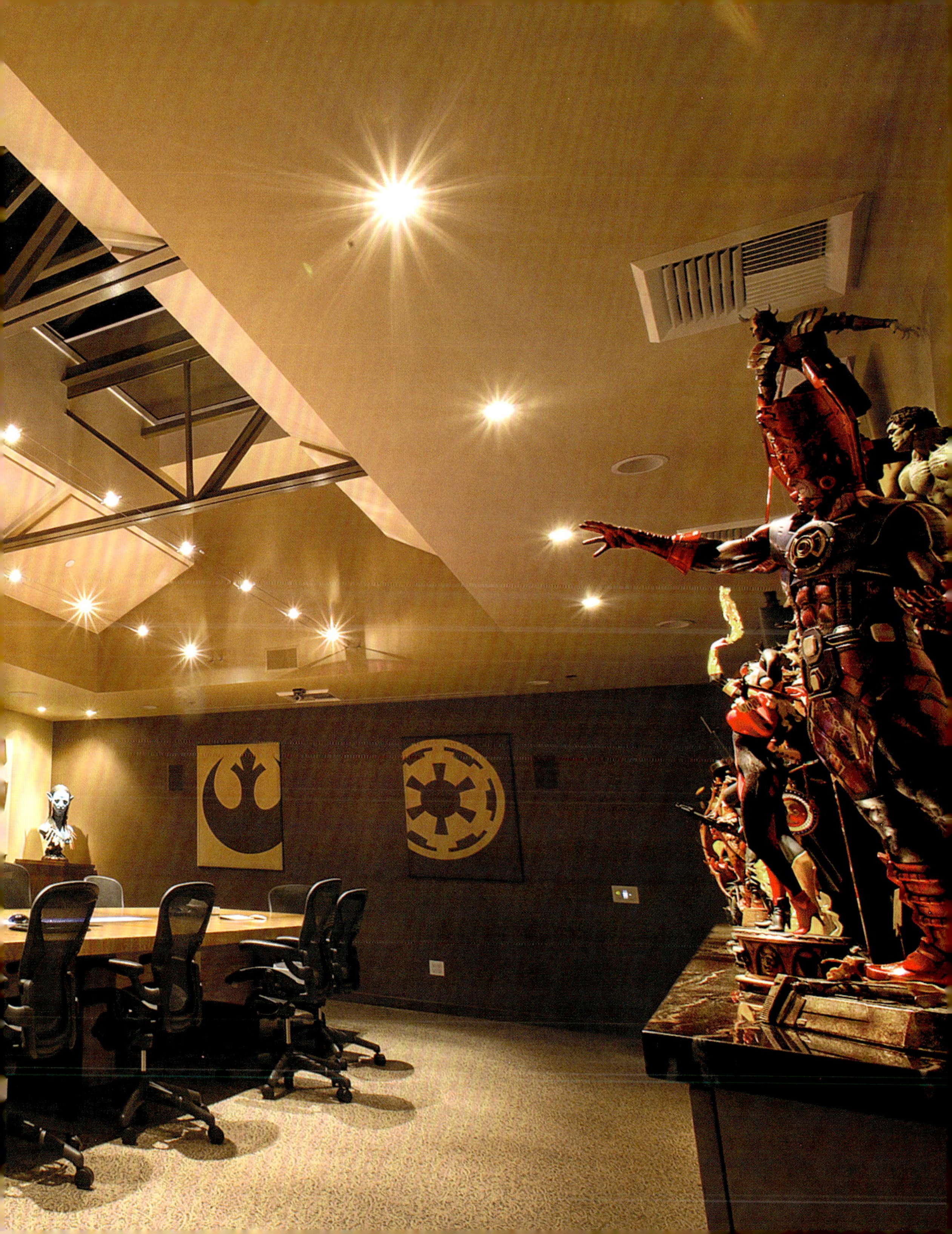

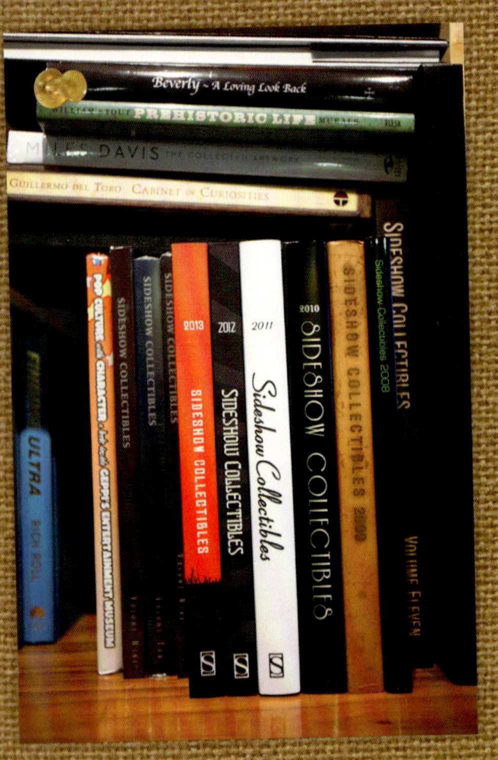

Beverly ~ A Loving Look Back
PREHISTORIC LIFE MURALS
MILES DAVIS THE COLLECTED ARTWORK
GUILLERMO DEL TORO CABINET OF CURIOSITIES
ULTRA
POP CULTURE with CHARACTER a look inside GEPPI'S ENTERTAINMENT MUSEUM
SIDESHOW COLLECTIBLES
SIDESHOW COLLECTIBLES
2013 SIDESHOW COLLECTIBLES
2012 SIDESHOW COLLECTIBLES
2011 Sideshow Collectibles
2010 SIDESHOW COLLECTIBLES
SIDESHOW COLLECTIBLES 2009
Sideshow Collectibles 2008
SIDESHOW COLLECTIBLES
VOLUME ELEVEN

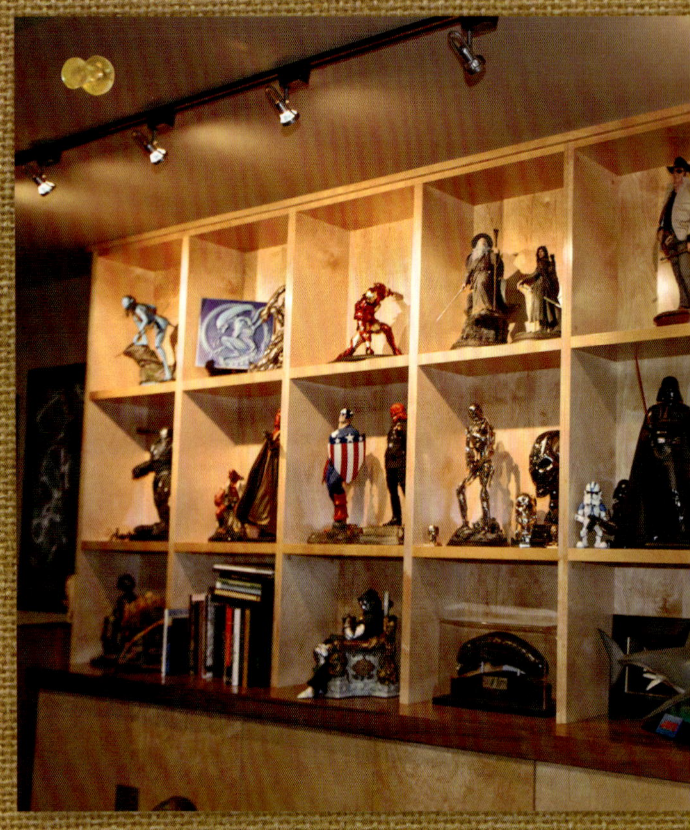

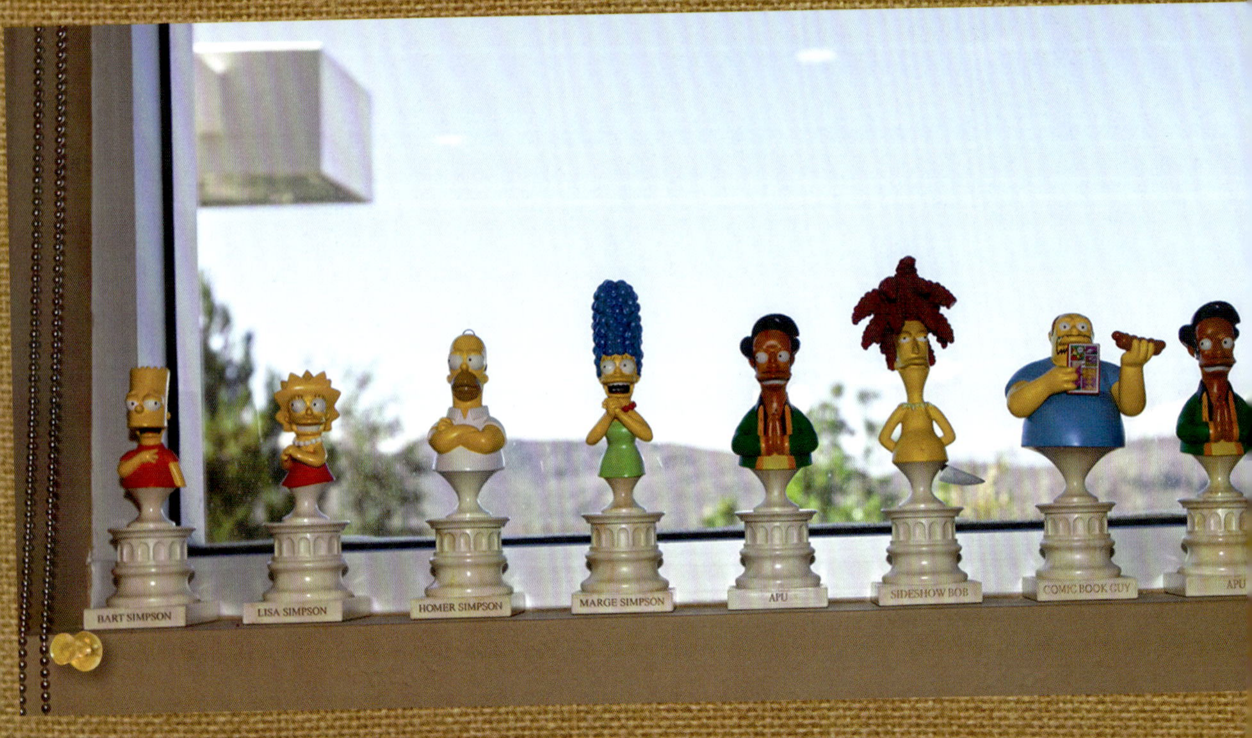

BART SIMPSON
LISA SIMPSON
HOMER SIMPSON
MARGE SIMPSON
APU
SIDESHOW BOB
COMIC BOOK GUY
APU

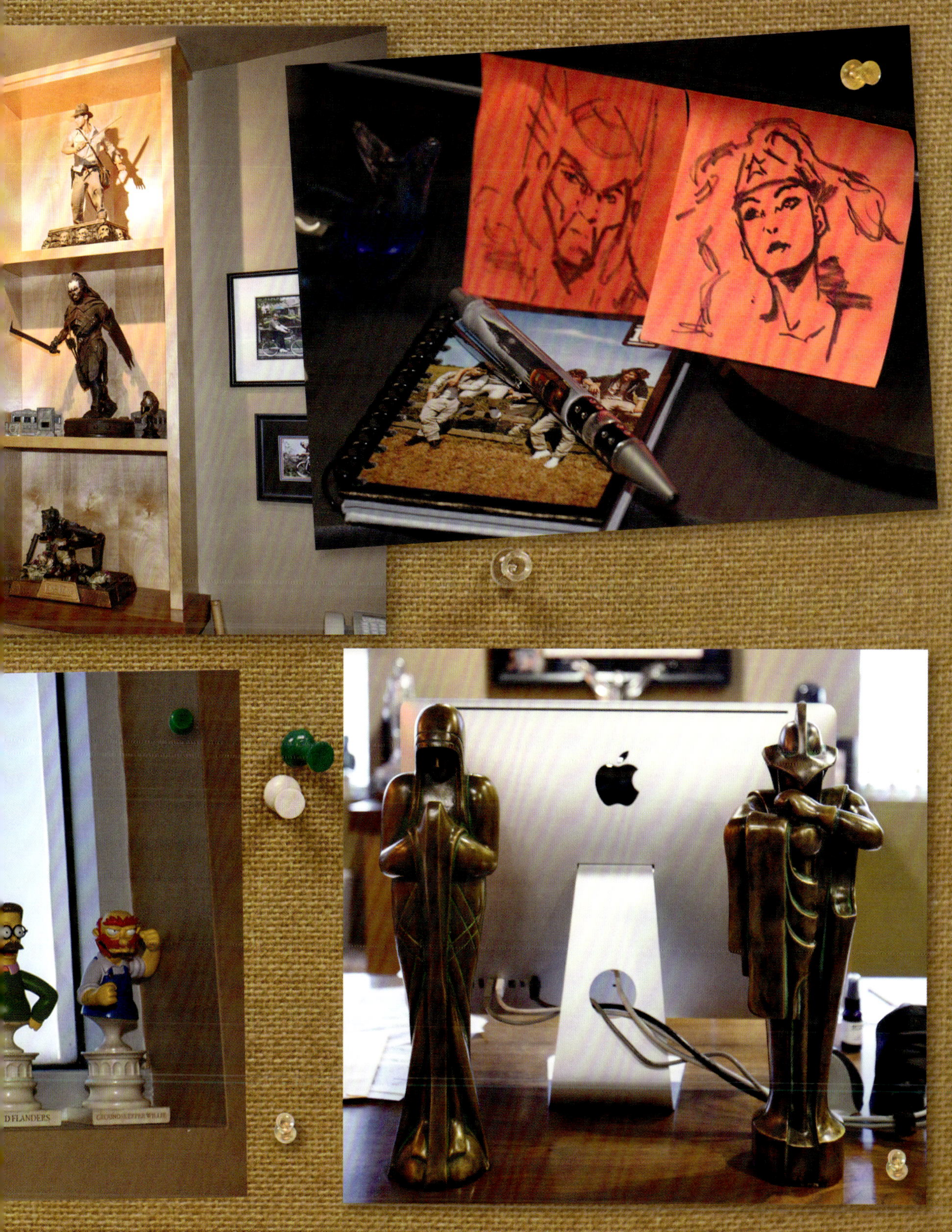

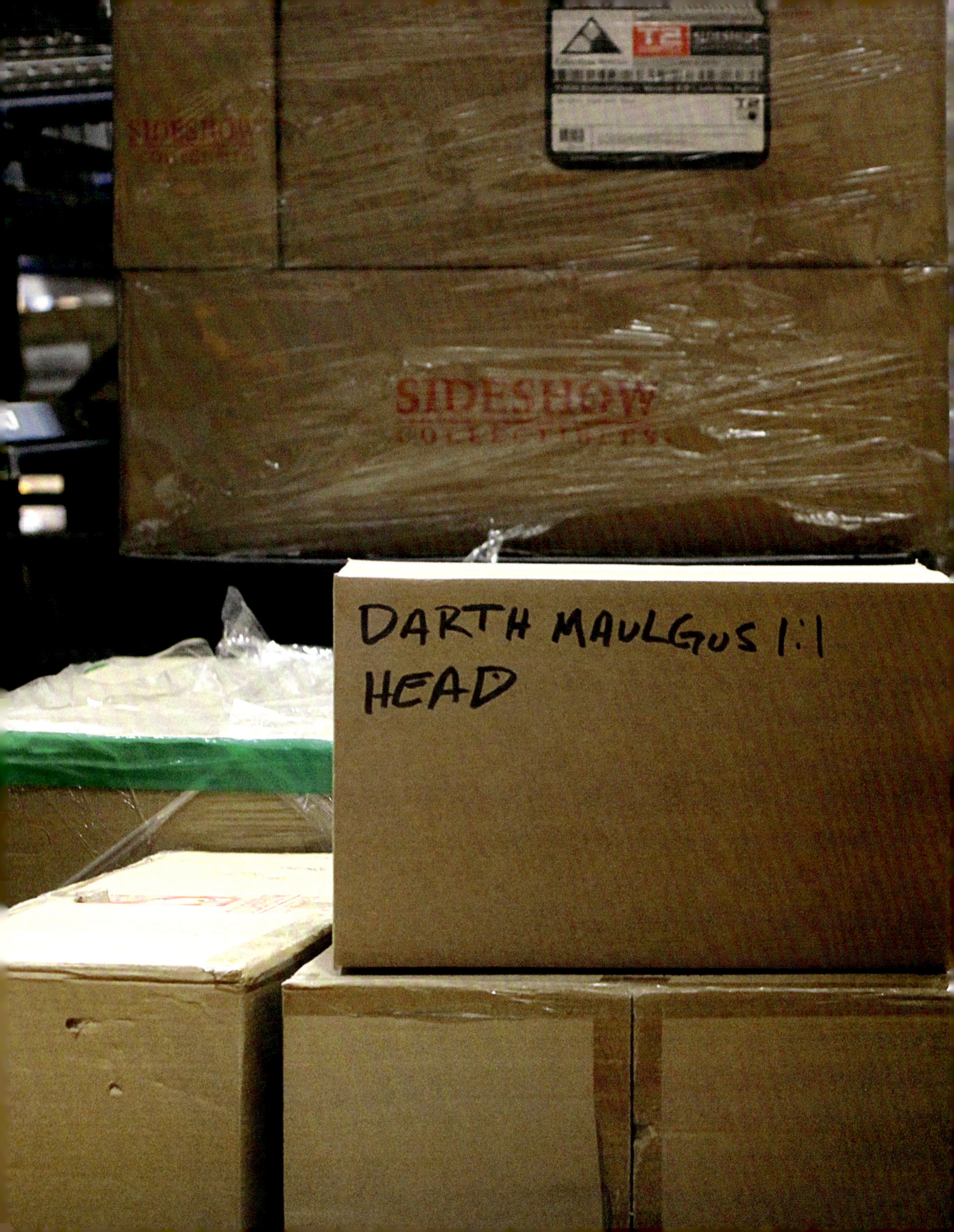
SIDESHOW
SIDESHOW
DARTH MAULGUS 1:1
HEAD

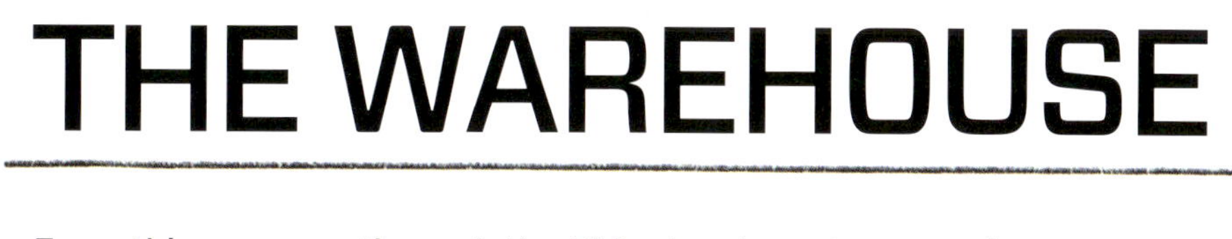

THE WAREHOUSE

Everything passes through the Shipping department on its way to or from the factories, the outside vendors, and our customers. It's the last stop in the product cycle—invoicing the orders and shipping customers their product. But it's also a support department providing a wide variety of services to the entire company, such as helping resolve customer complaints, overseeing quality control of goods, shipping personal packages, assembling furniture, and assisting with party setup and teardown, right down to moving office personnel from one office to the next as well as from one residence to the next. The Shipping team strikes a nice balance between having fun at work and being extremely productive. This year the department will not only ship well over a hundred thousand packages, it will also tell plenty of daily jokes, play the best and most varied selection of music in the building, and continue the tradition of Team Shipping dominating at poker.

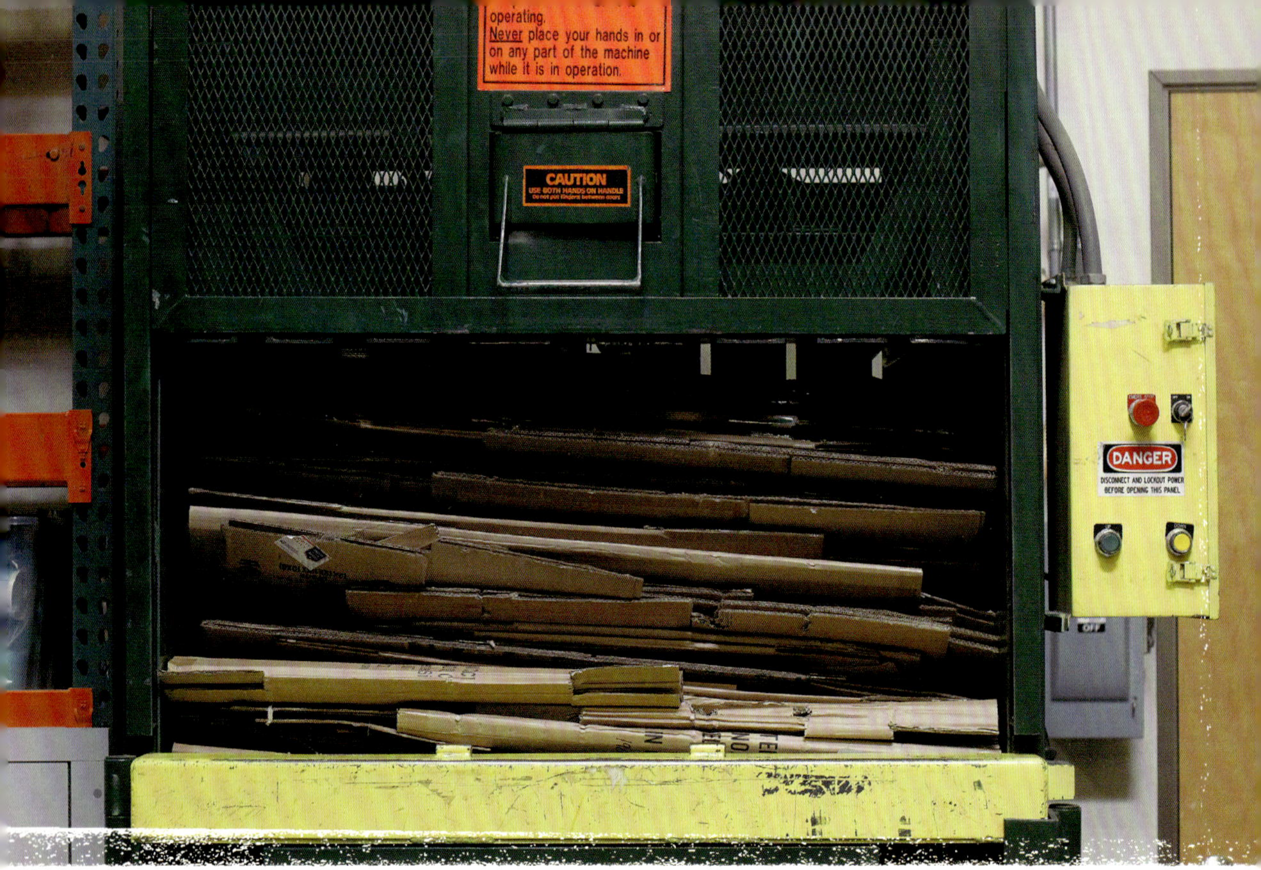

operating.
Never place your hands in or on any part of the machine while it is in operation.
CAUTION
USE BOTH HANDS ON HANDLE
Do not put fingers between doors
DANGER
DISCONNECT AND LOCKOUT POWER
BEFORE OPENING THIS PANEL
OFF

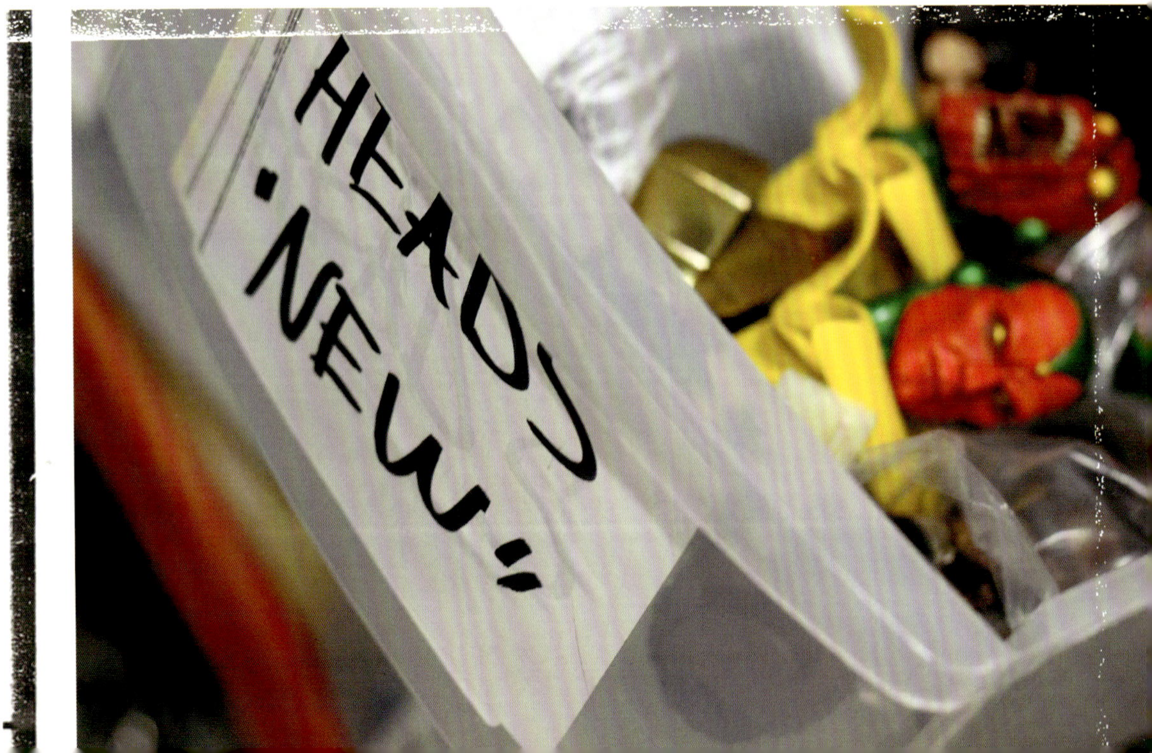

HEADS
.NEW"

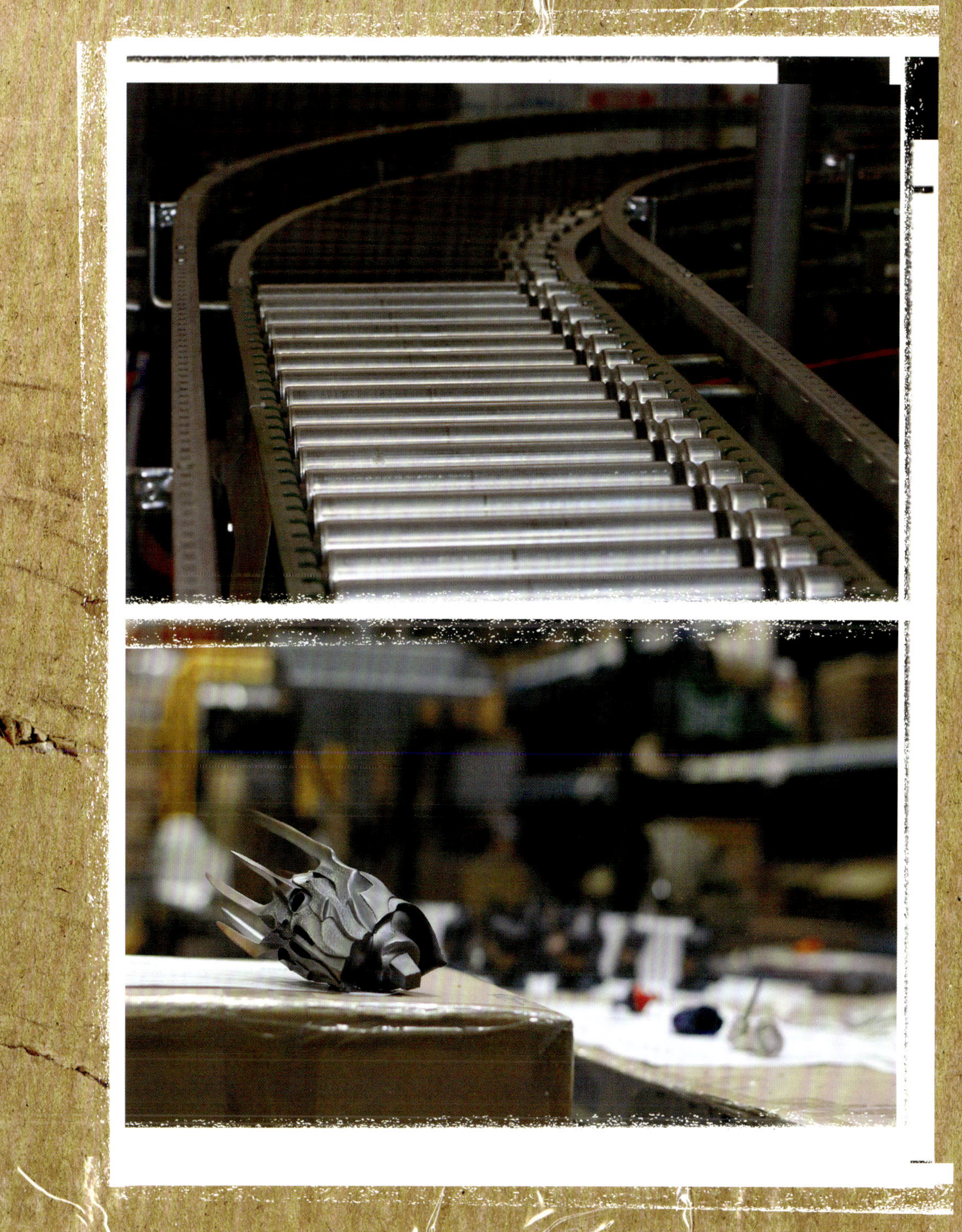

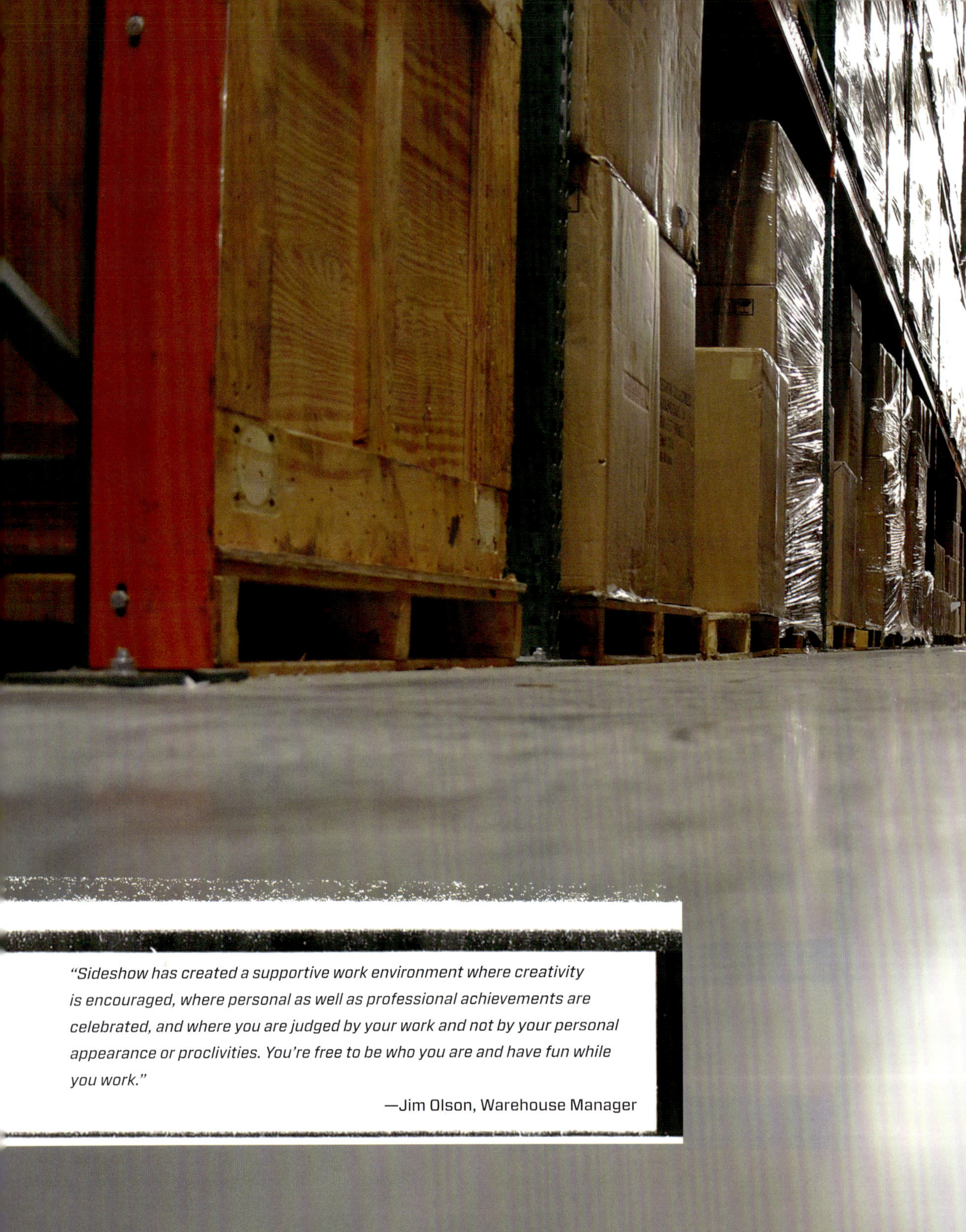

"Sideshow has created a supportive work environment where creativity is encouraged, where personal as well as professional achievements are celebrated, and where you are judged by your work and not by your personal appearance or proclivities. You're free to be who you are and have fun while you work."

—Jim Olson, Warehouse Manager

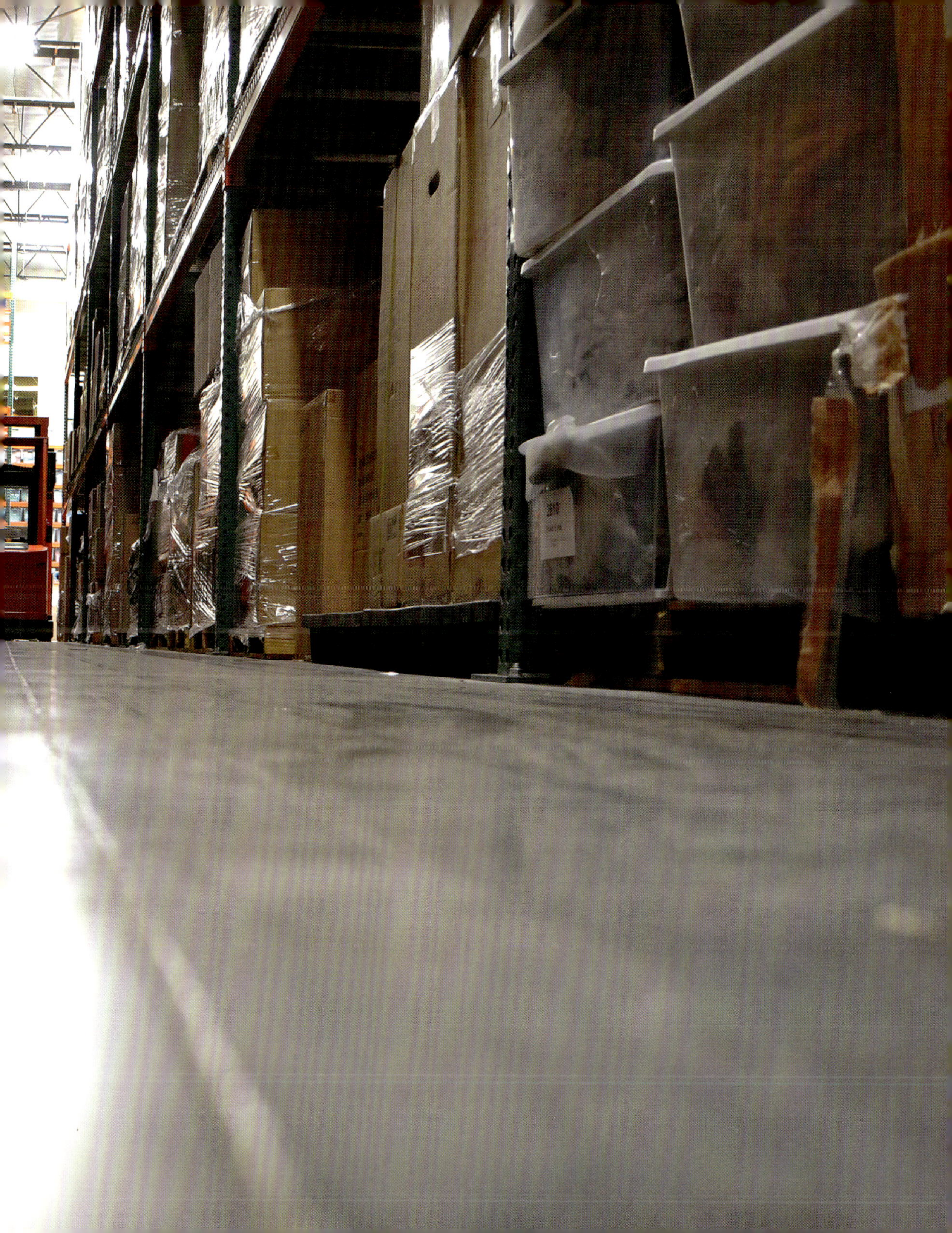

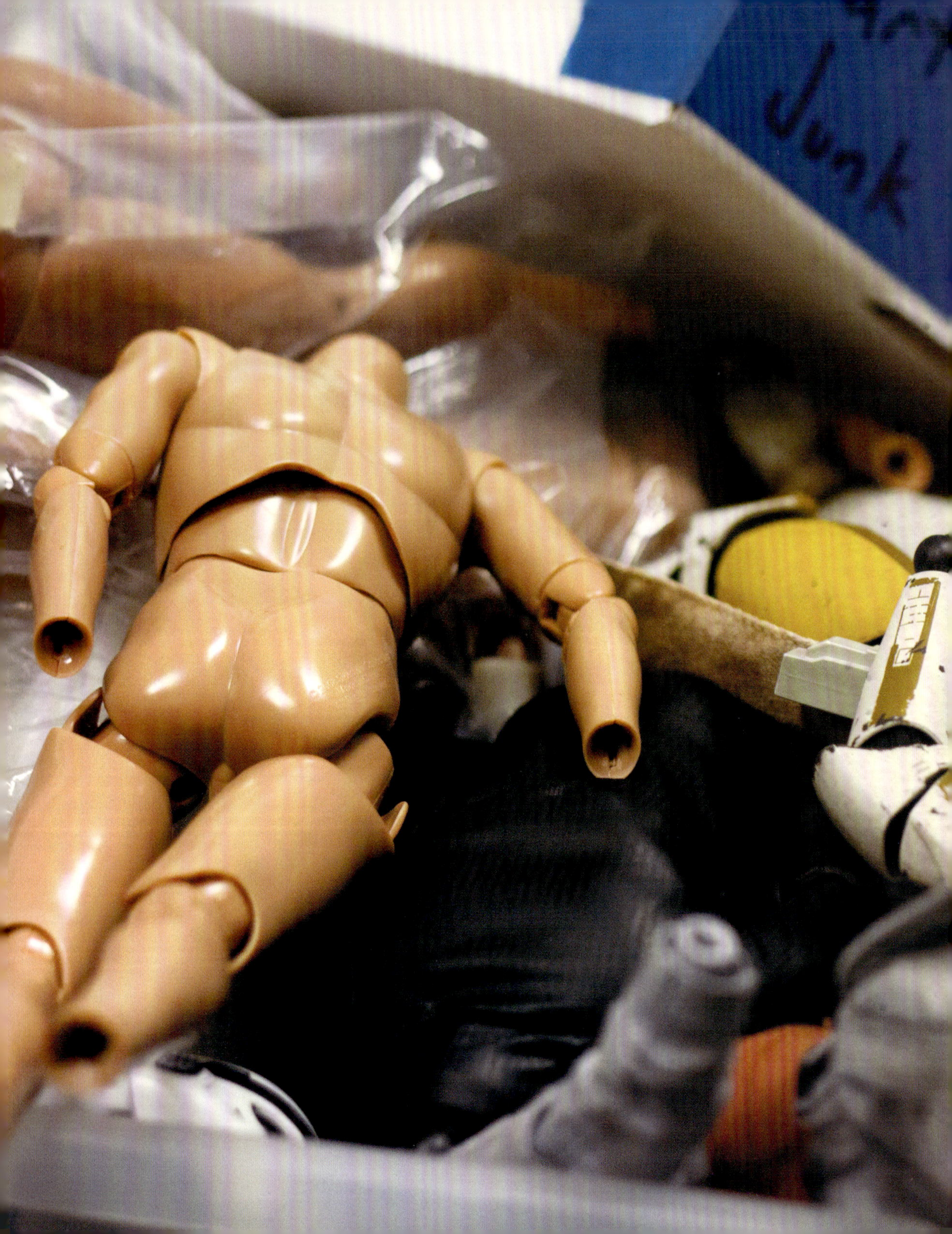
Junk

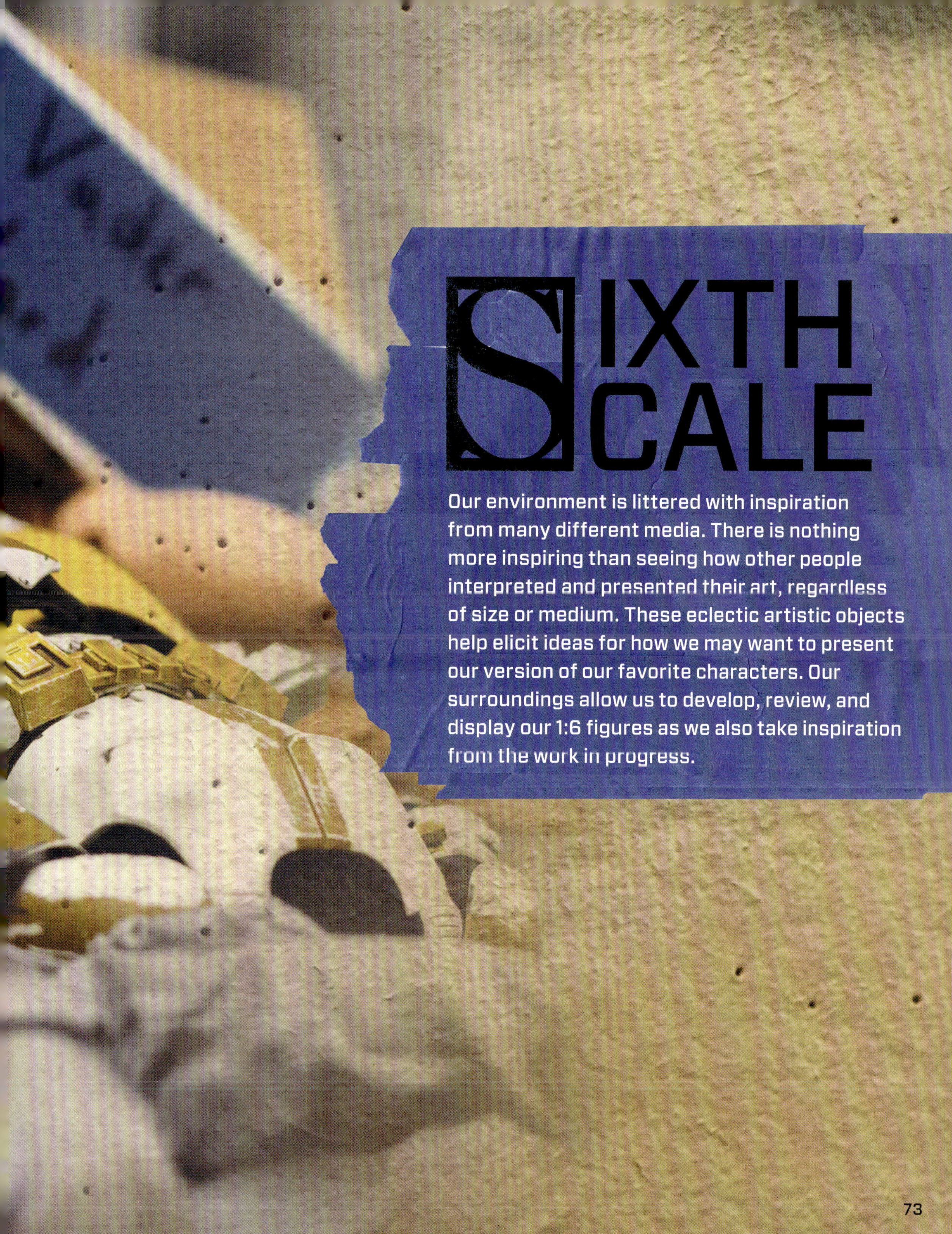

SIXTH SCALE

Our environment is littered with inspiration from many different media. There is nothing more inspiring than seeing how other people interpreted and presented their art, regardless of size or medium. These eclectic artistic objects help elicit ideas for how we may want to present our version of our favorite characters. Our surroundings allow us to develop, review, and display our 1:6 figures as we also take inspiration from the work in progress.

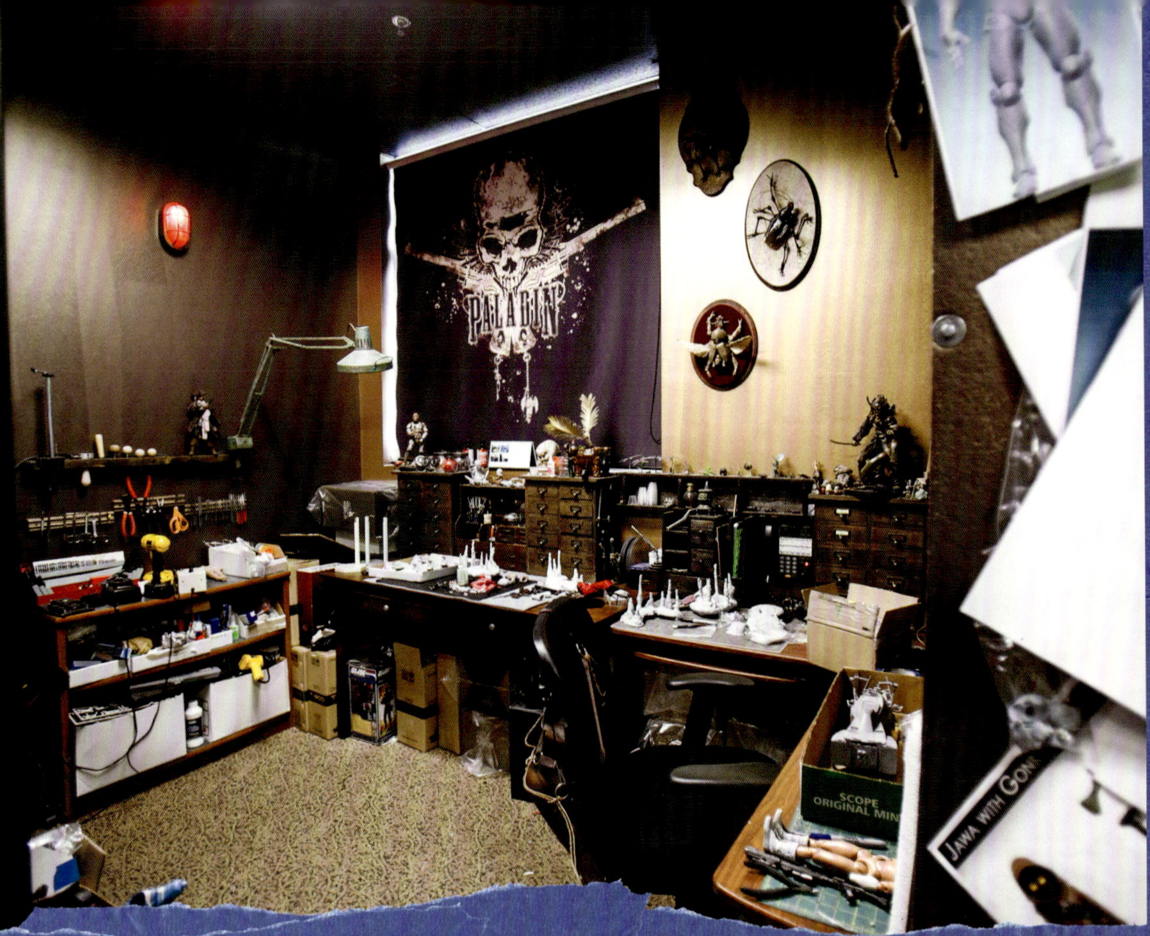

PALADIN
SCOPE
ORIGINAL MIN
JAWA WITH GONE

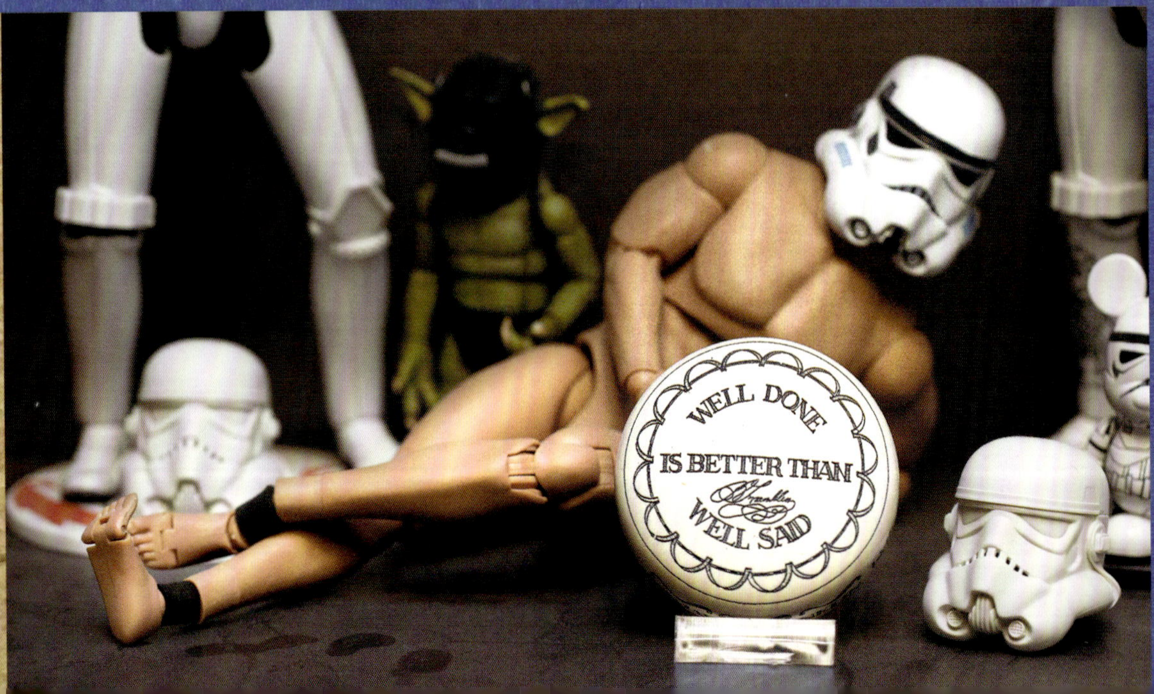

WELL DONE
IS BETTER THAN
WELL SAID

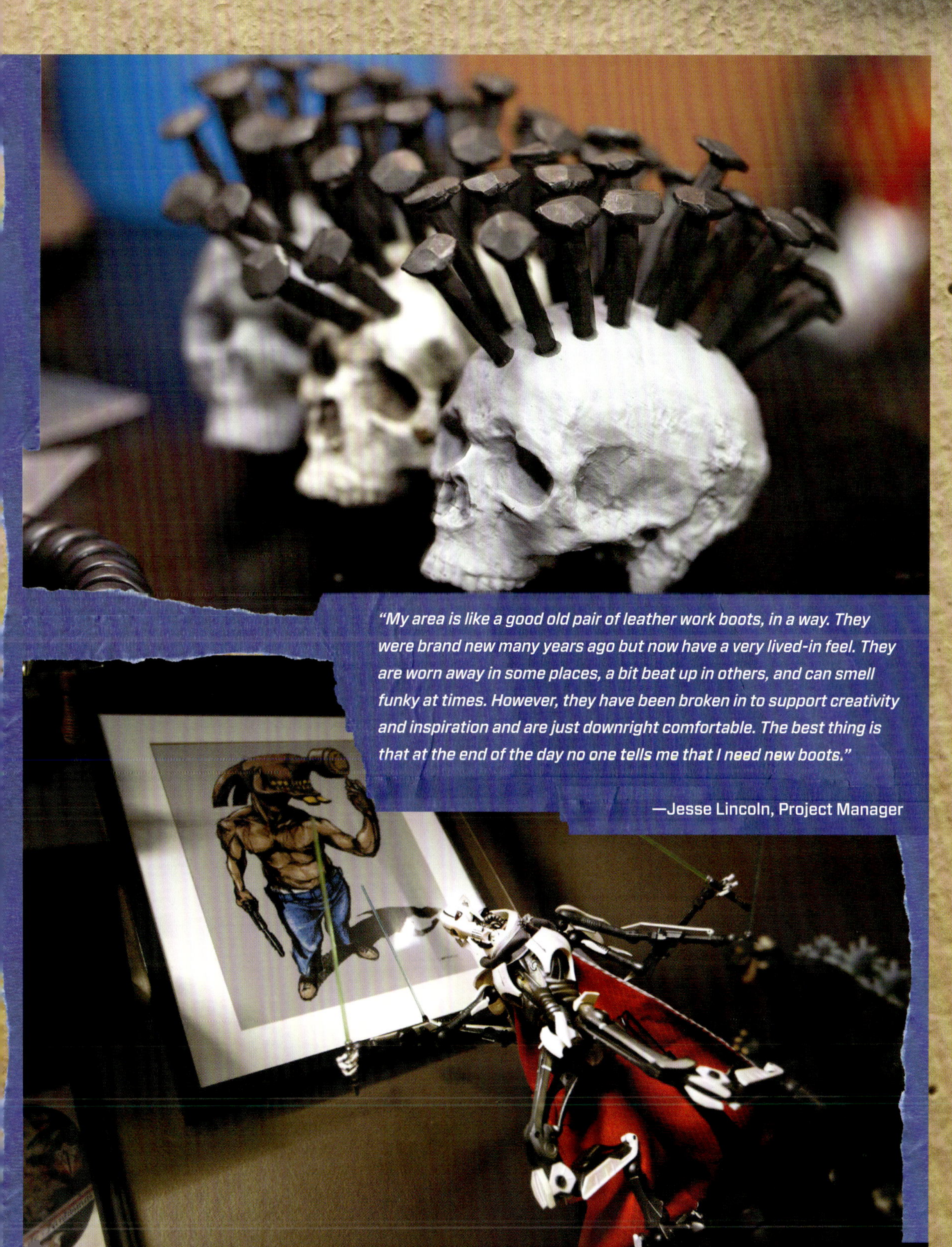

"My area is like a good old pair of leather work boots, in a way. They were brand new many years ago but now have a very lived-in feel. They are worn away in some places, a bit beat up in others, and can smell funky at times. However, they have been broken in to support creativity and inspiration and are just downright comfortable. The best thing is that at the end of the day no one tells me that I need new boots."

—Jesse Lincoln, Project Manager

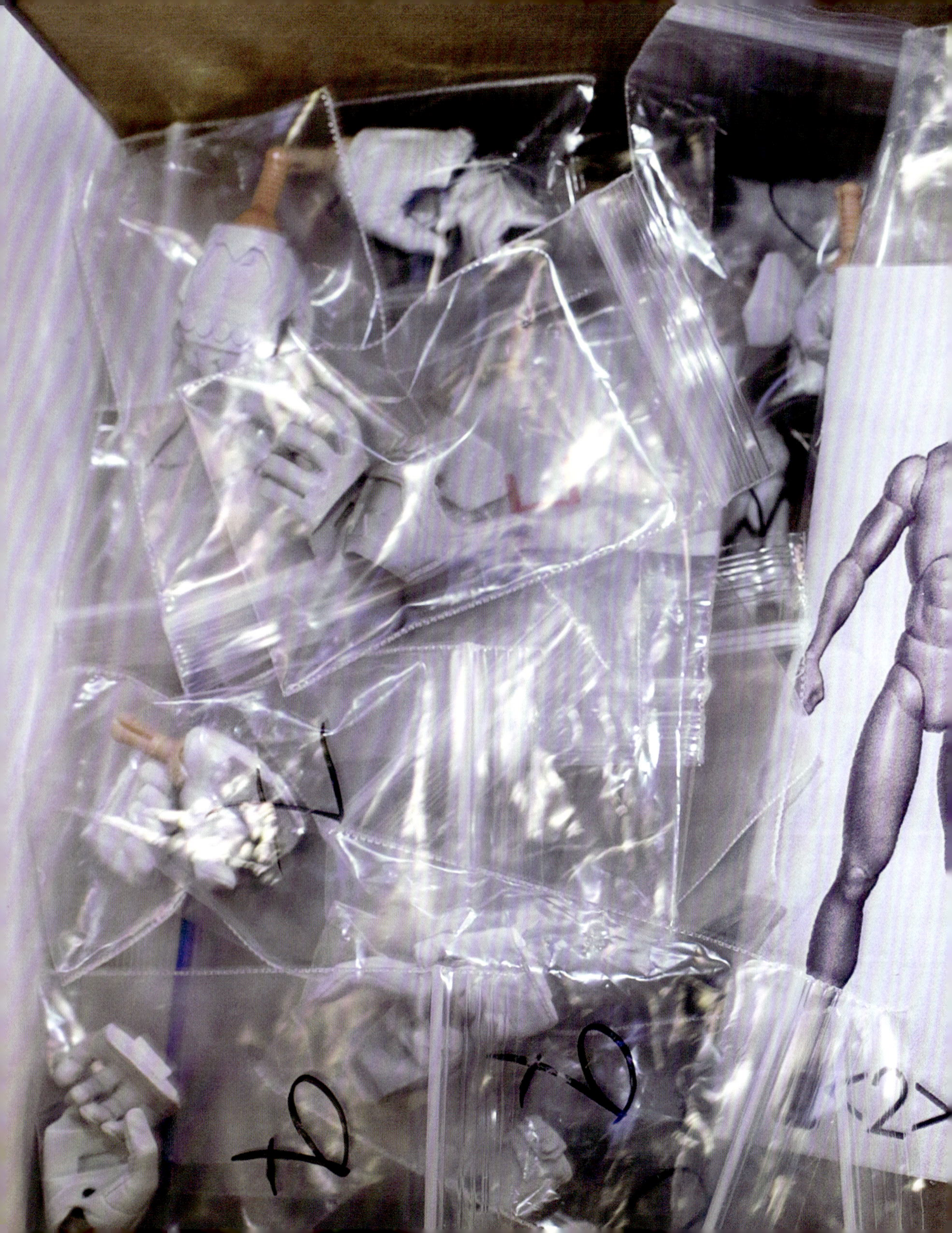

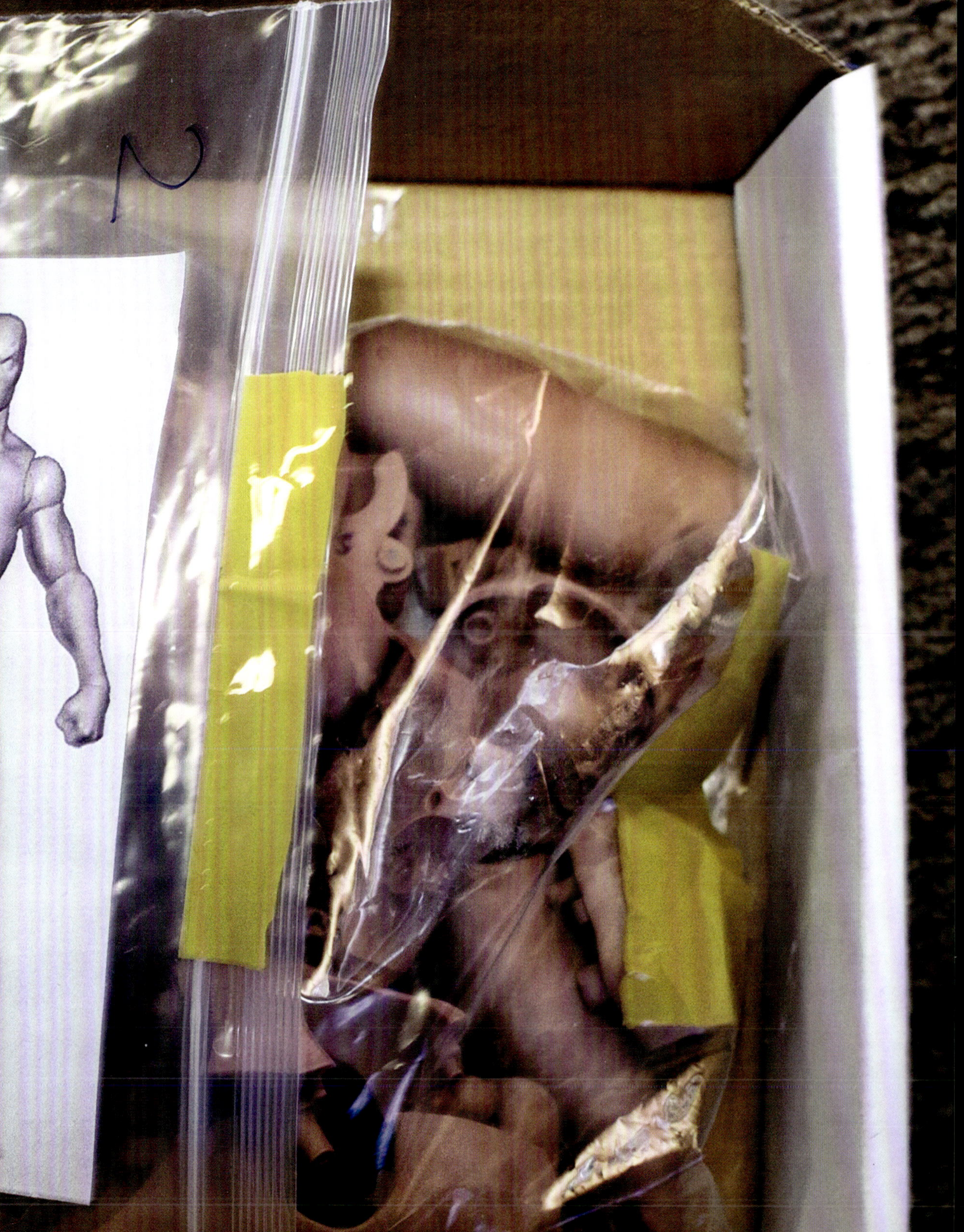

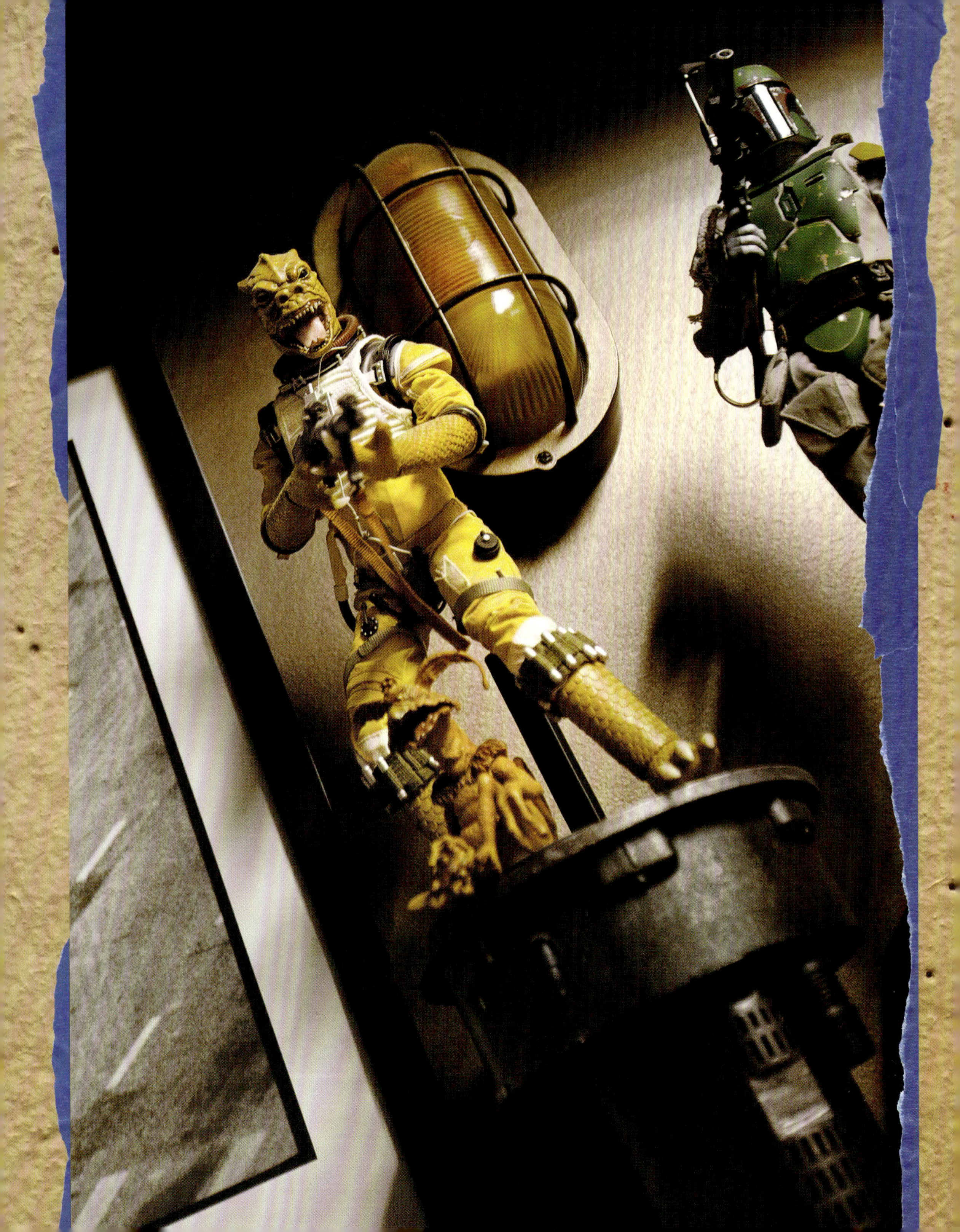

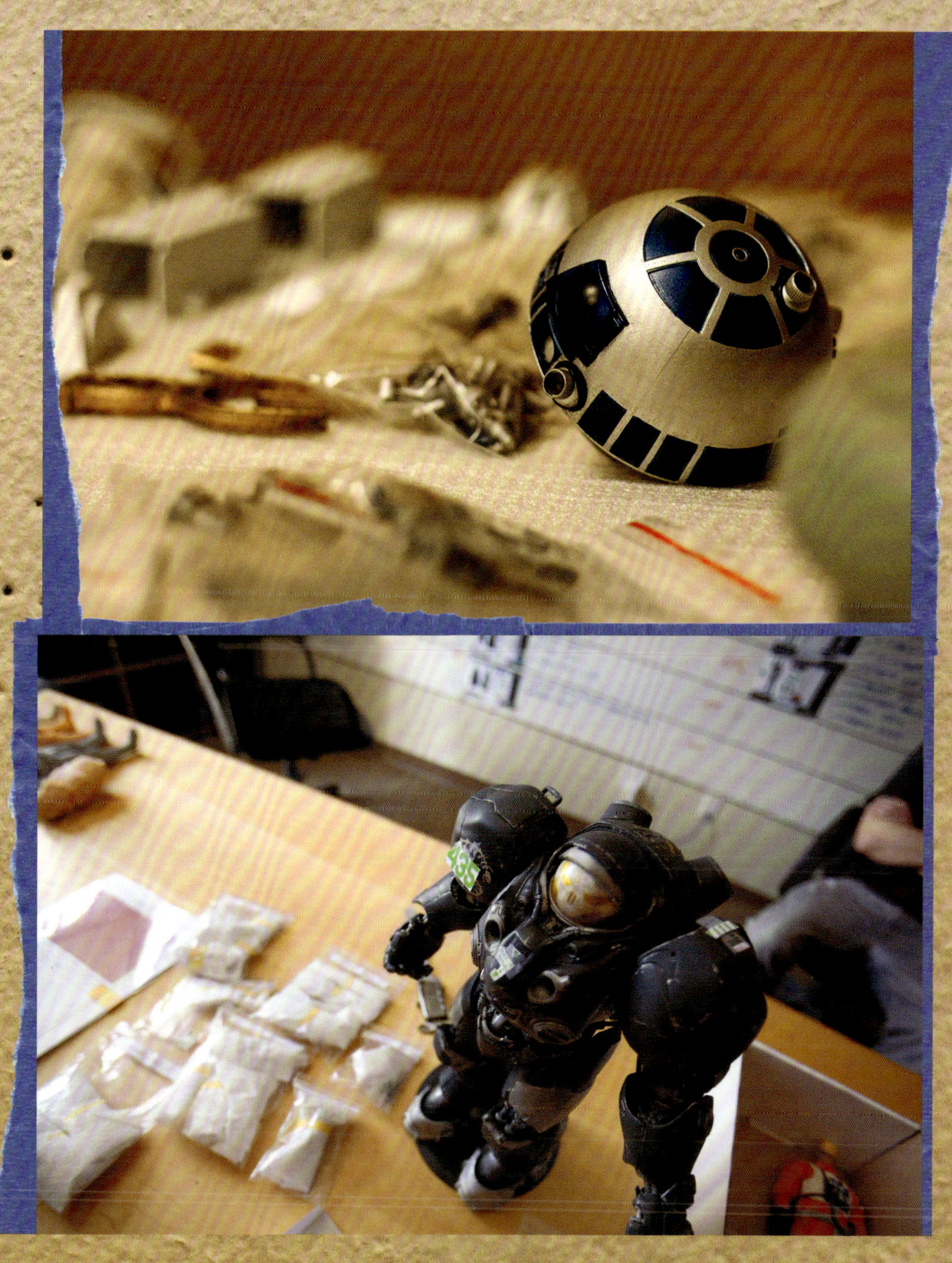

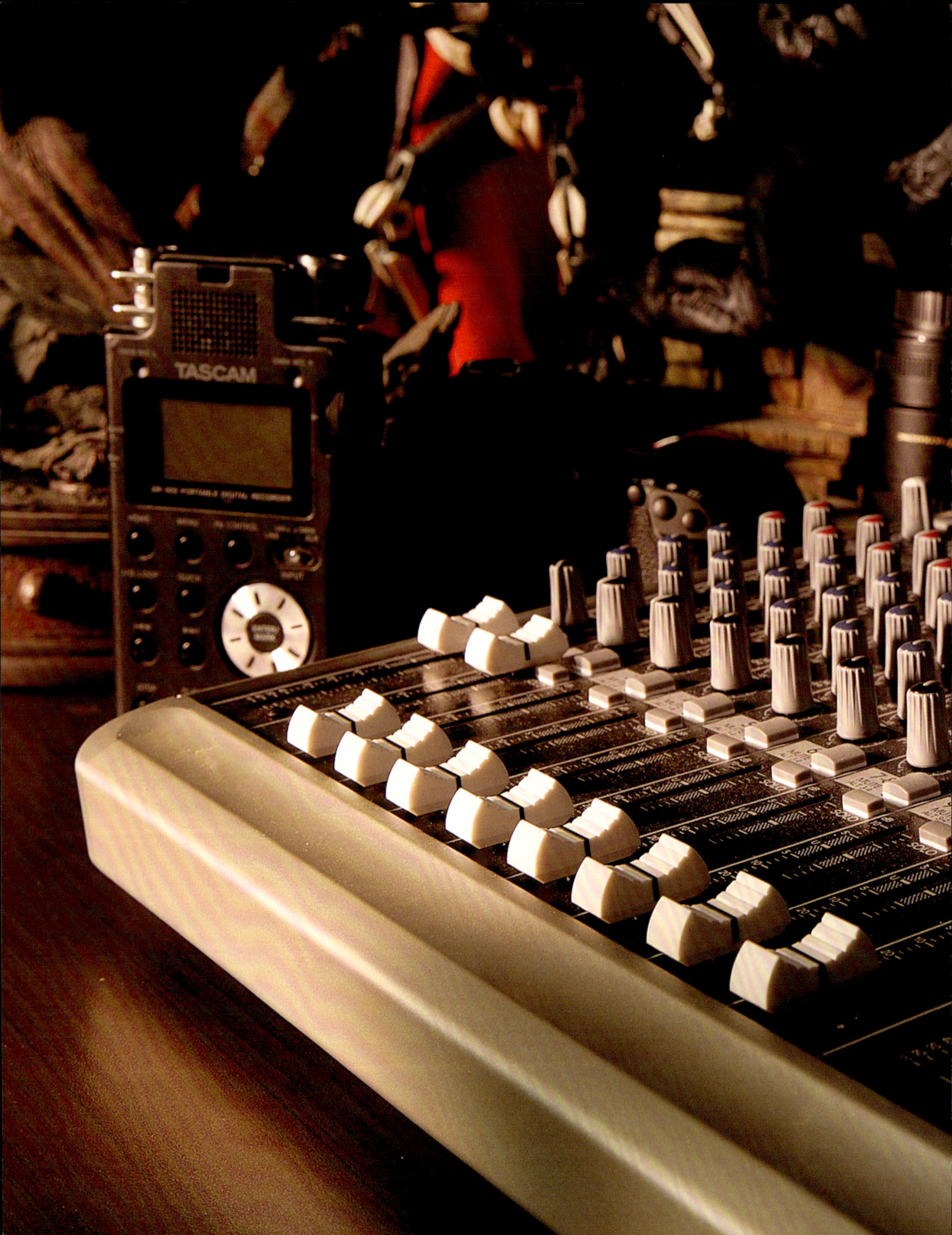
TASCAM

MULTIMEDIA

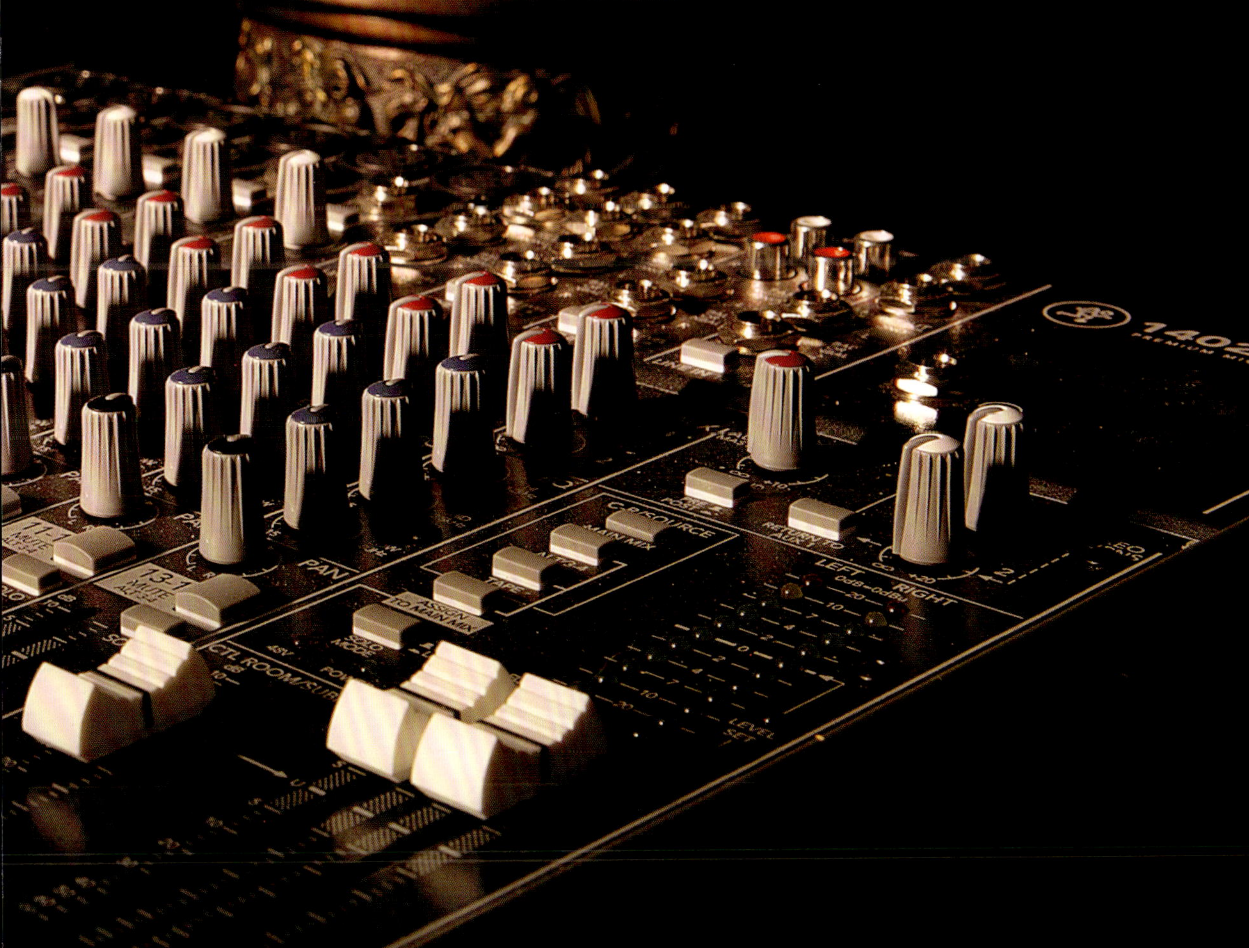

Composed of animators, editors, and cinematographers, Multimedia's role is to give audiences a glimpse behind the curtain here at Sideshow. We take viewers well beyond the confines of our office and give them a peek into the lives of artists, collectors, and many of the visionaries behind popular culture. As a team, we know that good storytelling is the key to success, and we plan on sticking to that motto. So take a seat, grab some popcorn, and enjoy.

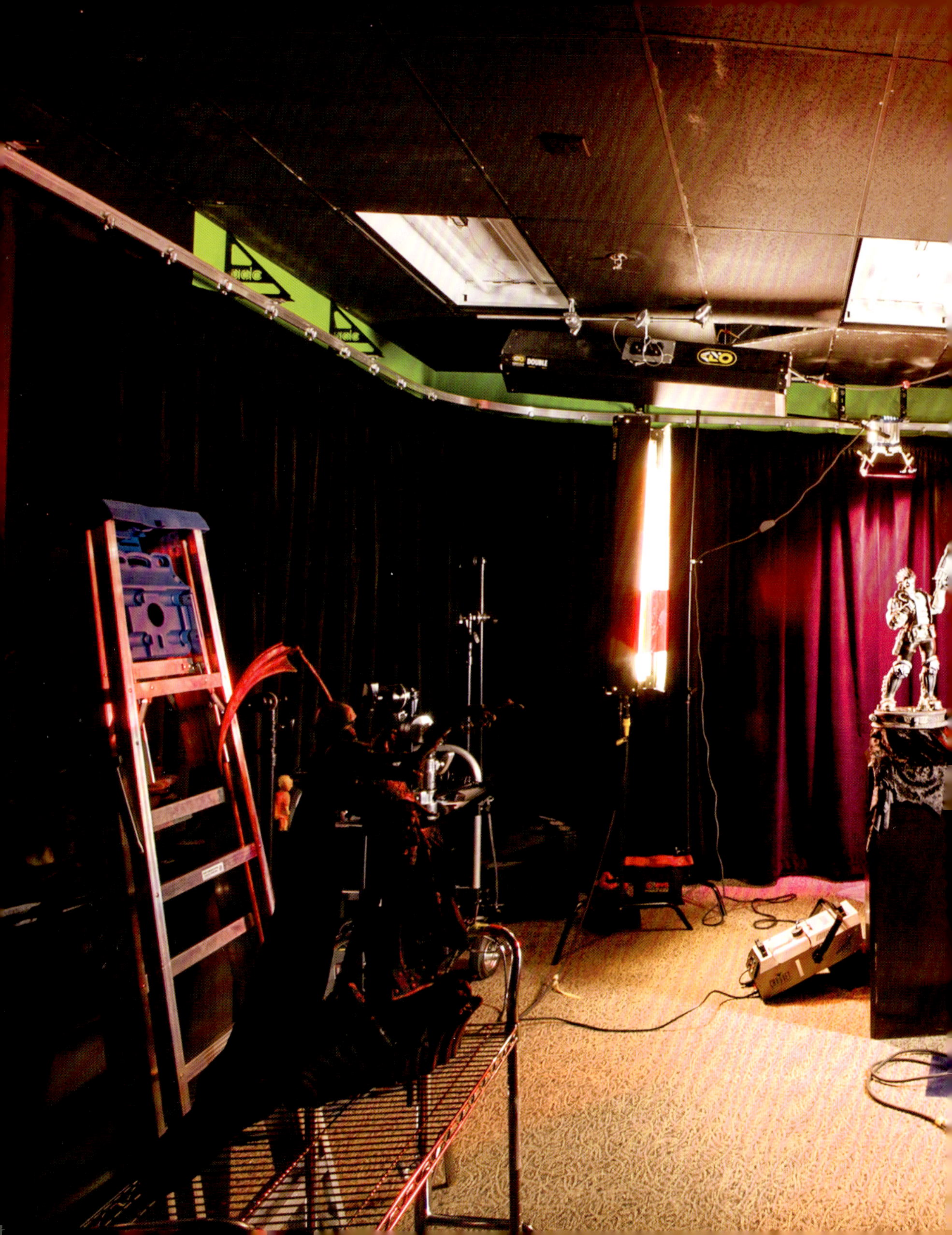

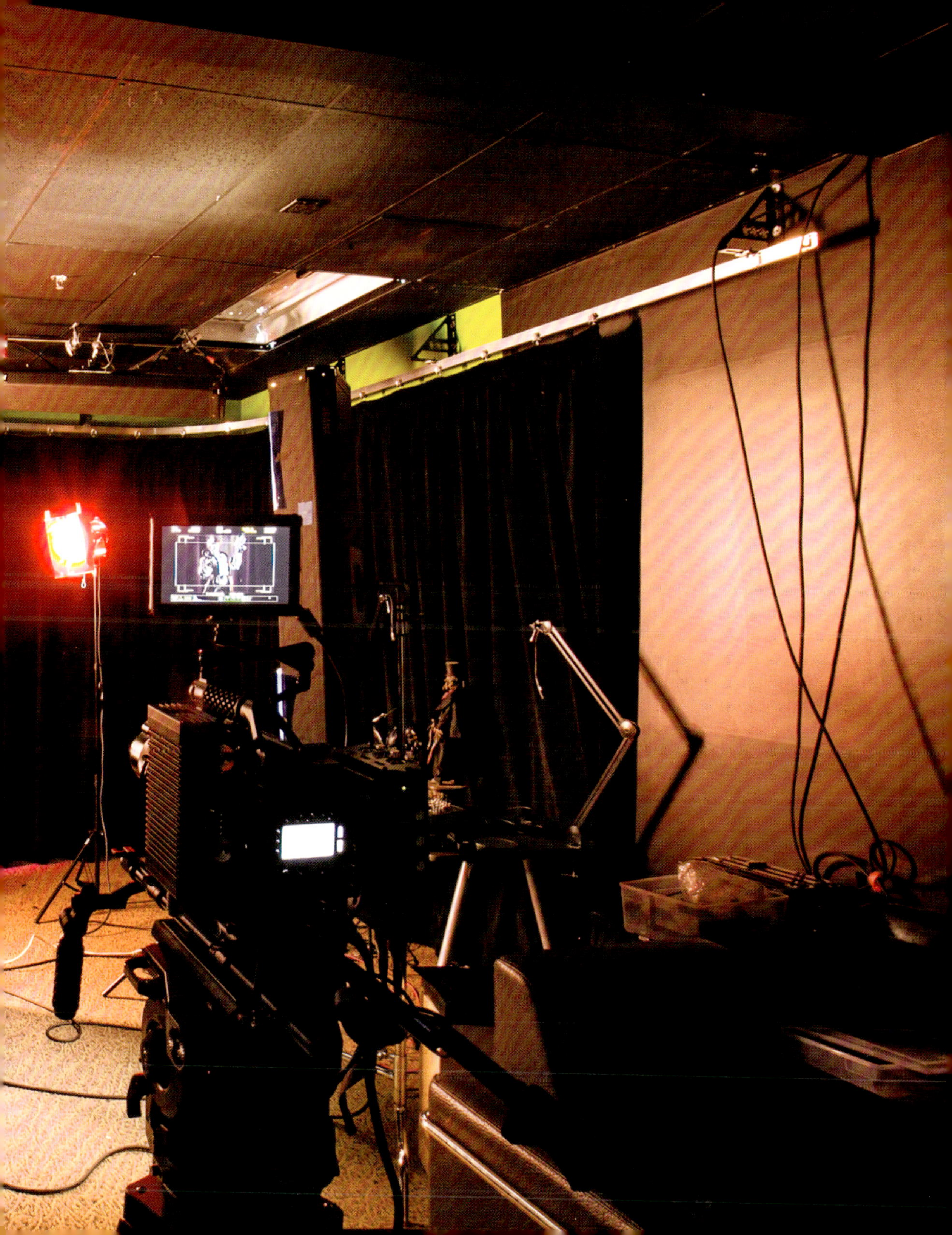

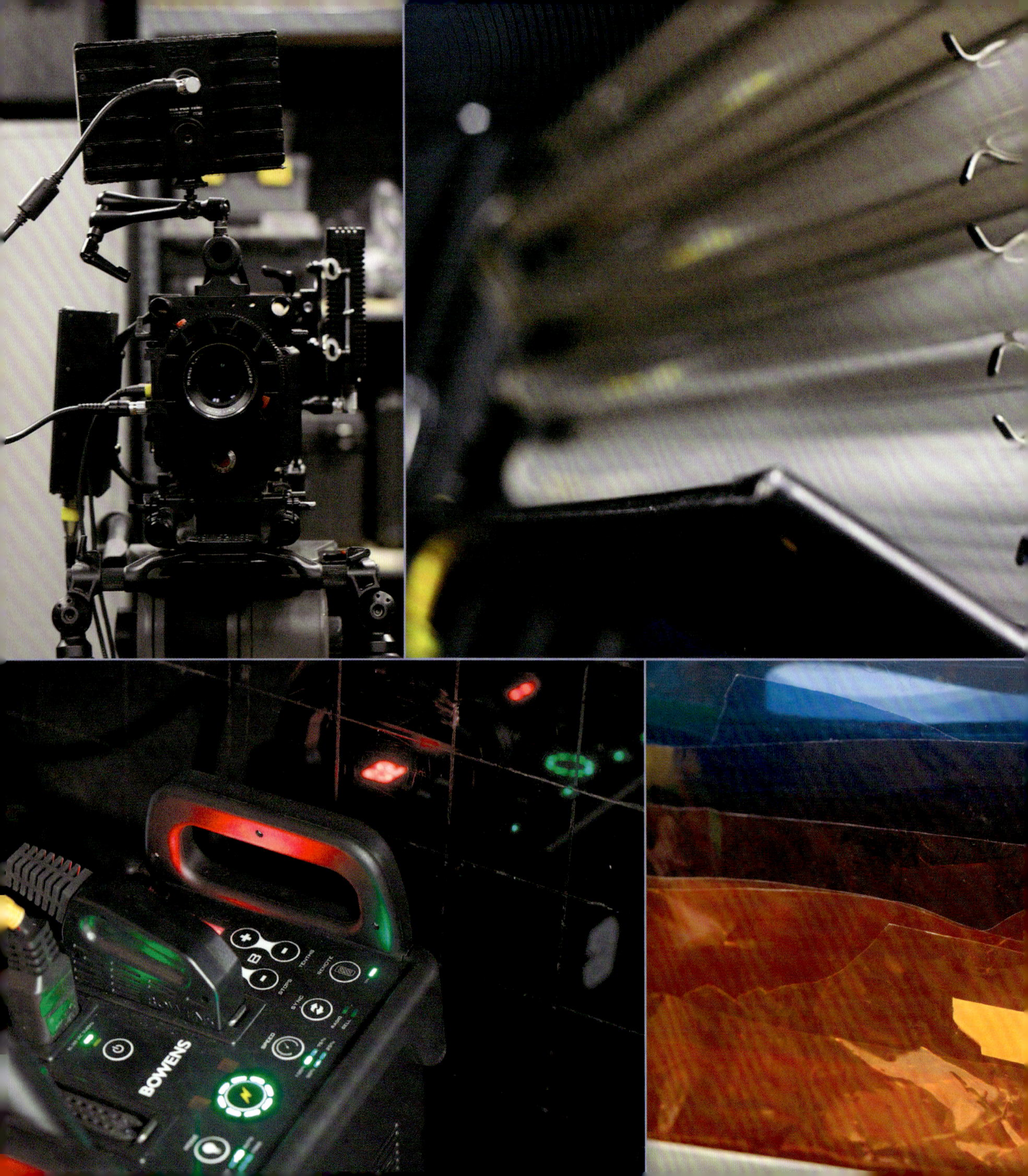
BOWENS

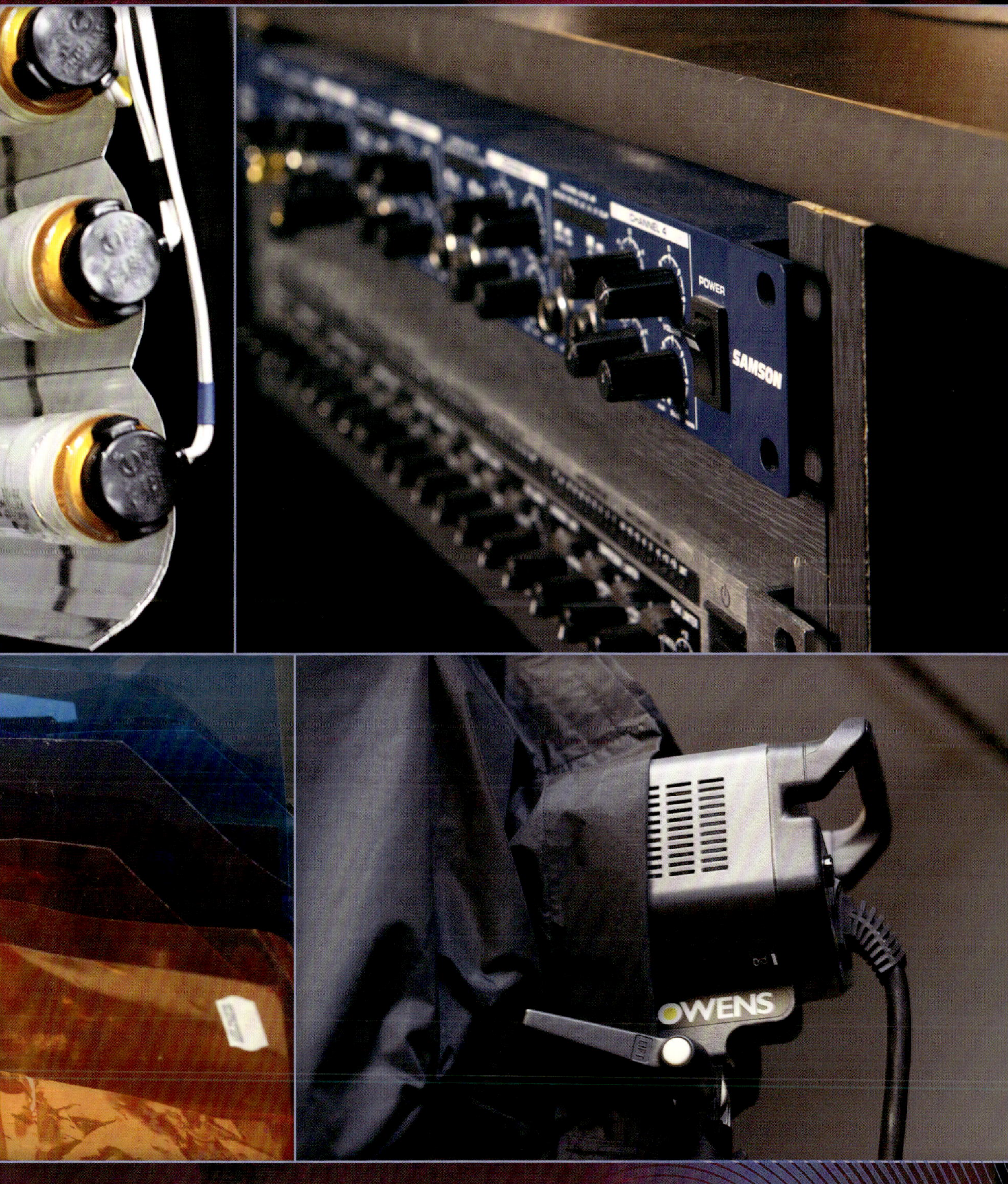
CHANNEL 4
POWER
SAMSON
OWENS
LIFT

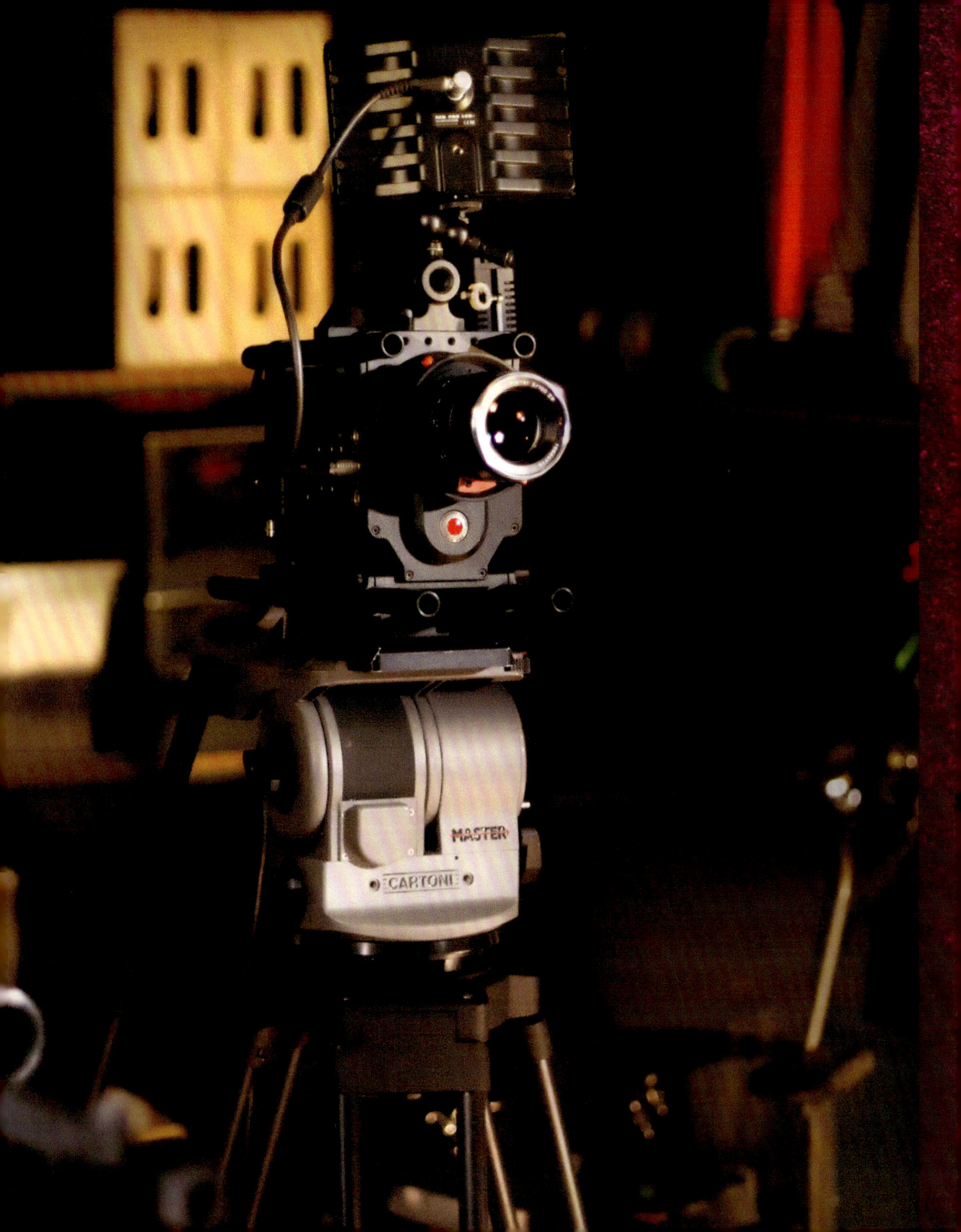
MASTER
CARTONI

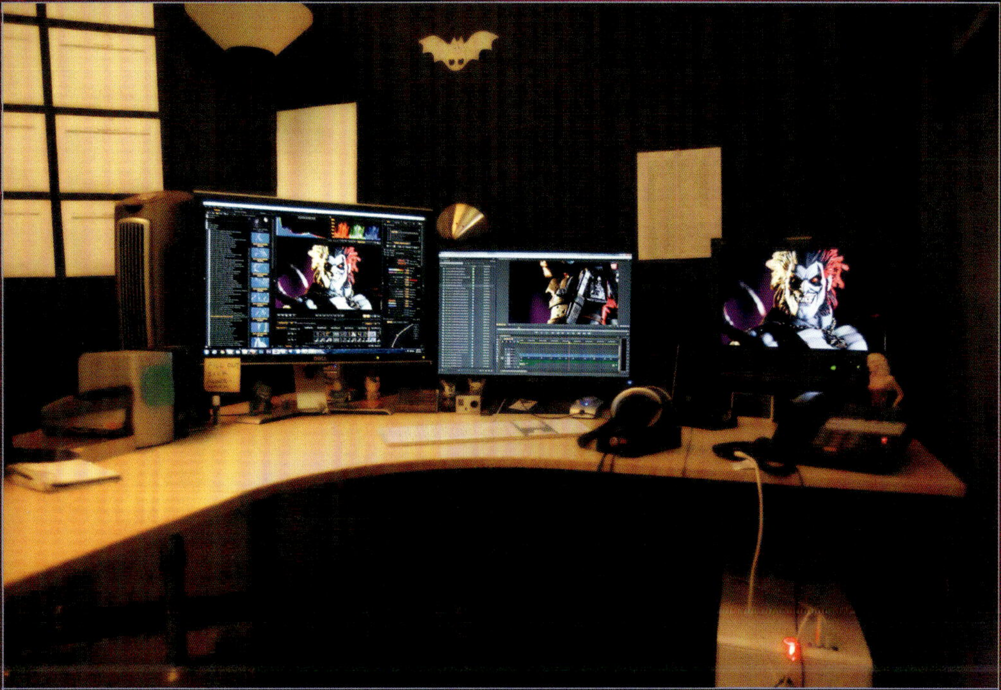

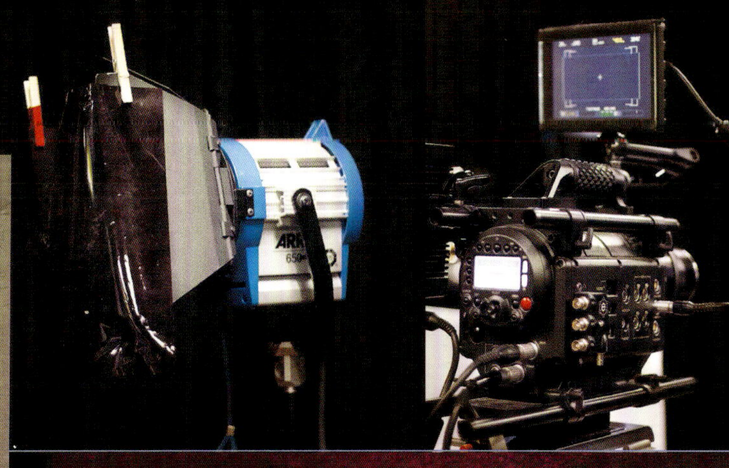

"It's a privilege to be
working in such a creative
and inspiring atmosphere.
Looking at all the eclectic
workstations really gives
insight into each person's
unique personality. You're
kind of the odd man out
if you do nothing to your
environment."

—Stephen Lubin,
Multimedia Manager

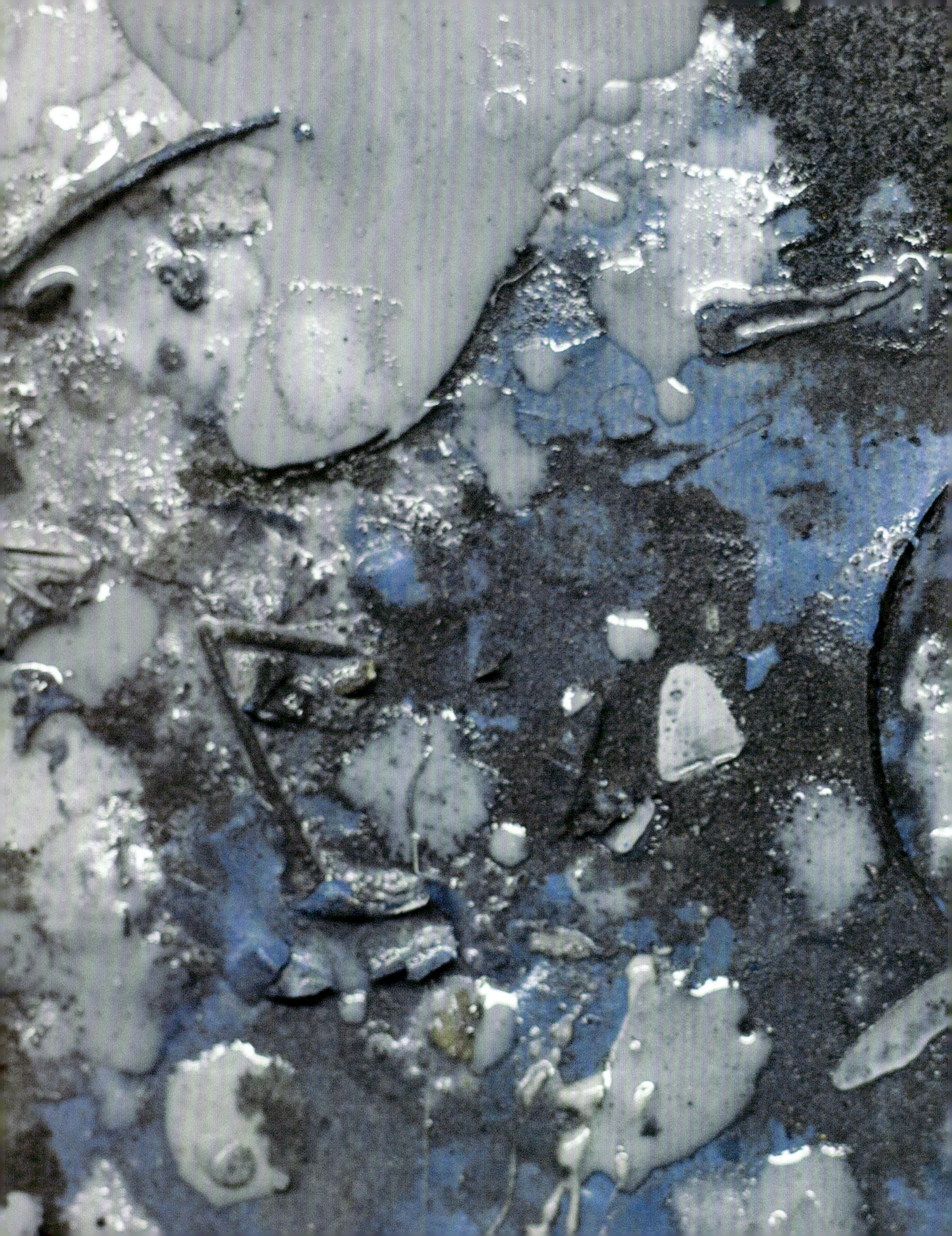

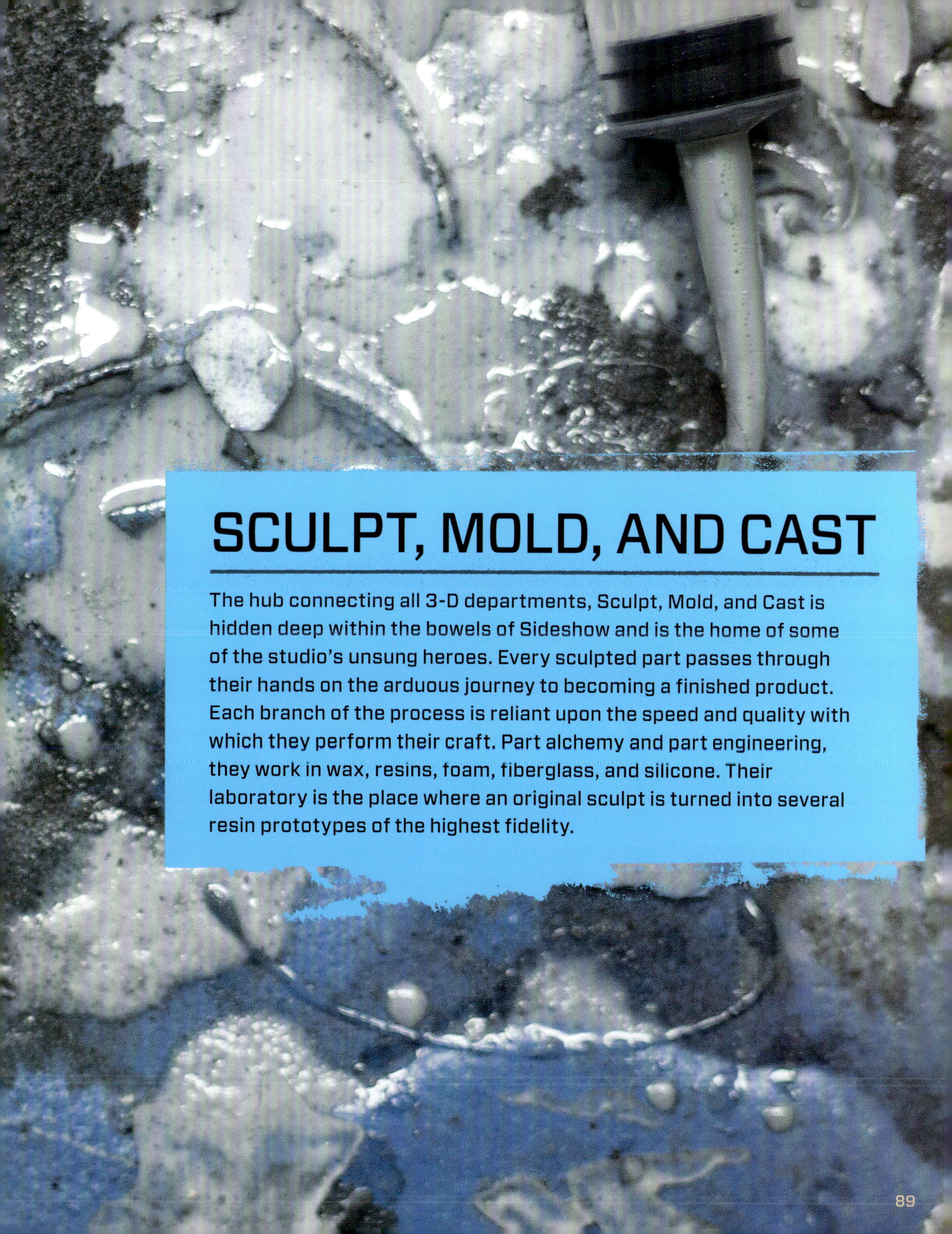

SCULPT, MOLD, AND CAST

The hub connecting all 3-D departments, Sculpt, Mold, and Cast is hidden deep within the bowels of Sideshow and is the home of some of the studio's unsung heroes. Every sculpted part passes through their hands on the arduous journey to becoming a finished product. Each branch of the process is reliant upon the speed and quality with which they perform their craft. Part alchemy and part engineering, they work in wax, resins, foam, fiberglass, and silicone. Their laboratory is the place where an original sculpt is turned into several resin prototypes of the highest fidelity.

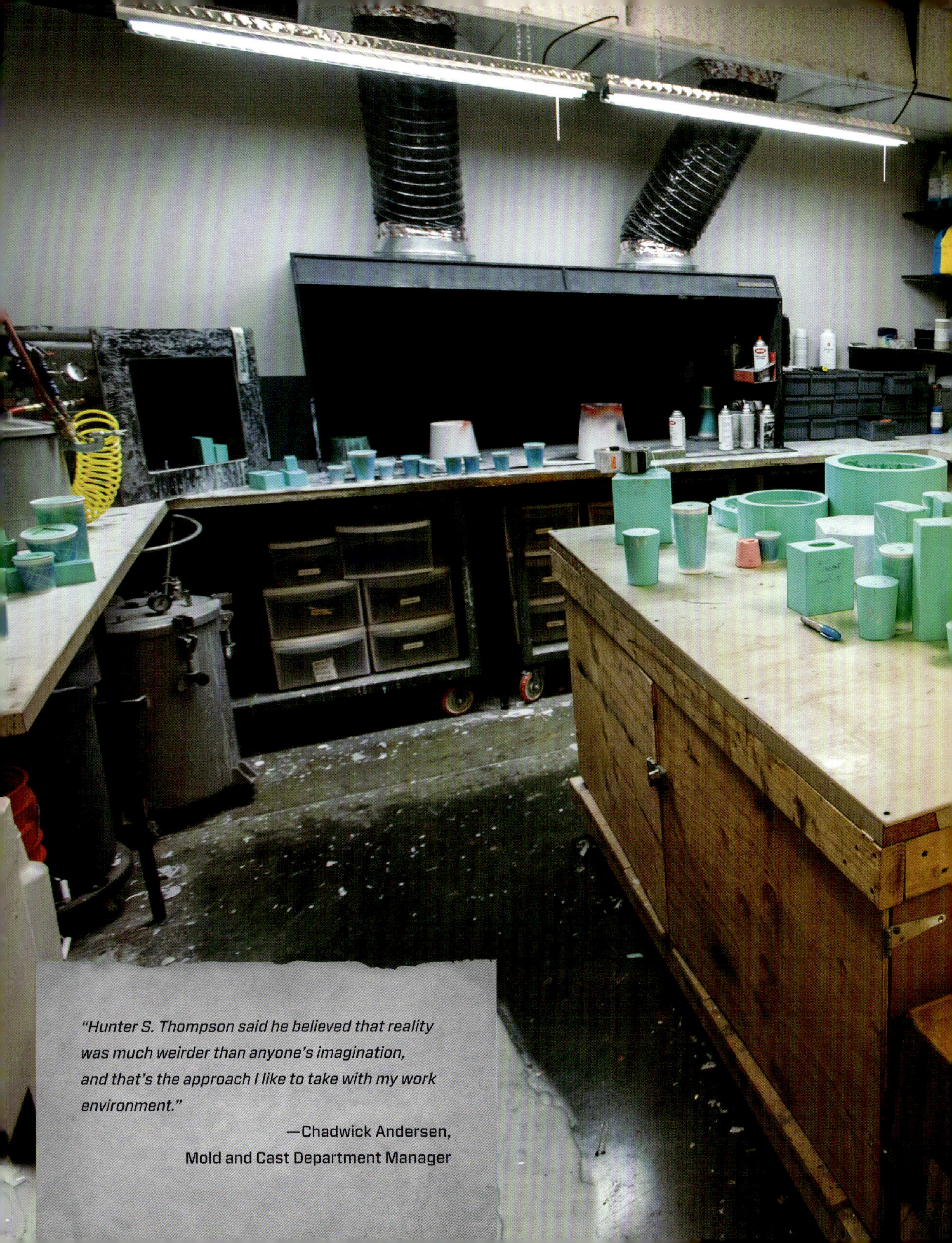

"Hunter S. Thompson said he believed that reality was much weirder than anyone's imagination, and that's the approach I like to take with my work environment."

—Chadwick Andersen,
Mold and Cast Department Manager

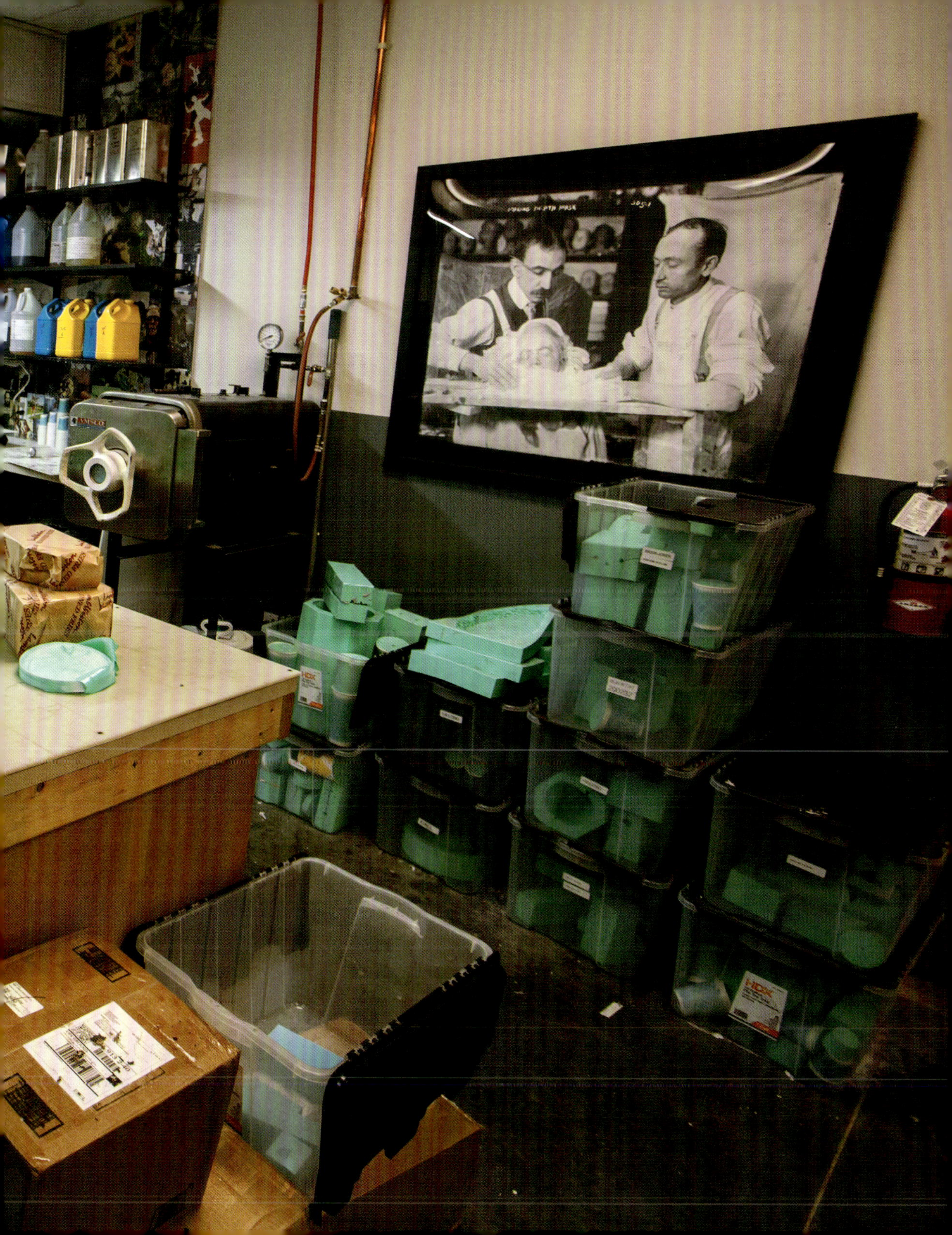

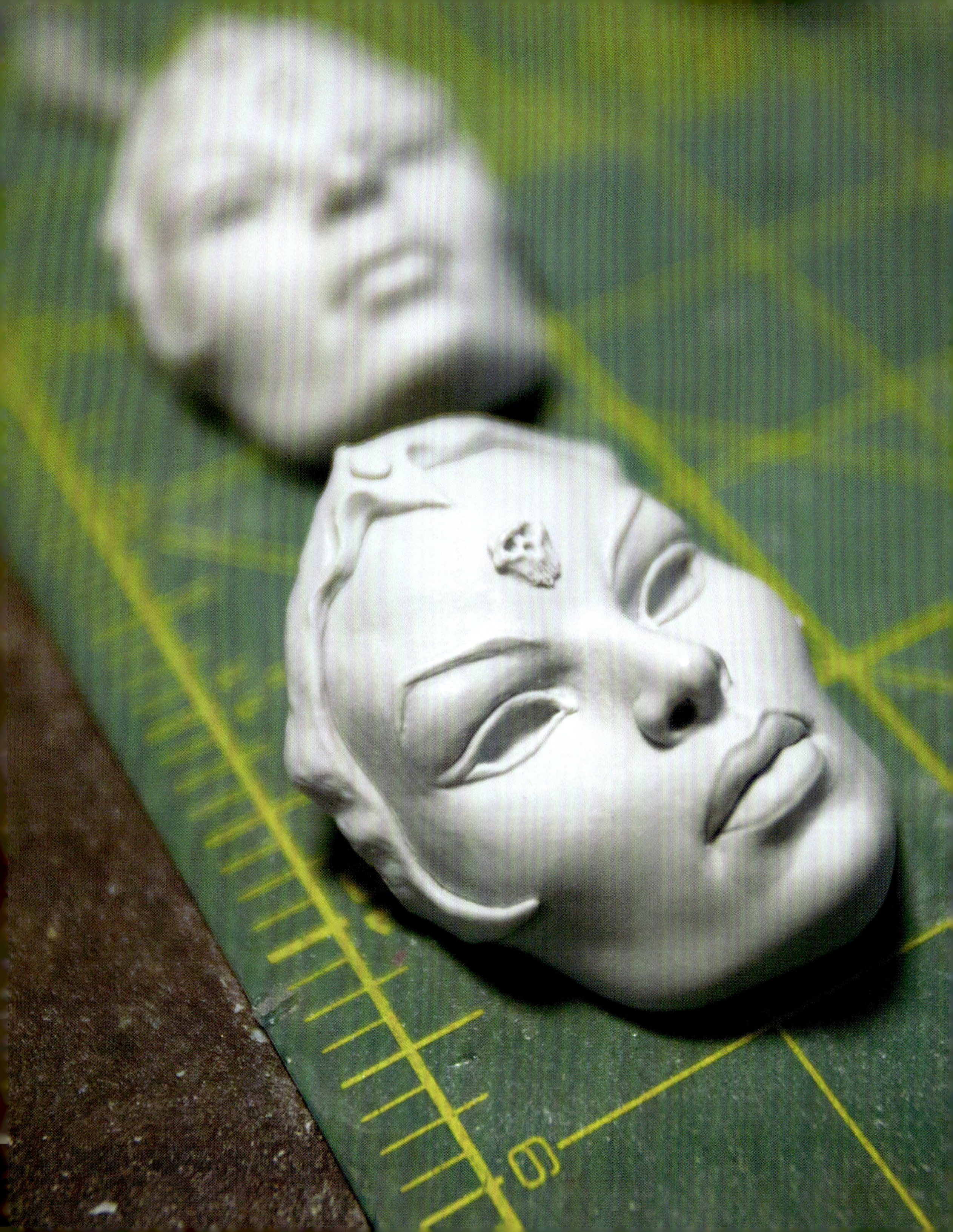

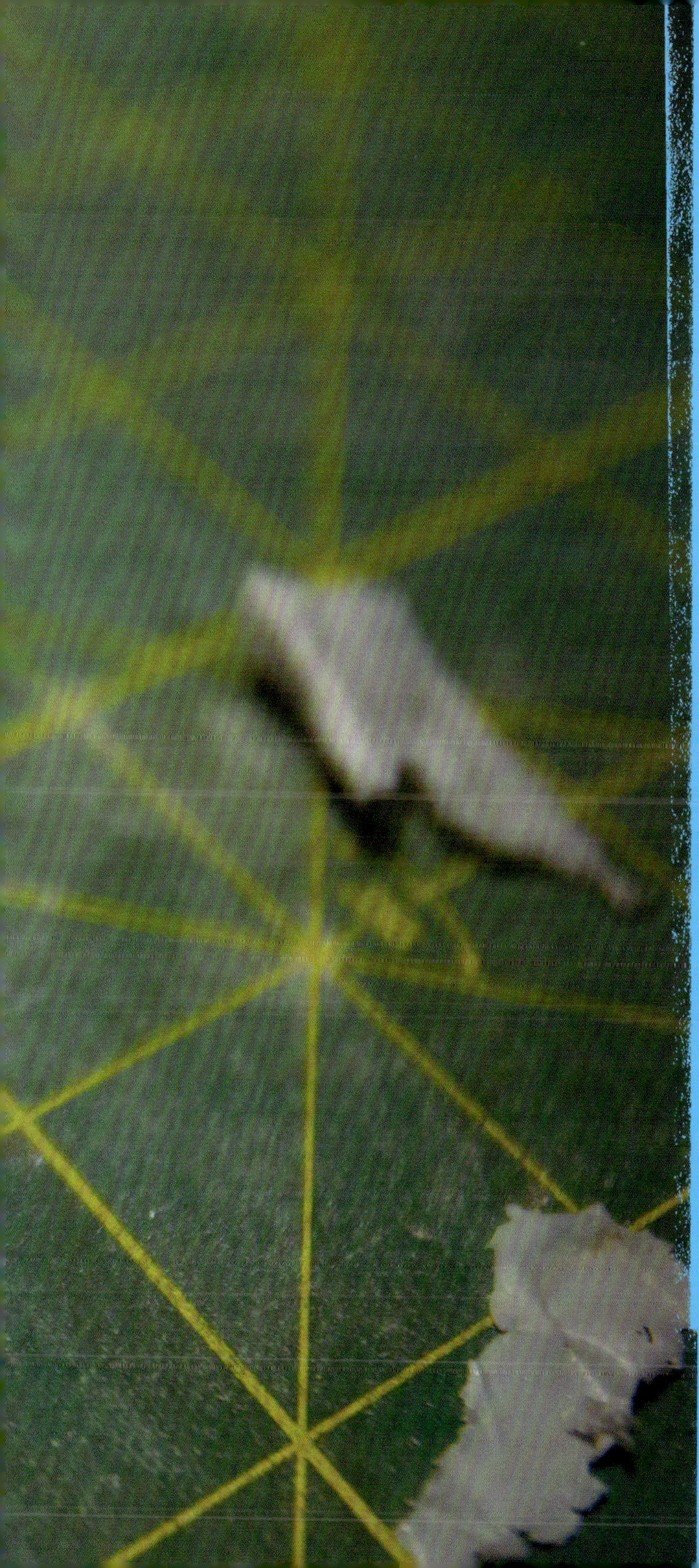

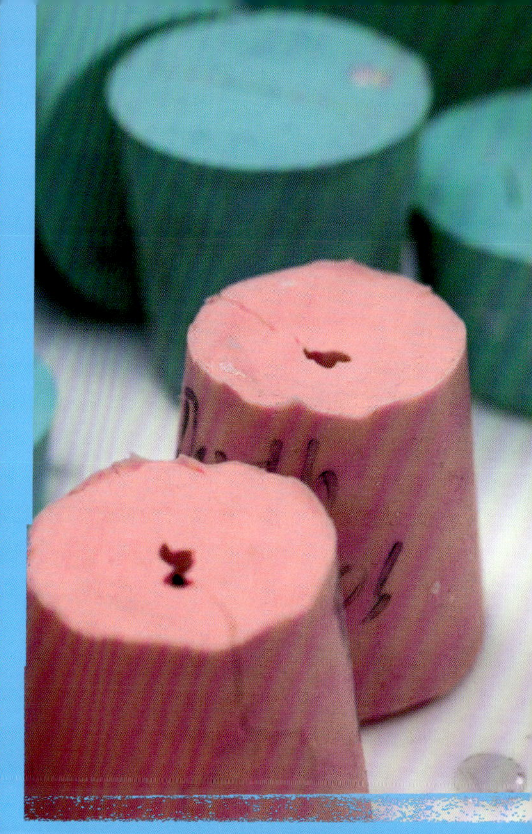
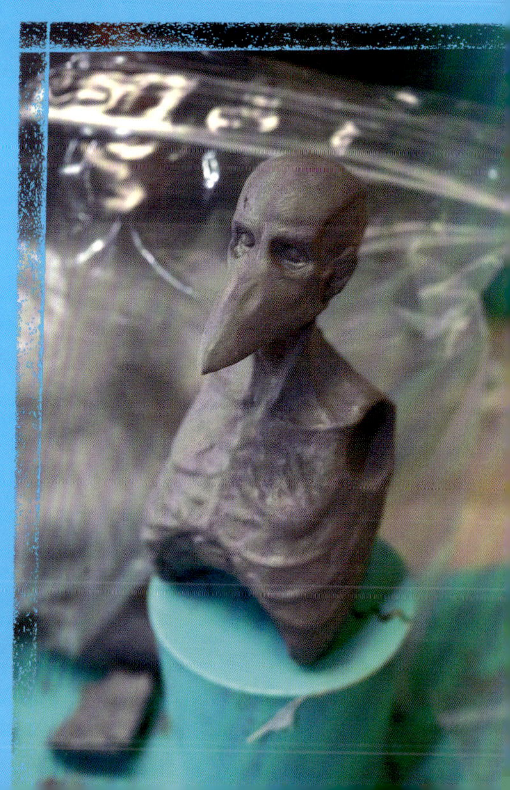

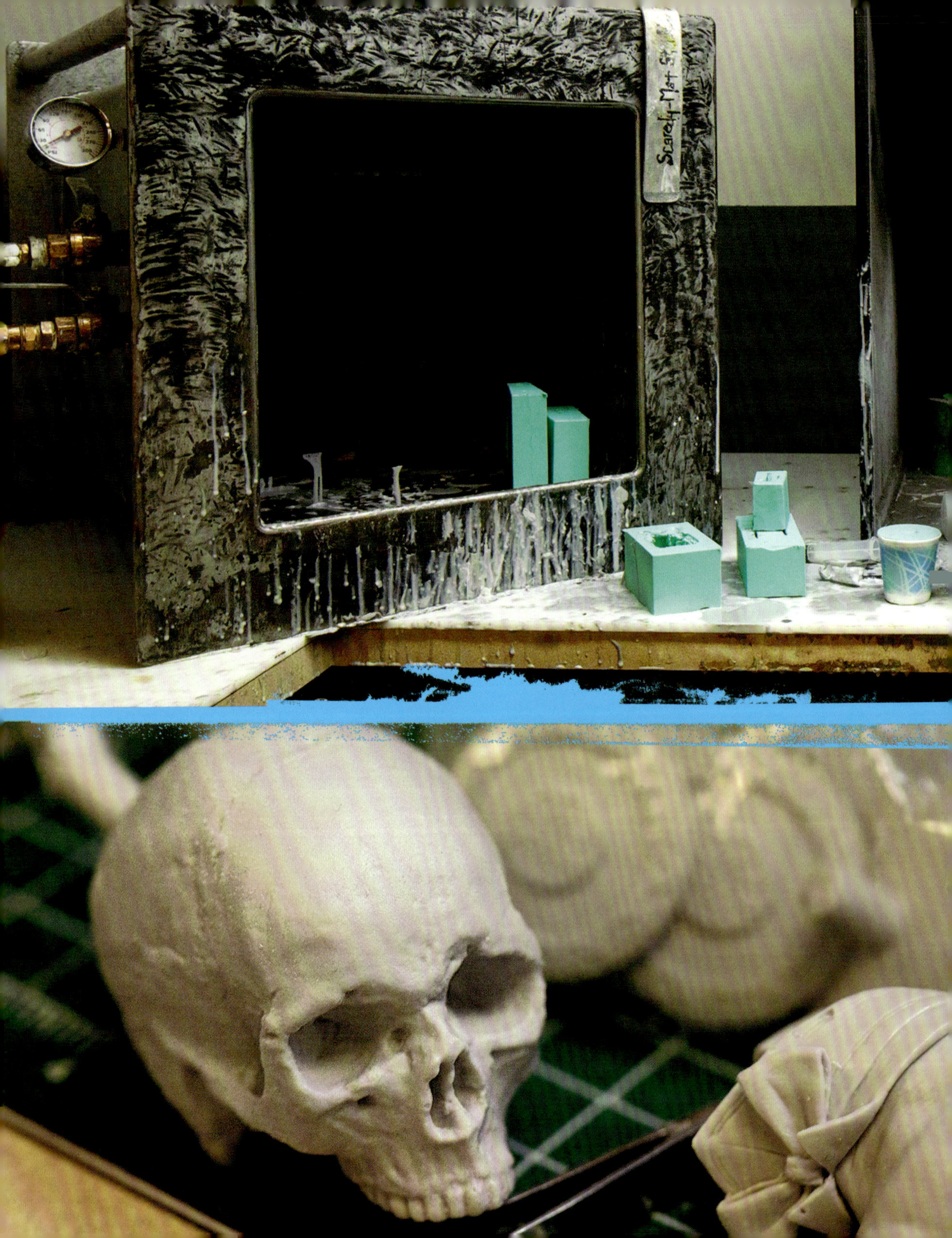

Scarch-Mat S

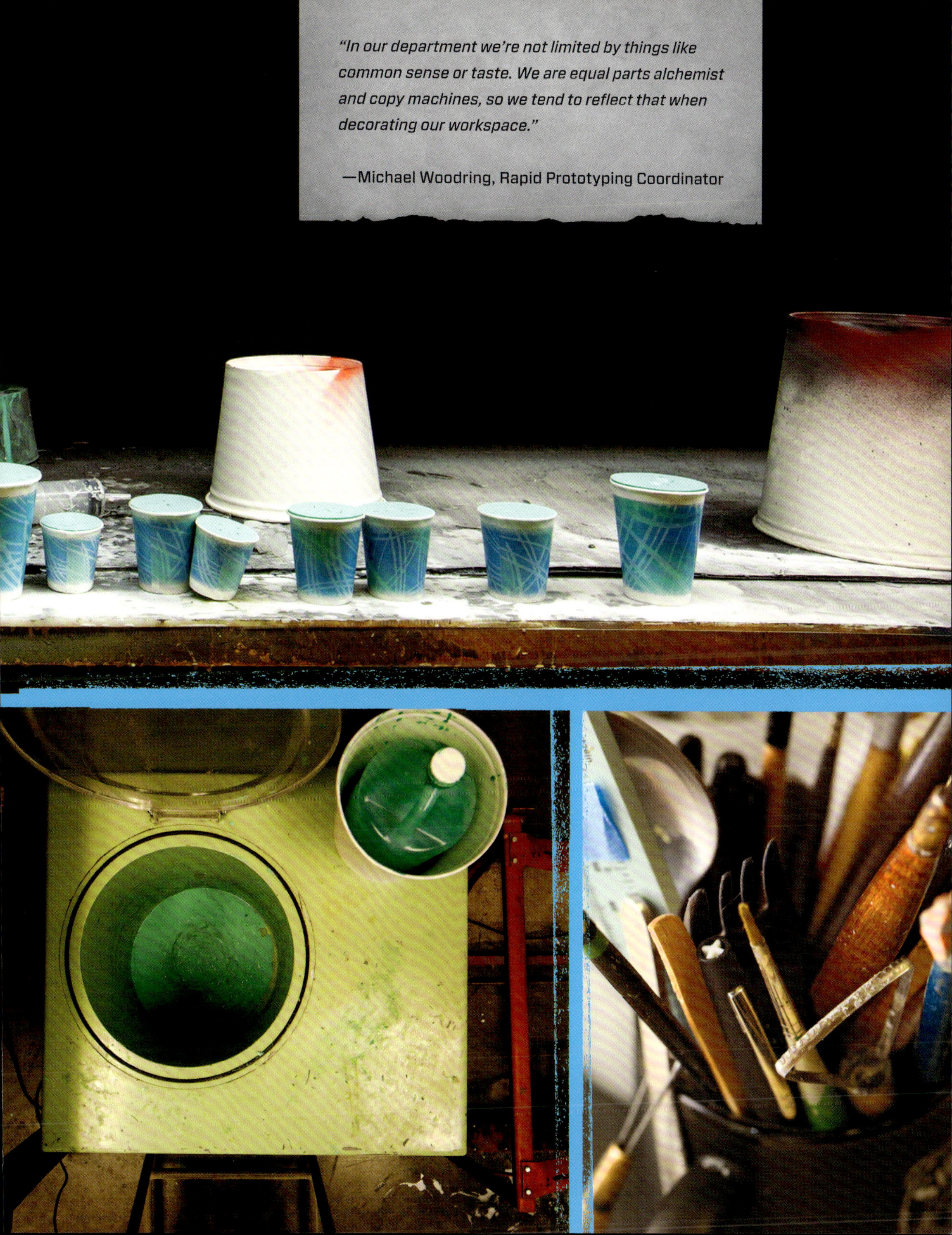
"In our department we're not limited by things like common sense or taste. We are equal parts alchemist and copy machines, so we tend to reflect that when decorating our workspace."

—Michael Woodring, Rapid Prototyping Coordinator

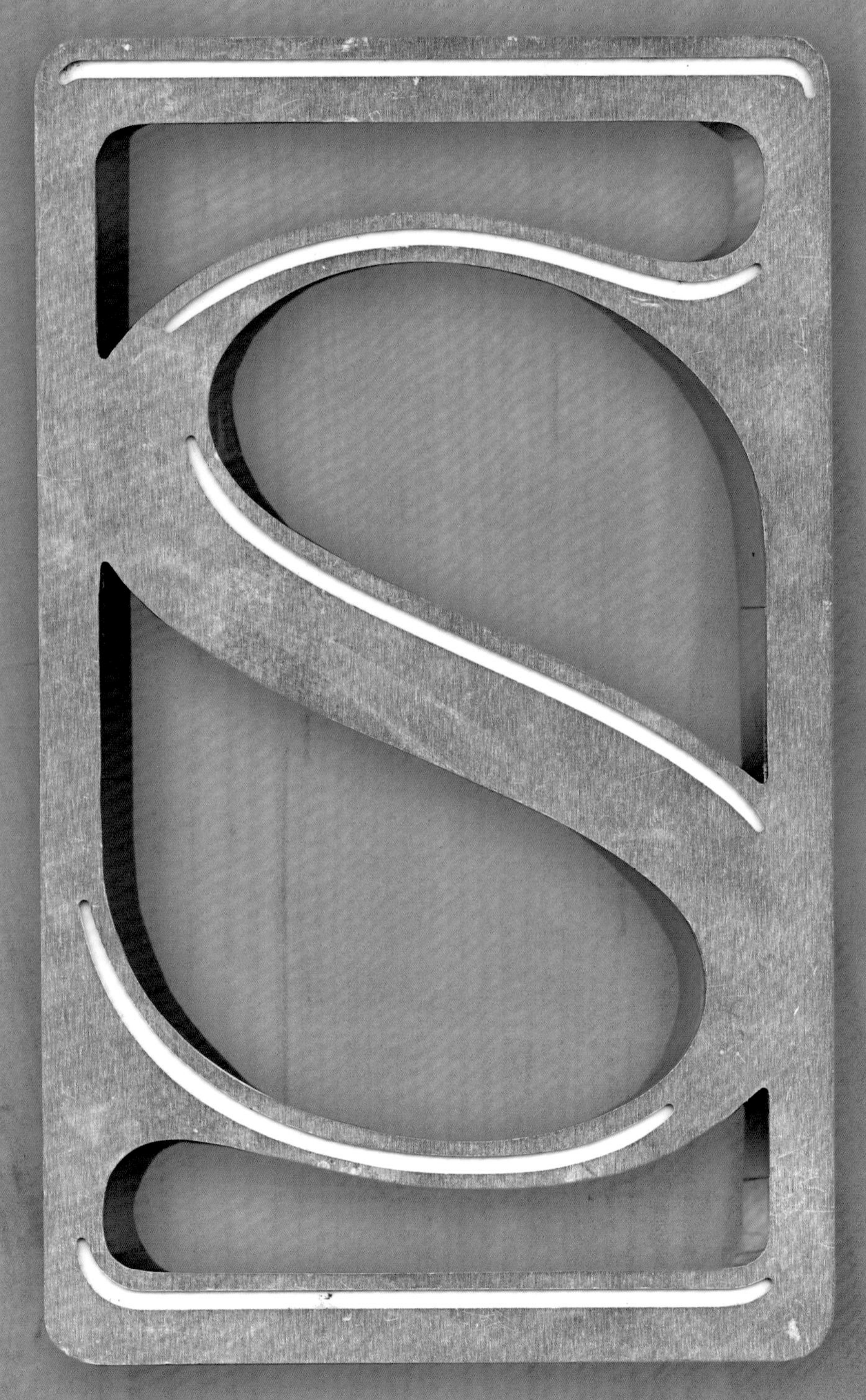

GRAPHICS

In the farthest depths of Sideshow lies a cave in which its dwellers are able to steal a layer of dimension and turn 3-D into 2-D. The inhabitants of these coordinates are responsible for the final package that houses each product before it can be called complete. They also work on a plethora of other design applications including (but not limited to) convention layouts, publishing, costuming, and anything else that the elders need. Though every day brings along many tasks, it's often accented with laughter, the background chatter of a film playing on the big screen, and an overall sense of camaraderie.

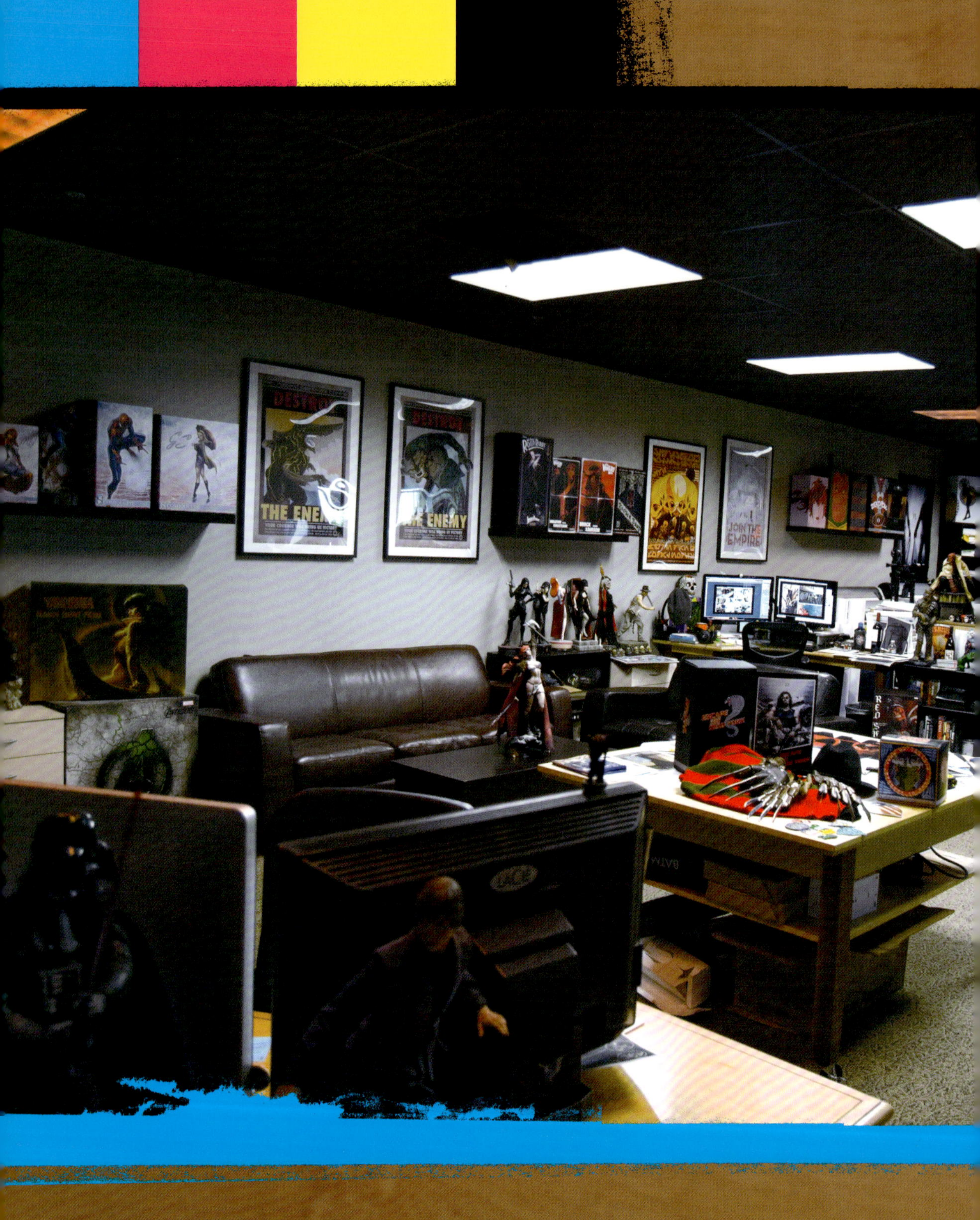

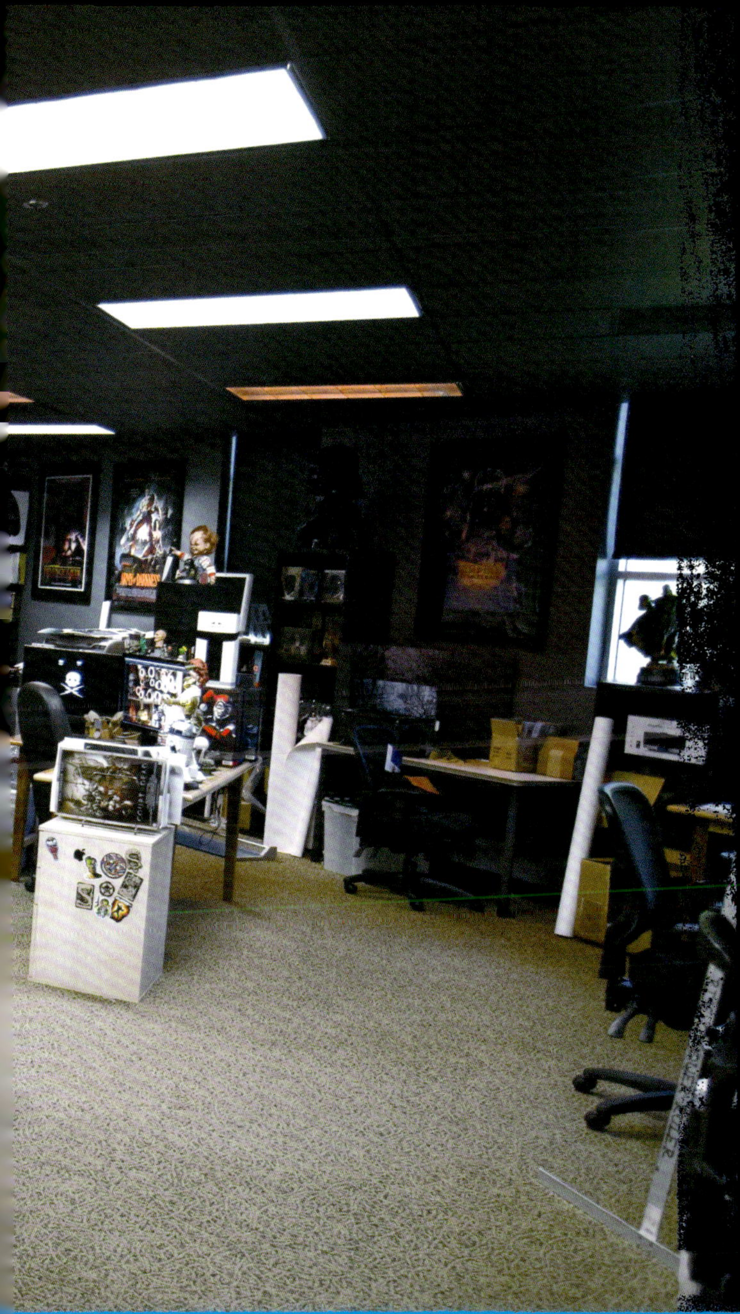

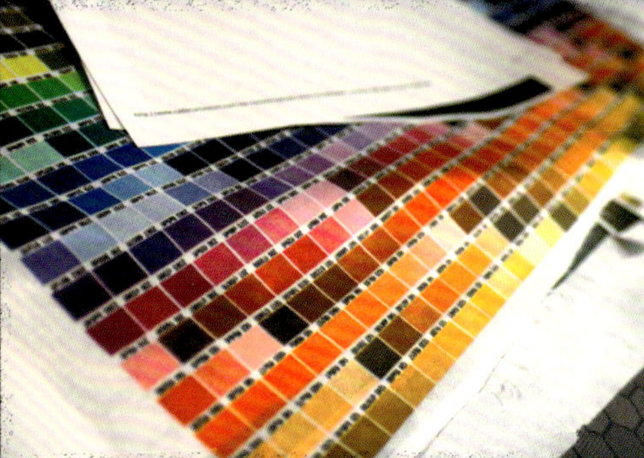

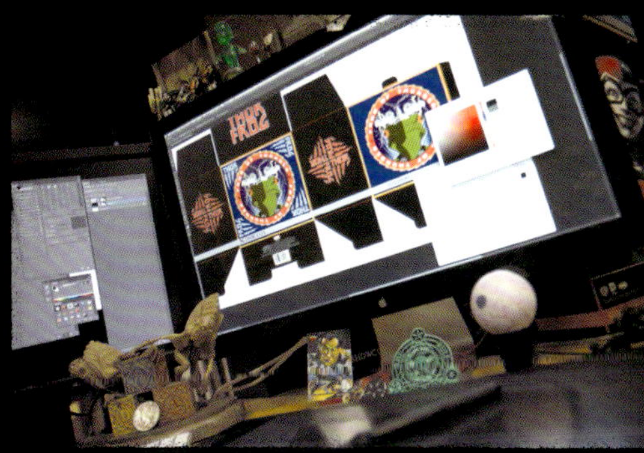

"The studio itself has a lot to do with the people and the way they keep it light and fun. We're all just big kids. Every day at the office we get the same feelings of wonder and excitement that we had back when we were growing up."

—Jennifer Garrett,
Sr. Graphic Designer

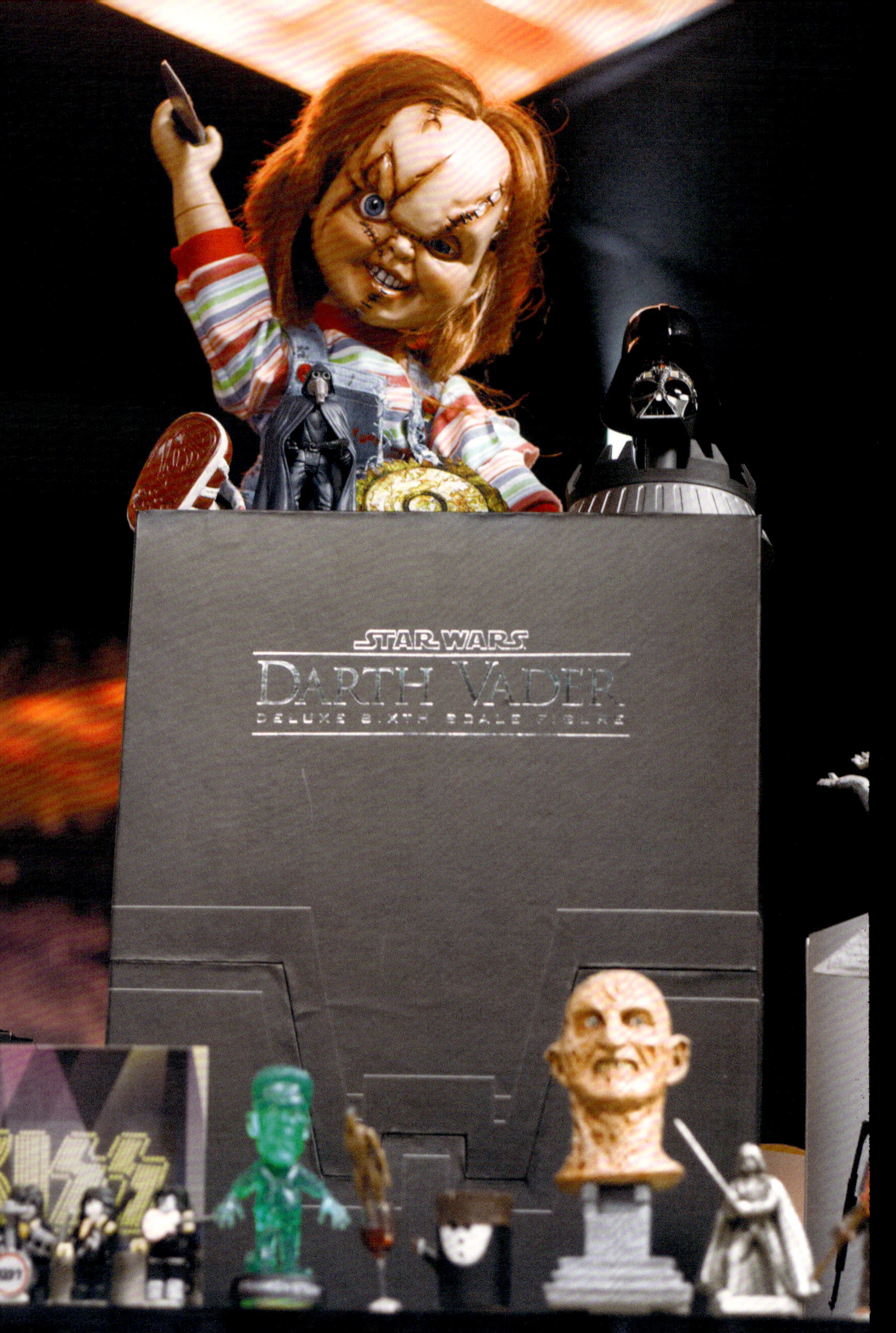

STAR WARS
DARTH VADER
DELUXE SIXTH SCALE FIGURE

"The environment here makes me aware of what's going on in the creative world. It causes you to never just accept where you are creatively, but instead, to keep constantly progressing and advancing. It keeps you from becoming stagnant; keeps you fresh and driven to grow, desire, and learn."

—Andrew McBride, Sr. Graphic Designer

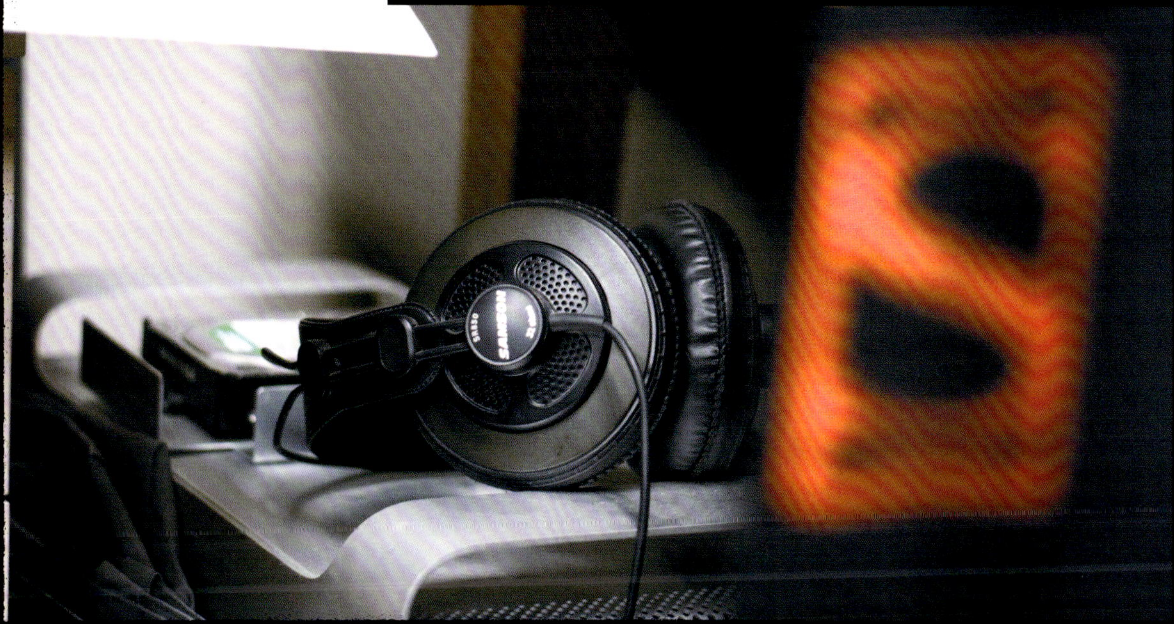

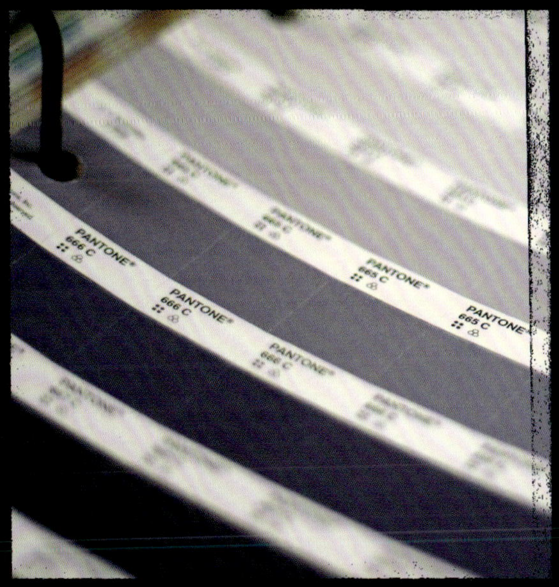

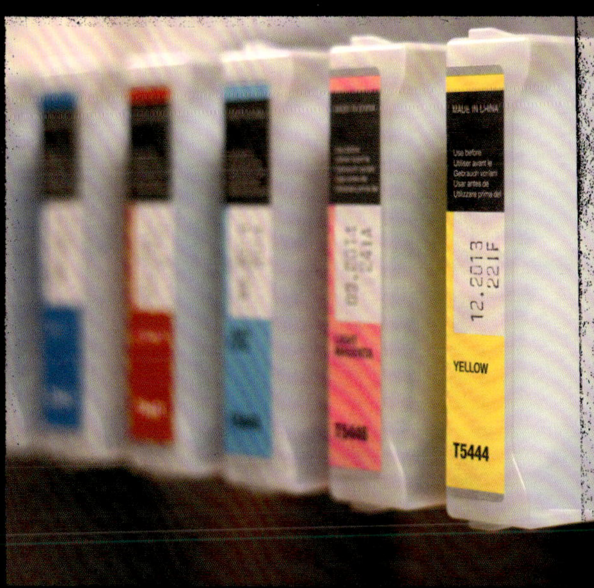

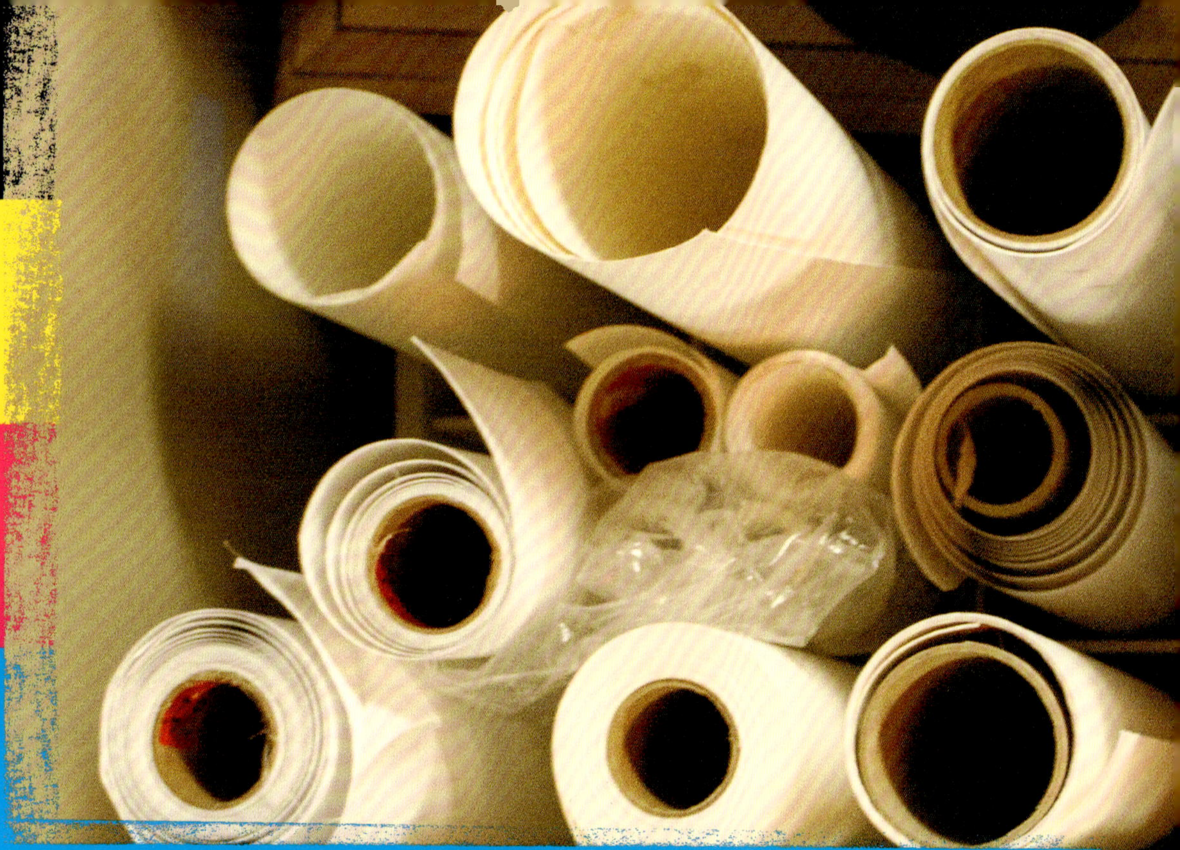

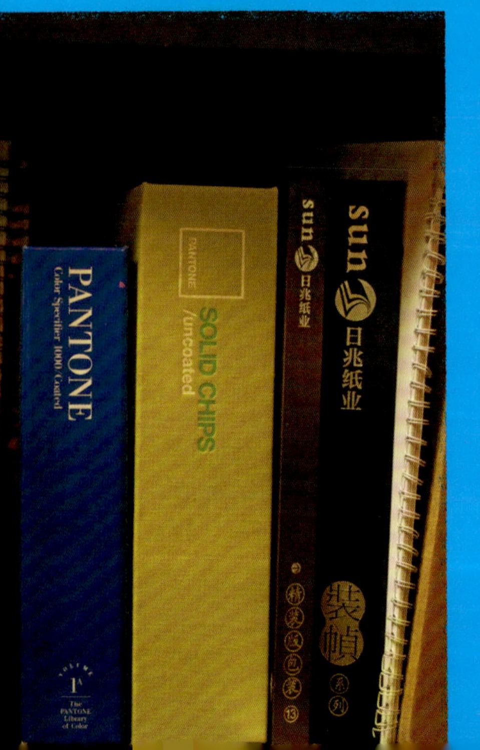
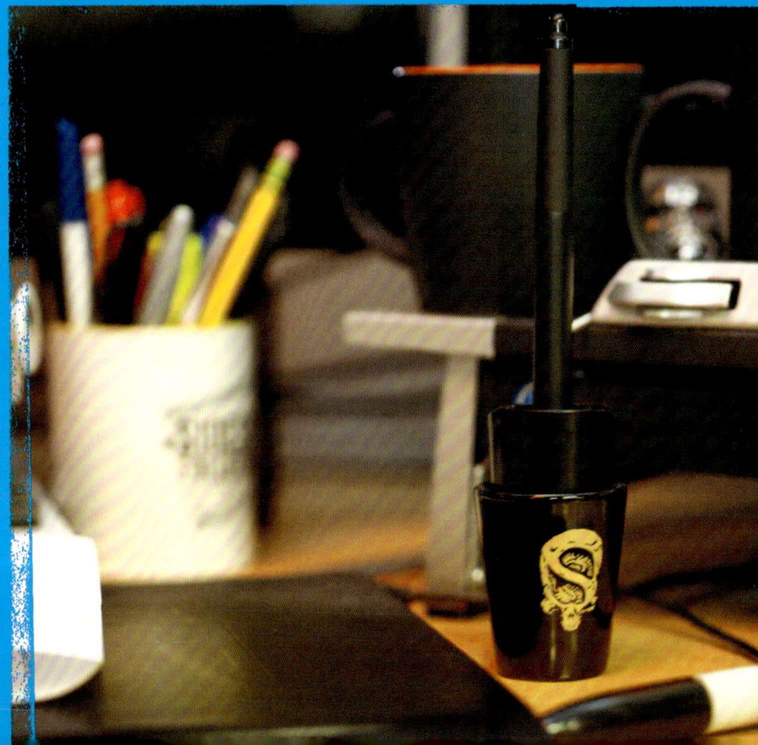
PANTONE
Color Specifier 1000 Coated
PANTONE
SOLID CHIPS
/Uncoated
sun
日兆纸业
sun
日兆纸业
装帧
系列
The PANTONE
Library of Color

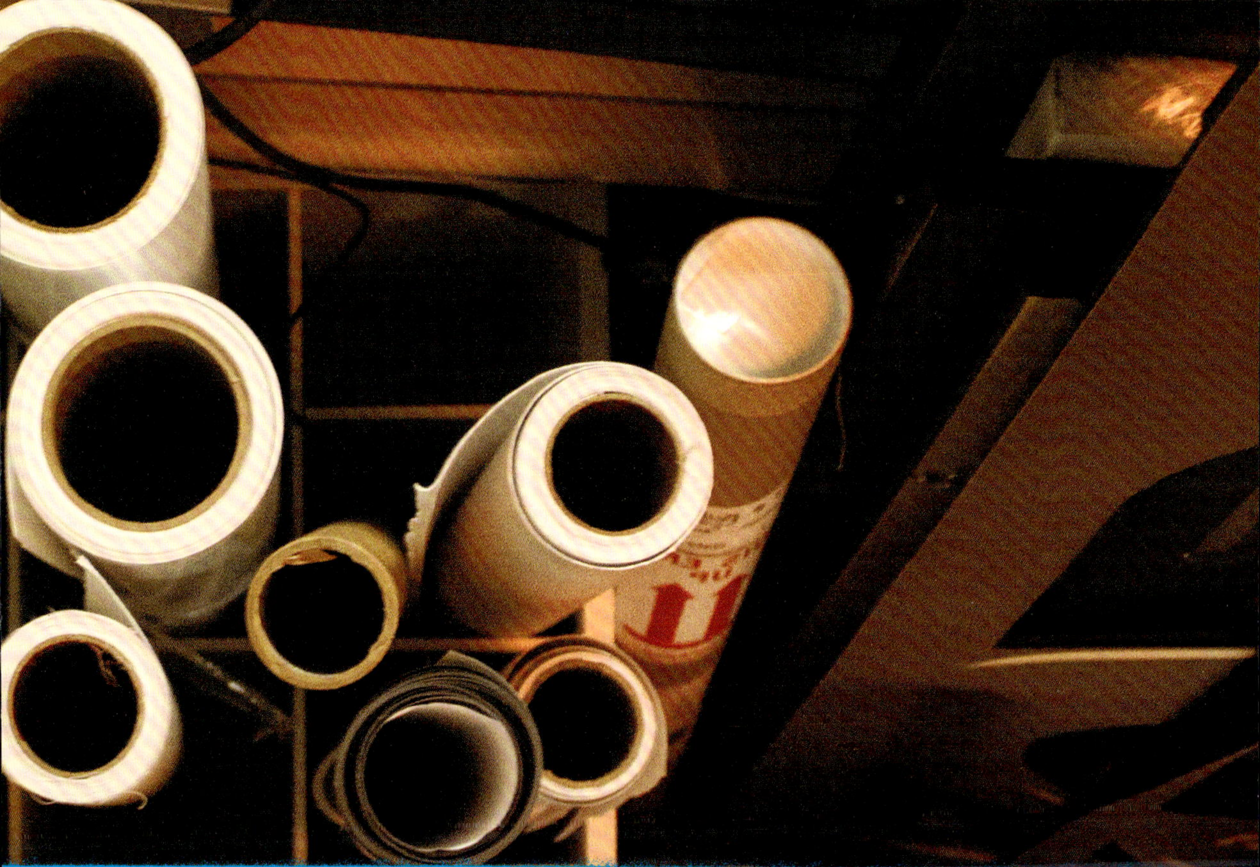

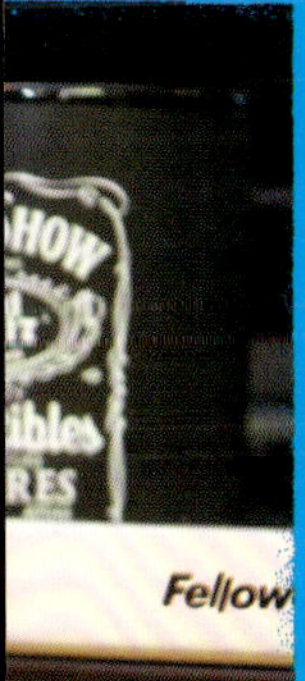

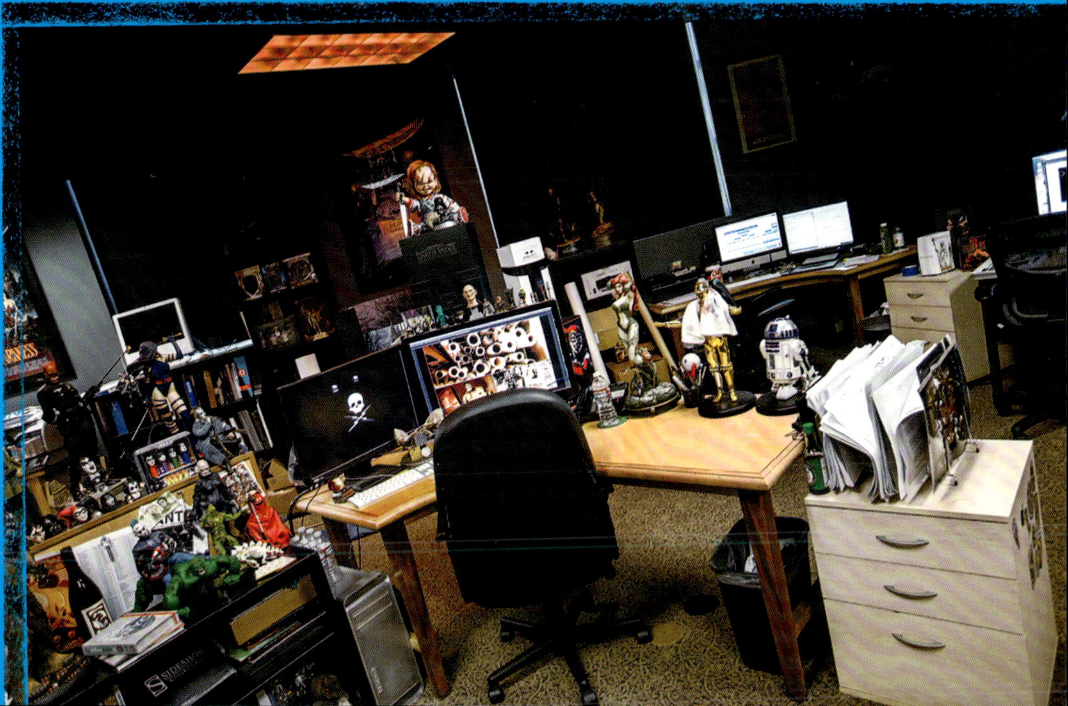

SHOW
ibles
RES
Fellow

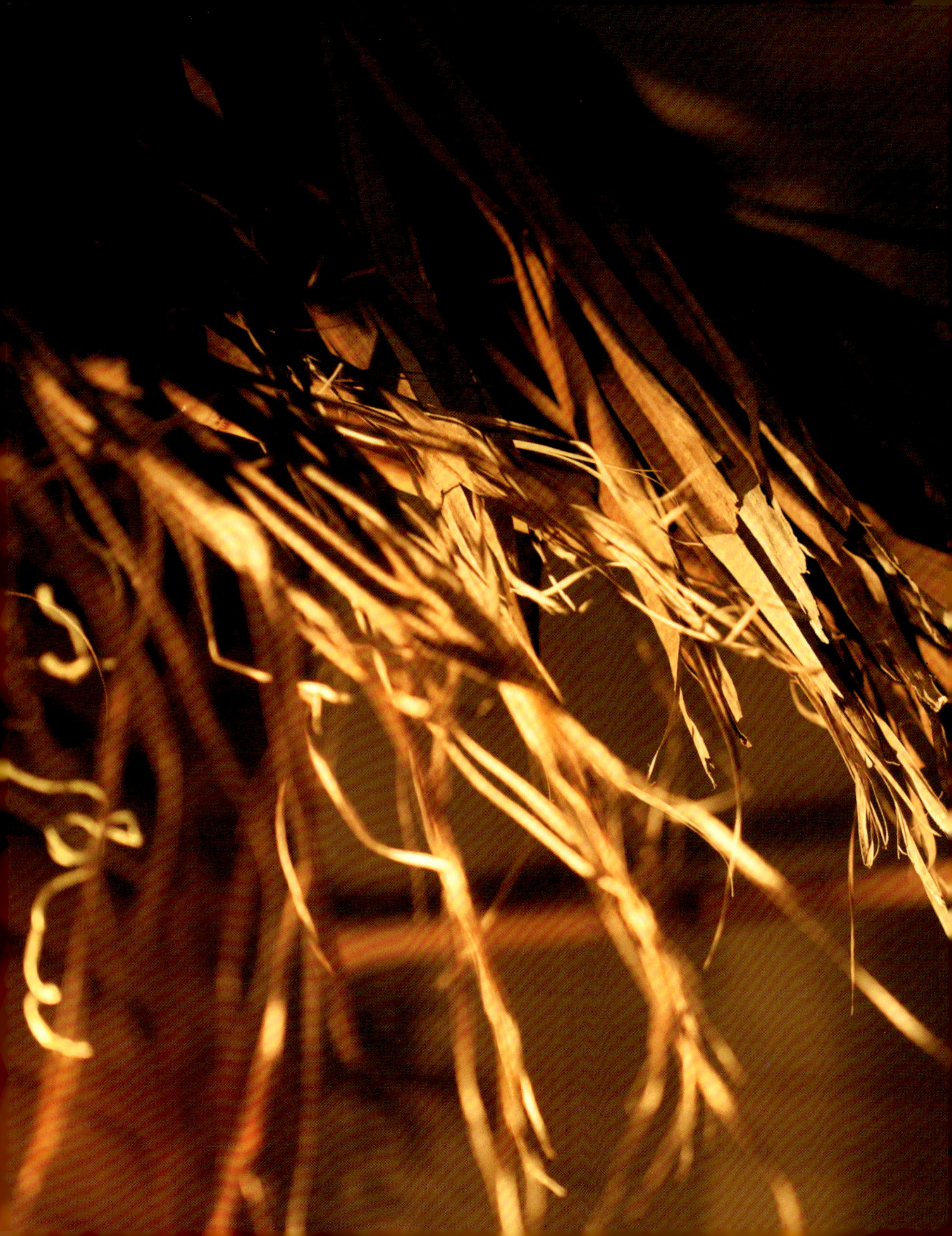

DESIGN AND DEVELOPMENT HEADQUARTERS

The development wing is quite literally a jungle. The Design and Development HQ is the "tour guide" for projects from the Design department to the Production department. In the development wing we "encounter" many different people, ideas, and mediums—from sculpt to cut and sew. These gifted individuals use their talents to enhance the project on its "journey," and it is their job to make sure it stays "on course."

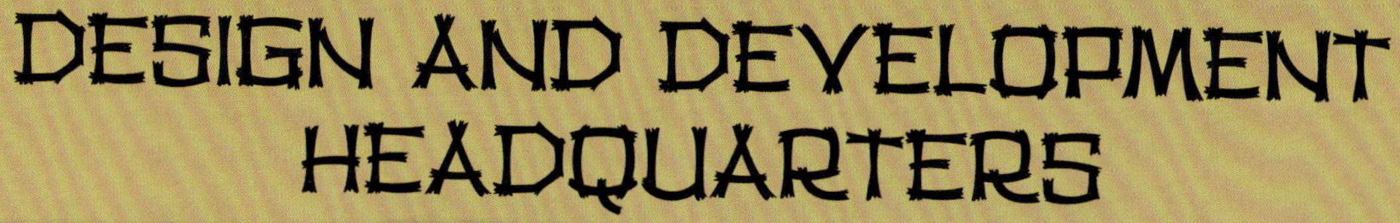

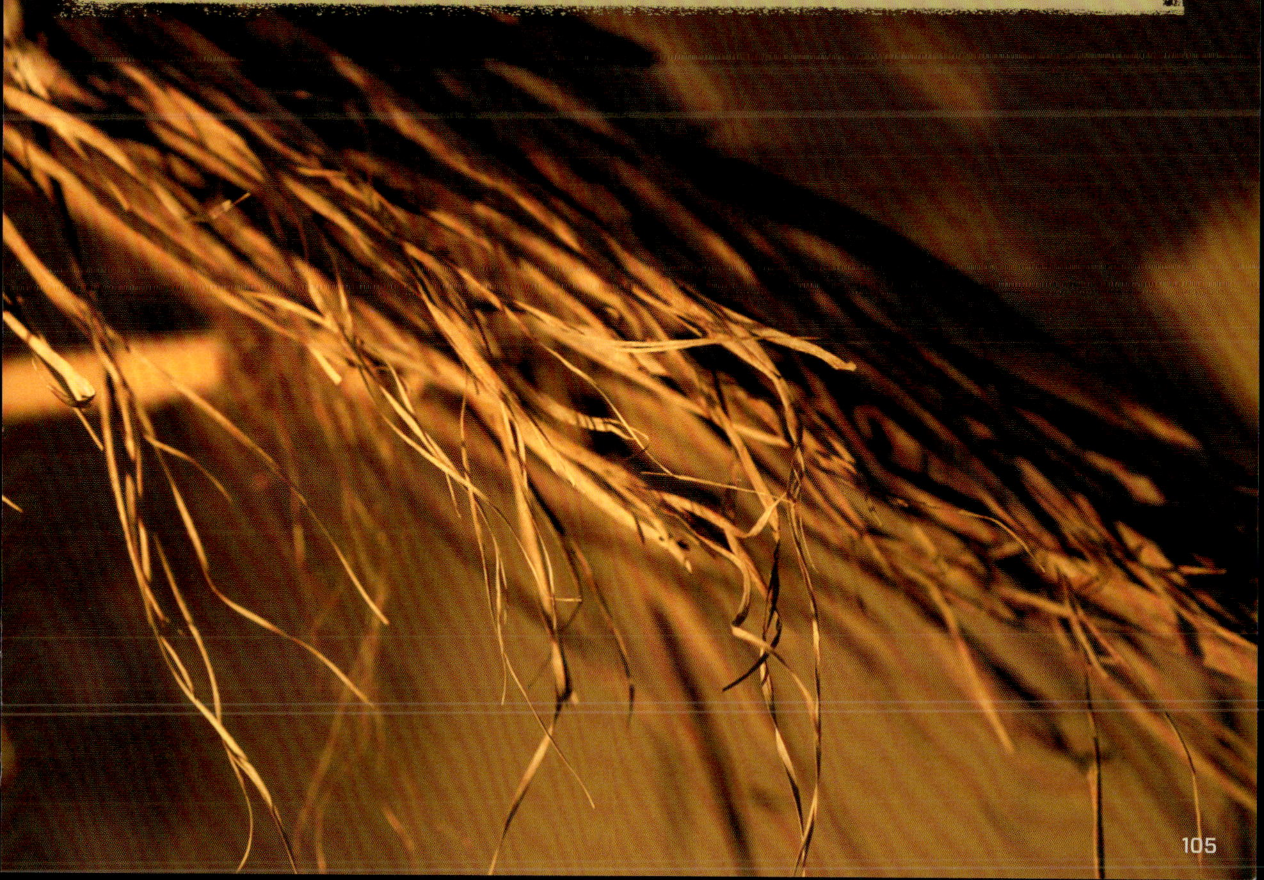

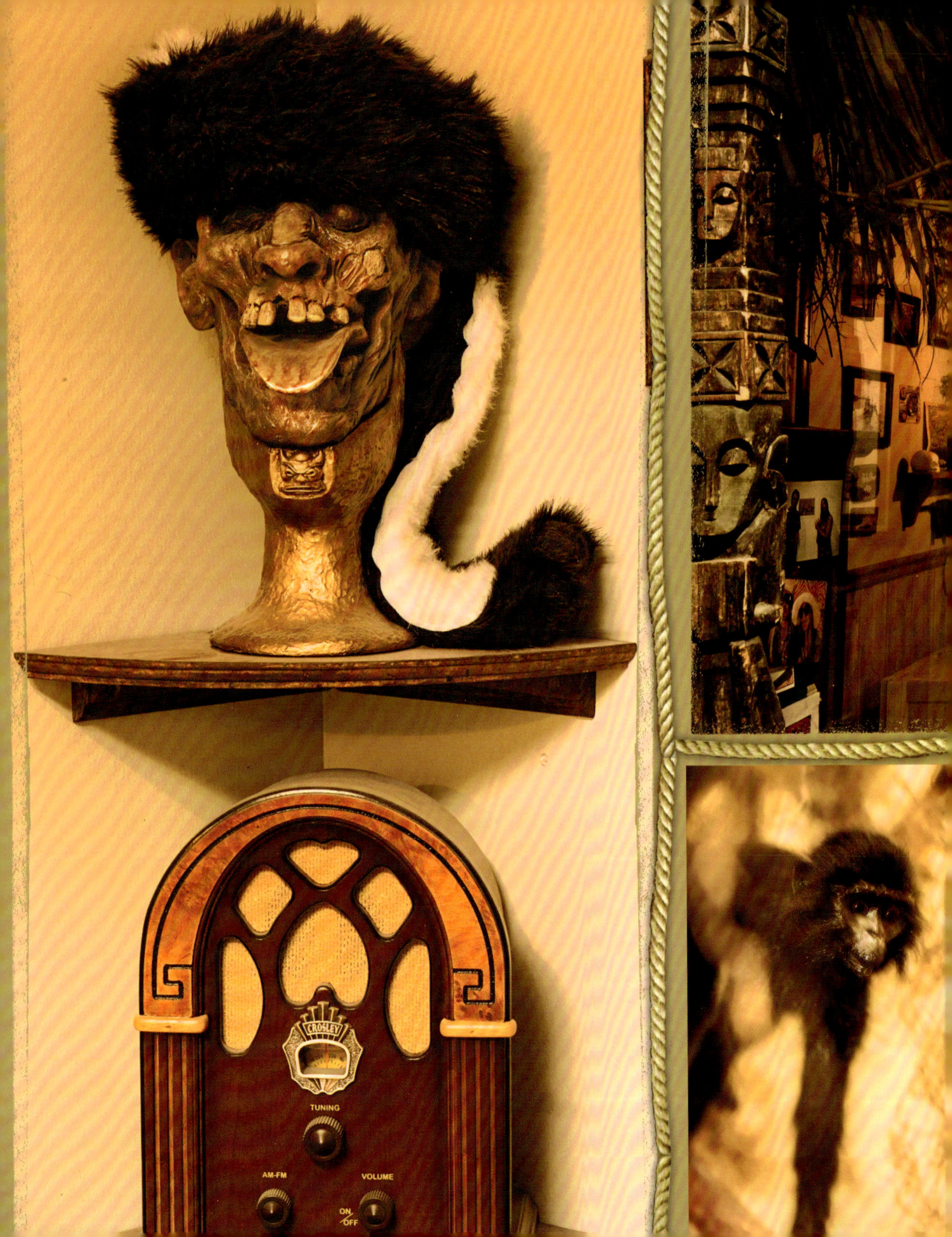

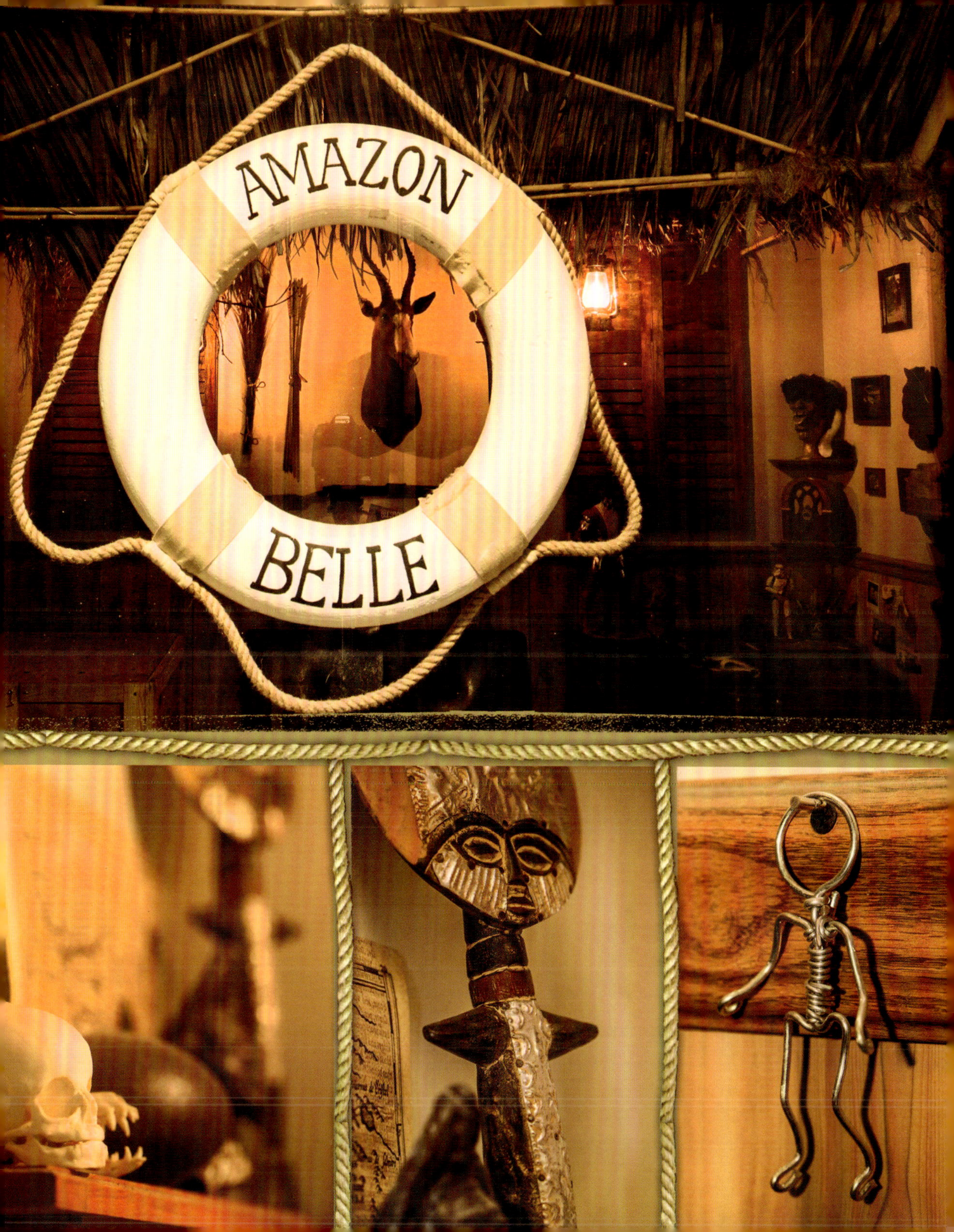

AMAZON
BELLE

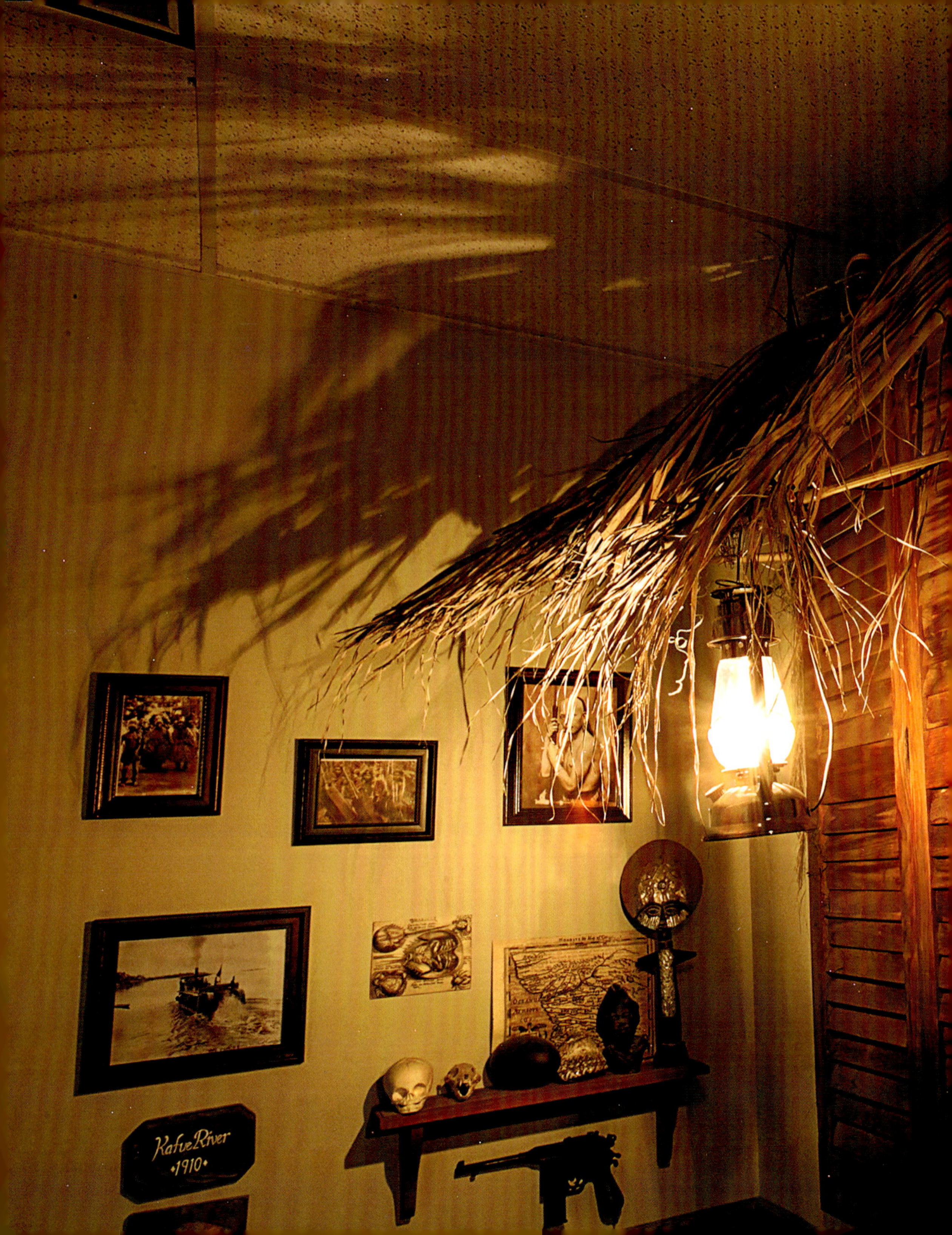
Katue River
•1910•

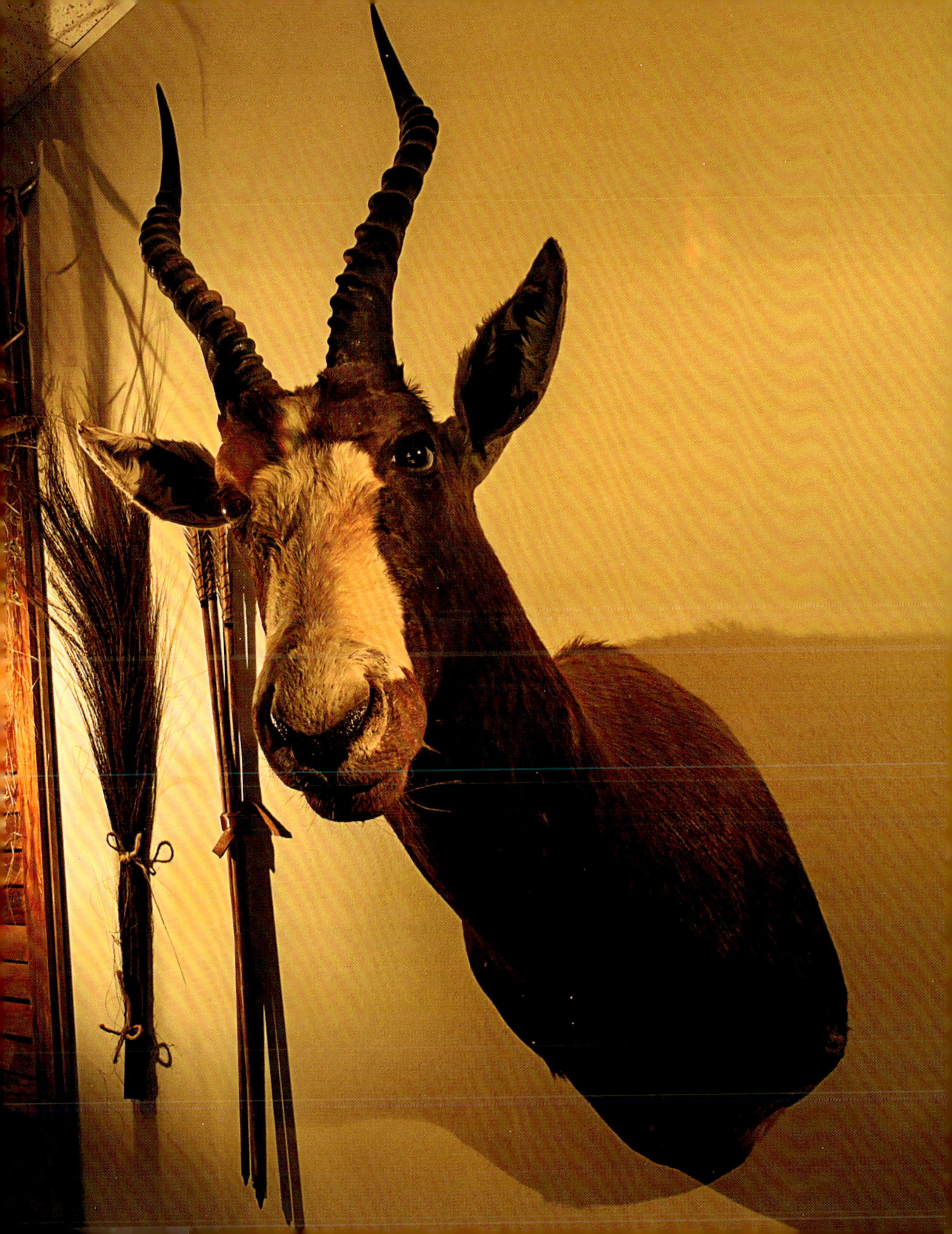

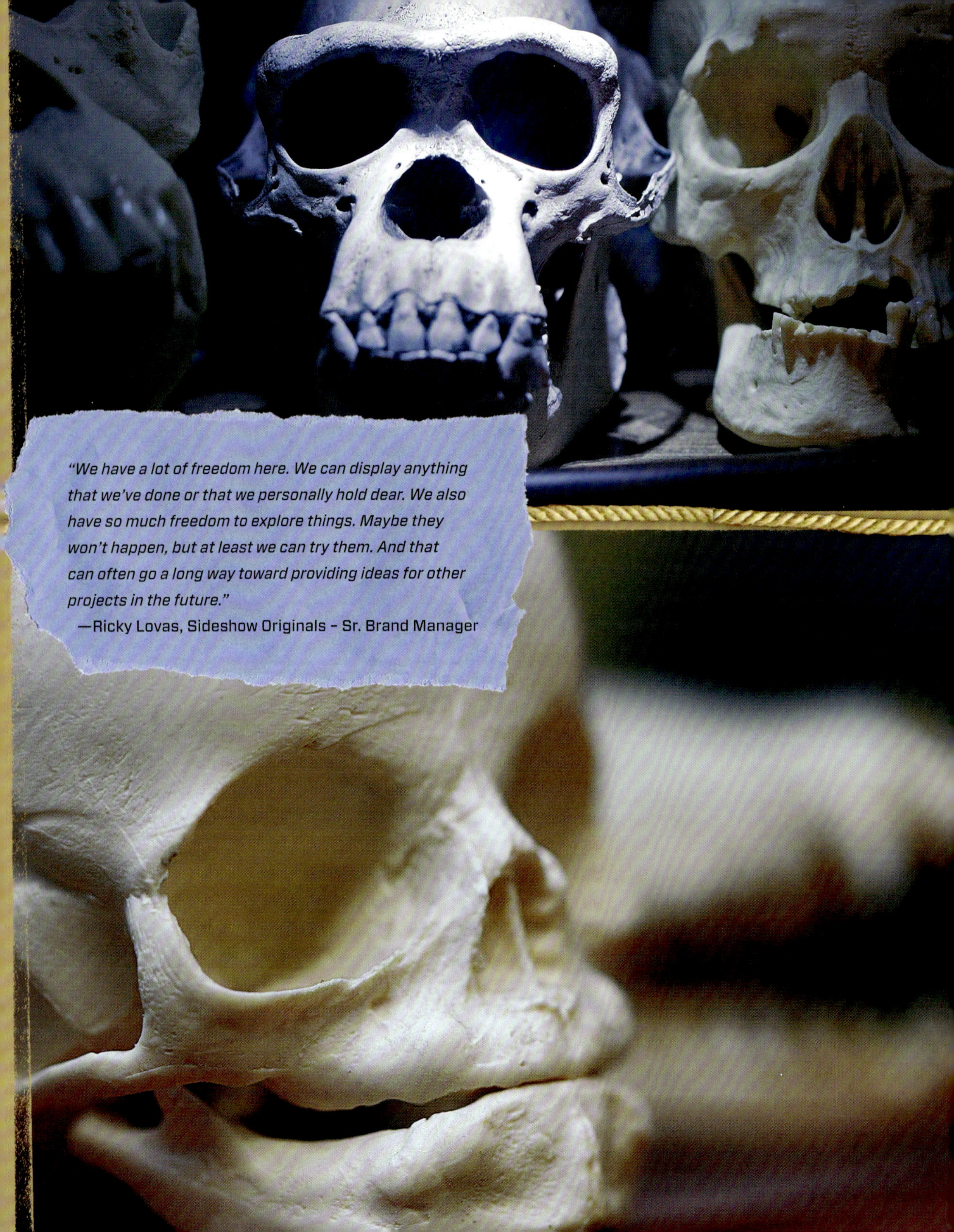
"We have a lot of freedom here. We can display anything that we've done or that we personally hold dear. We also have so much freedom to explore things. Maybe they won't happen, but at least we can try them. And that can often go a long way toward providing ideas for other projects in the future."
—Ricky Lovas, Sideshow Originals – Sr. Brand Manager

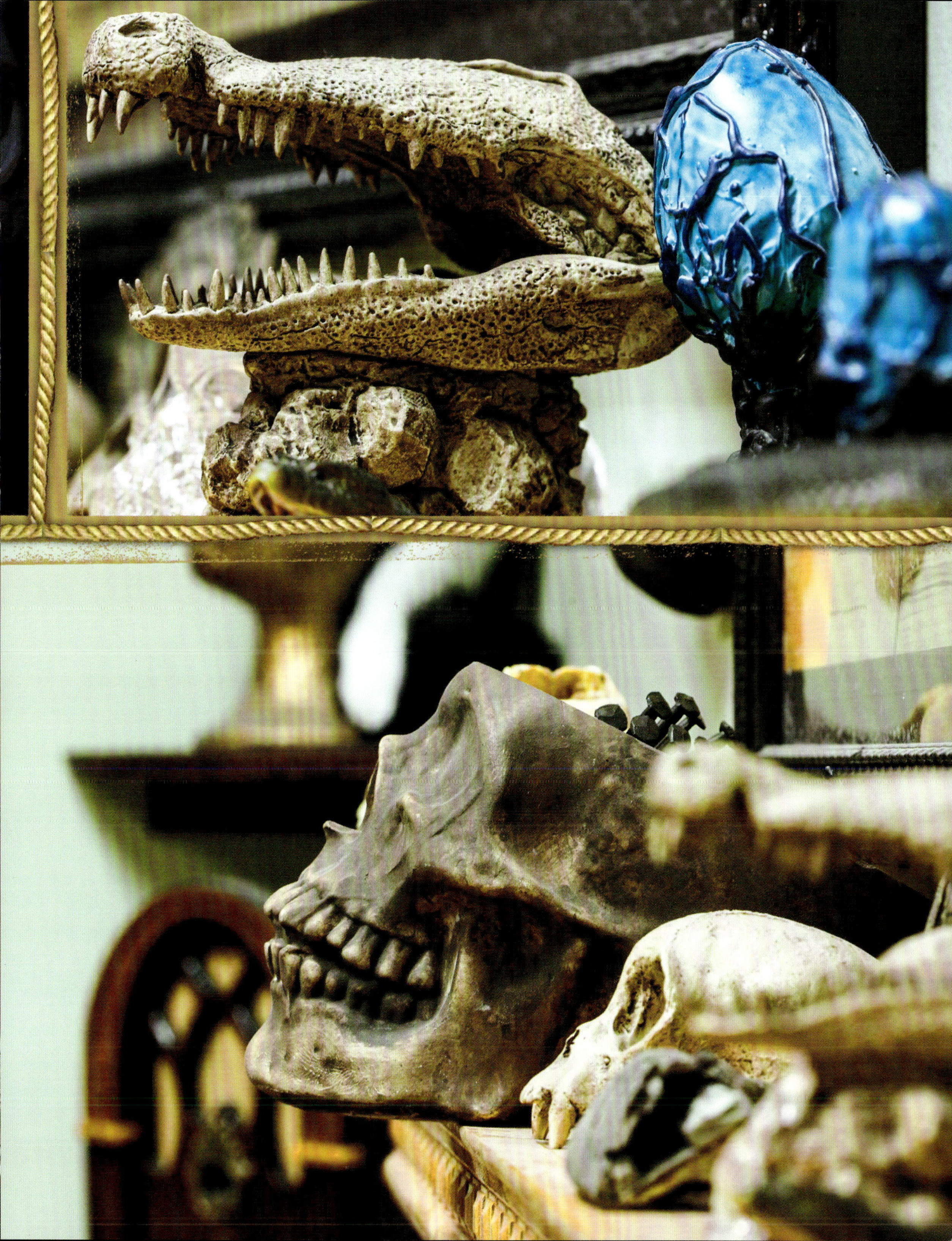

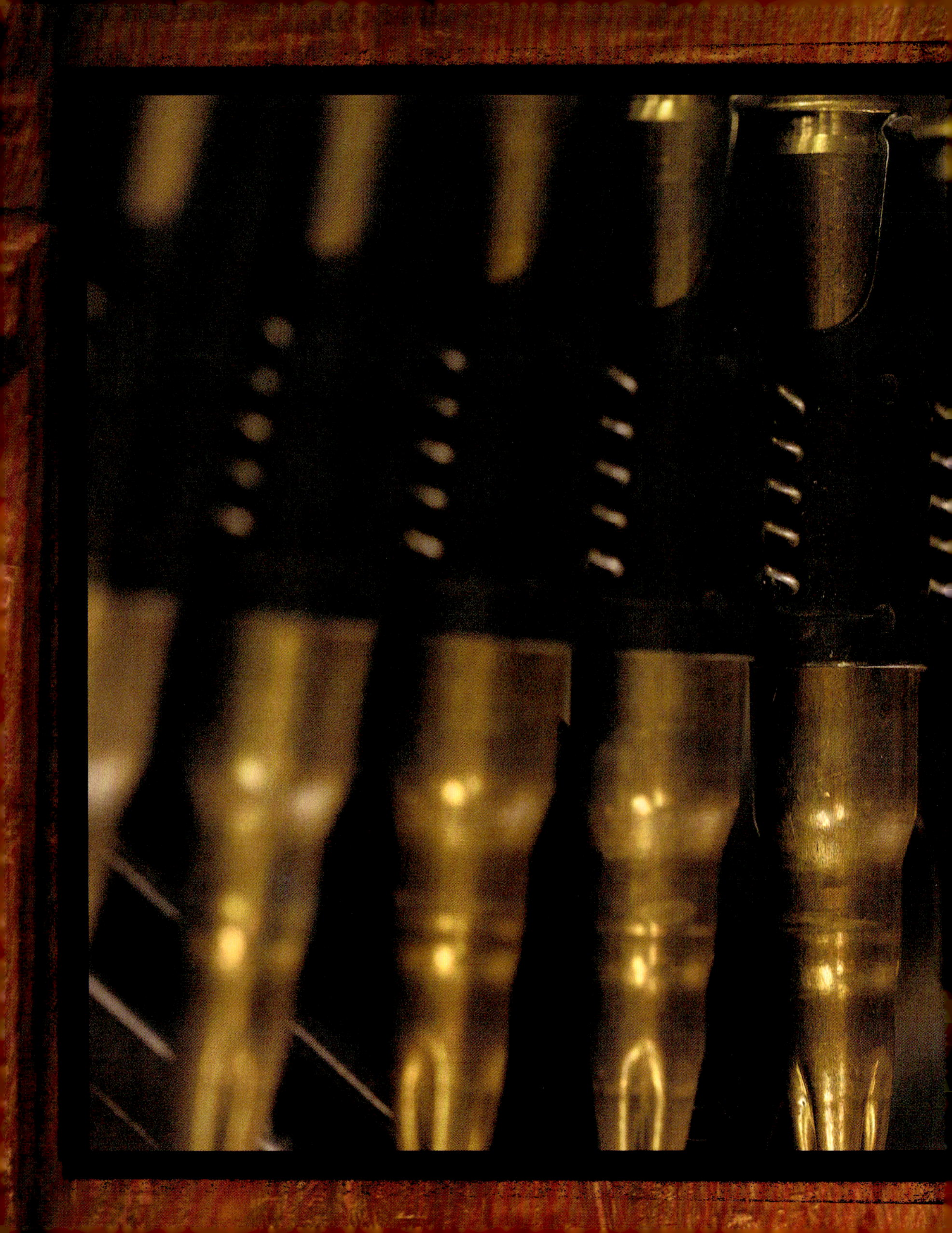

OFFICE OF THE
CREATIVE DIRECTOR

TOM GILLILAND

"My workspace is part time capsule, part museum, and all eclectic chaos in motion. Nothing ever sits long in one place, yet the artifacts gathered have collectively resided here for some time. They are forever shifting as I need to call upon some touchstone that takes me to a specific place or topic that embodies my inspirations. The poncho of The Man With No Name reminds me of the enigmatic quality of my antiheroes. The dark portraits of foreboding places and creatures remind me of the balance between the beatific and the horrific, while the warm autumn colors punctuated with raw wood, time-lost rust, and cold steel inhabit the small touches needed by the day's design challenges. In short, this is my sanctuary, where the rules and laws of our world fall away in a wash of fantasy and archetype ideals."

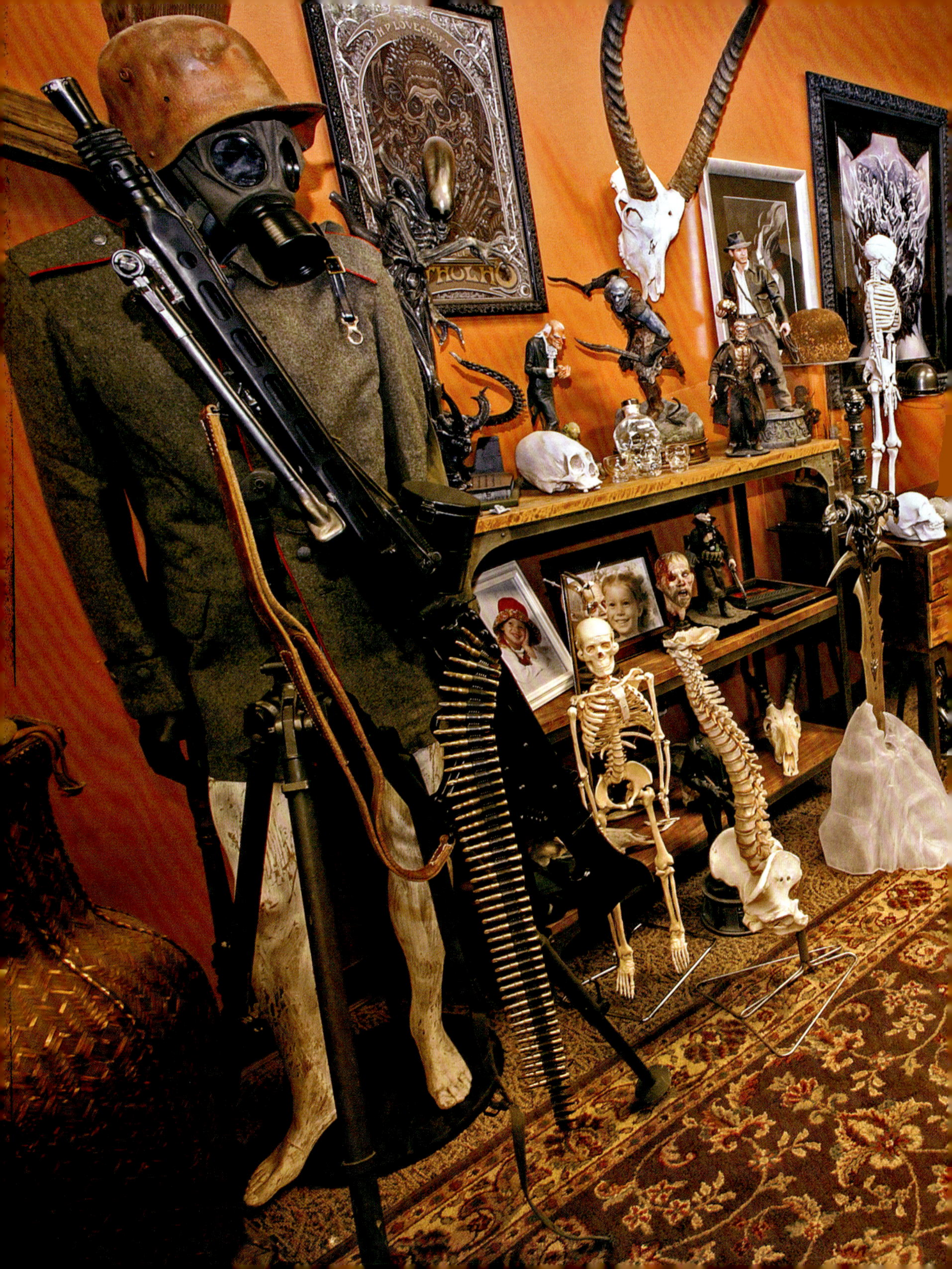

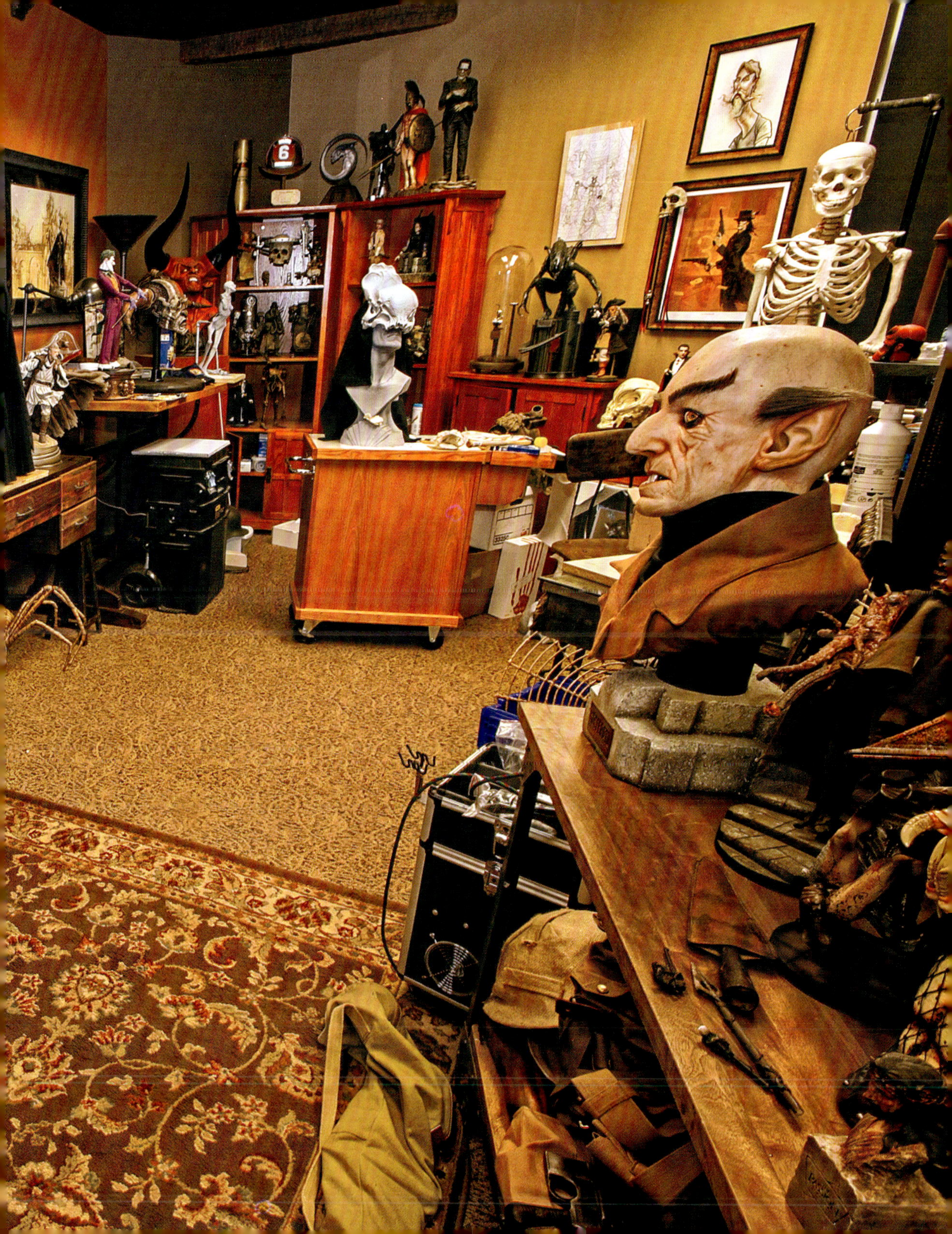

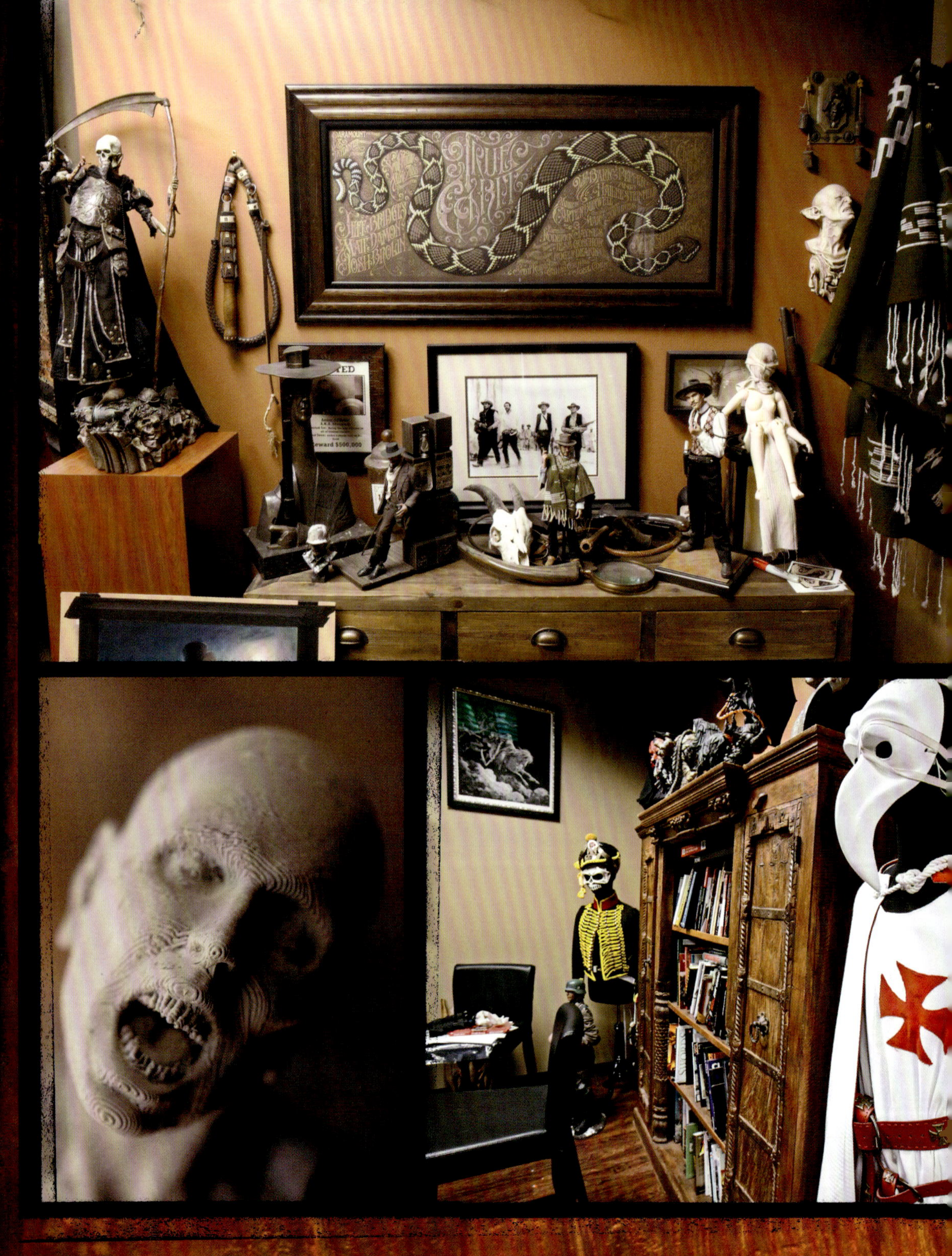

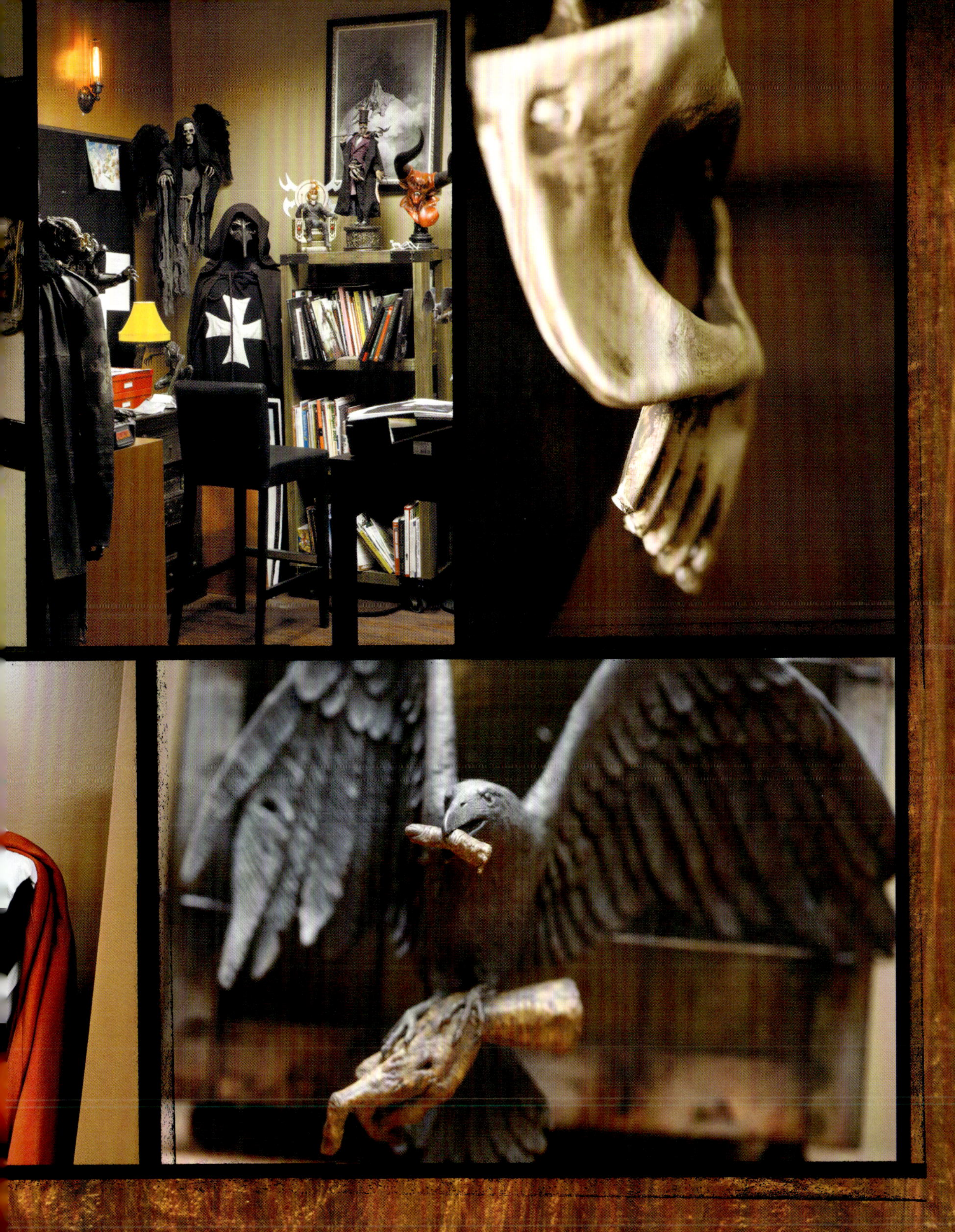

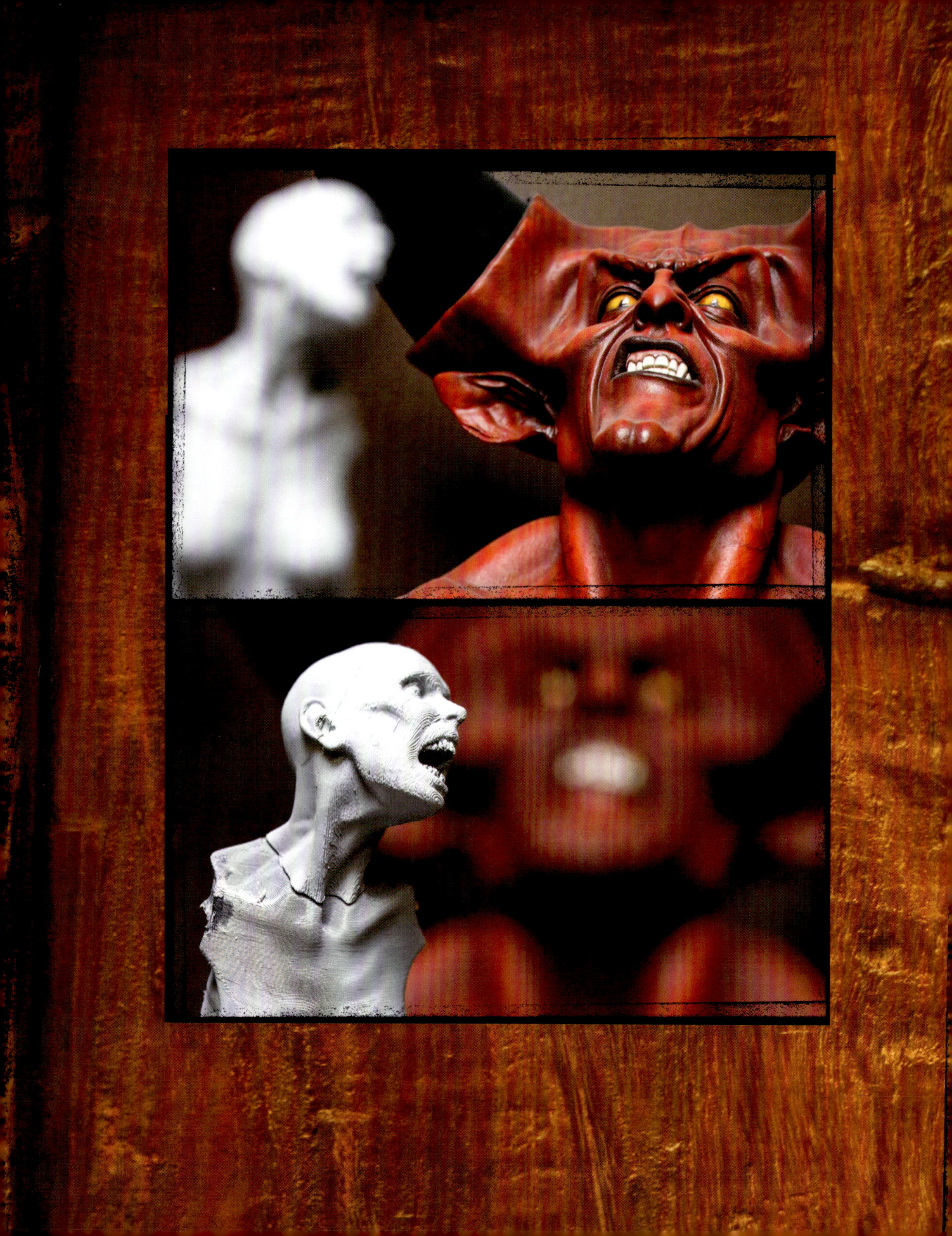

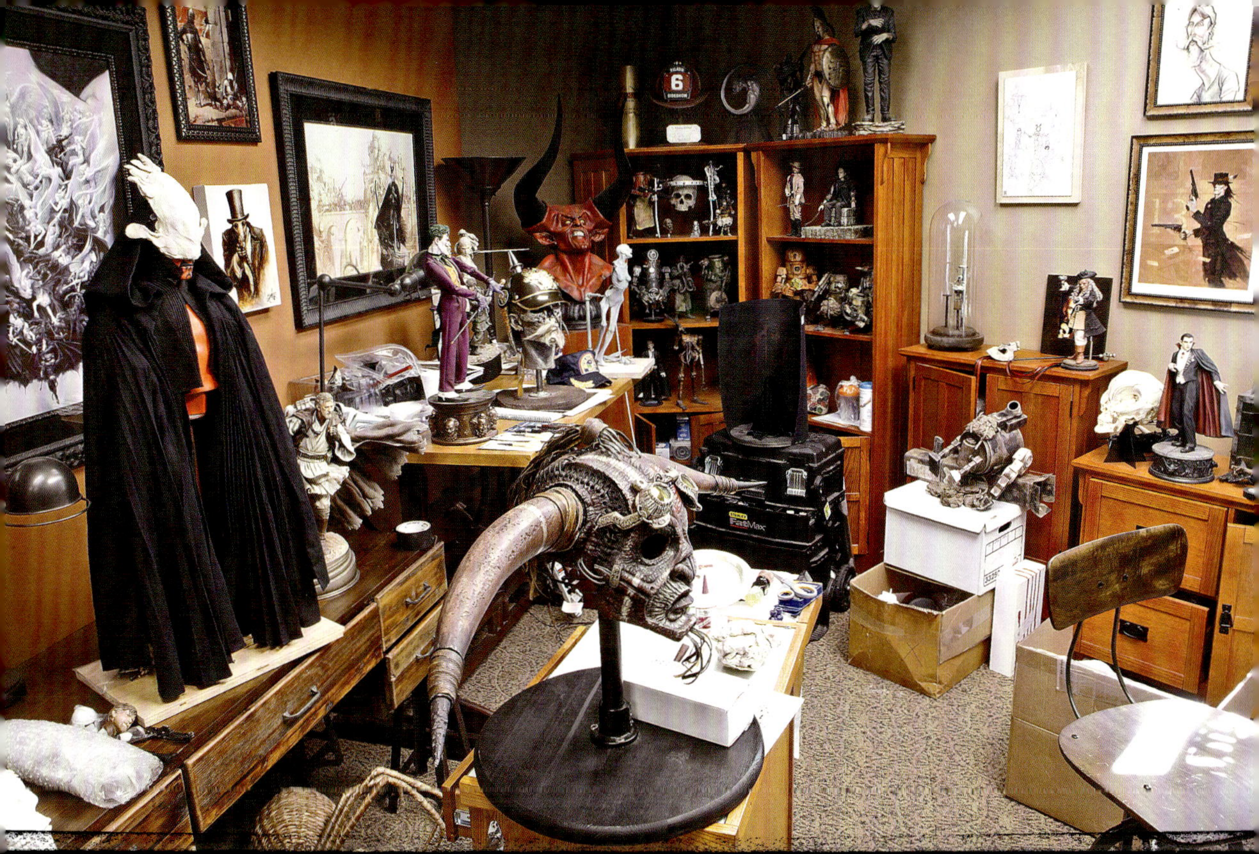

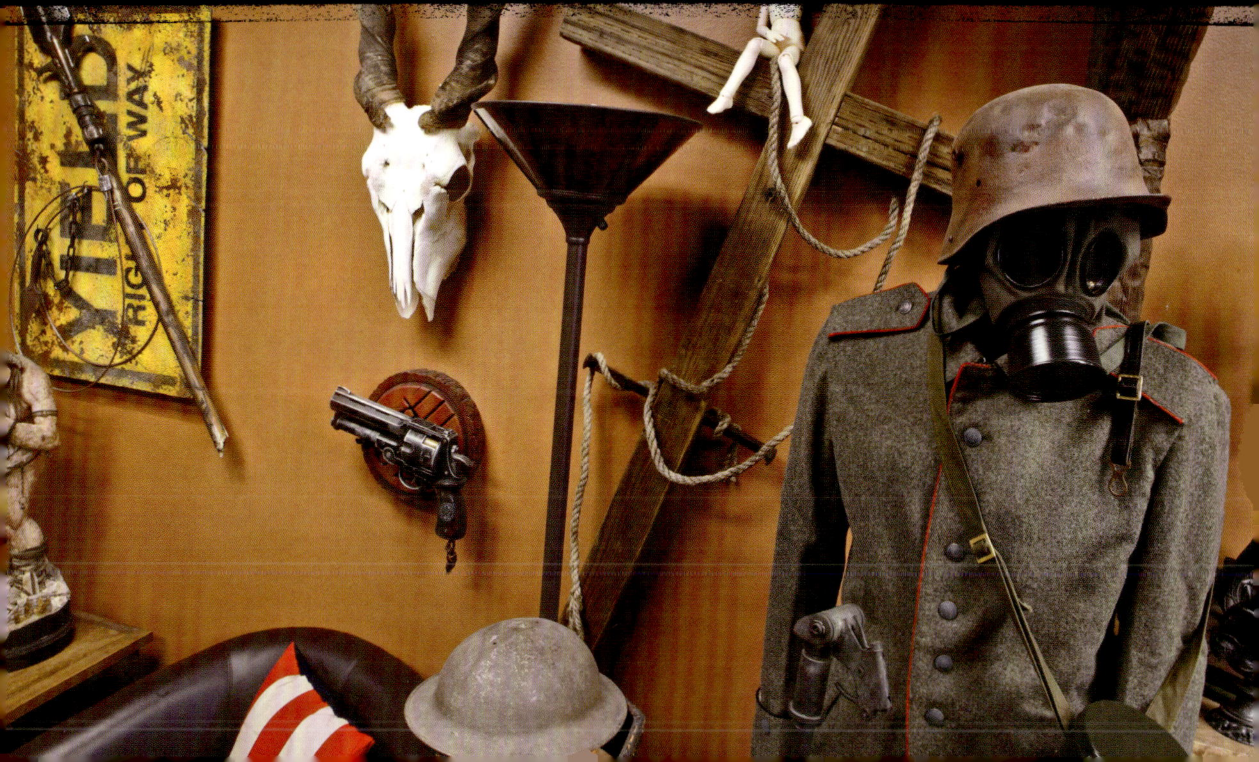

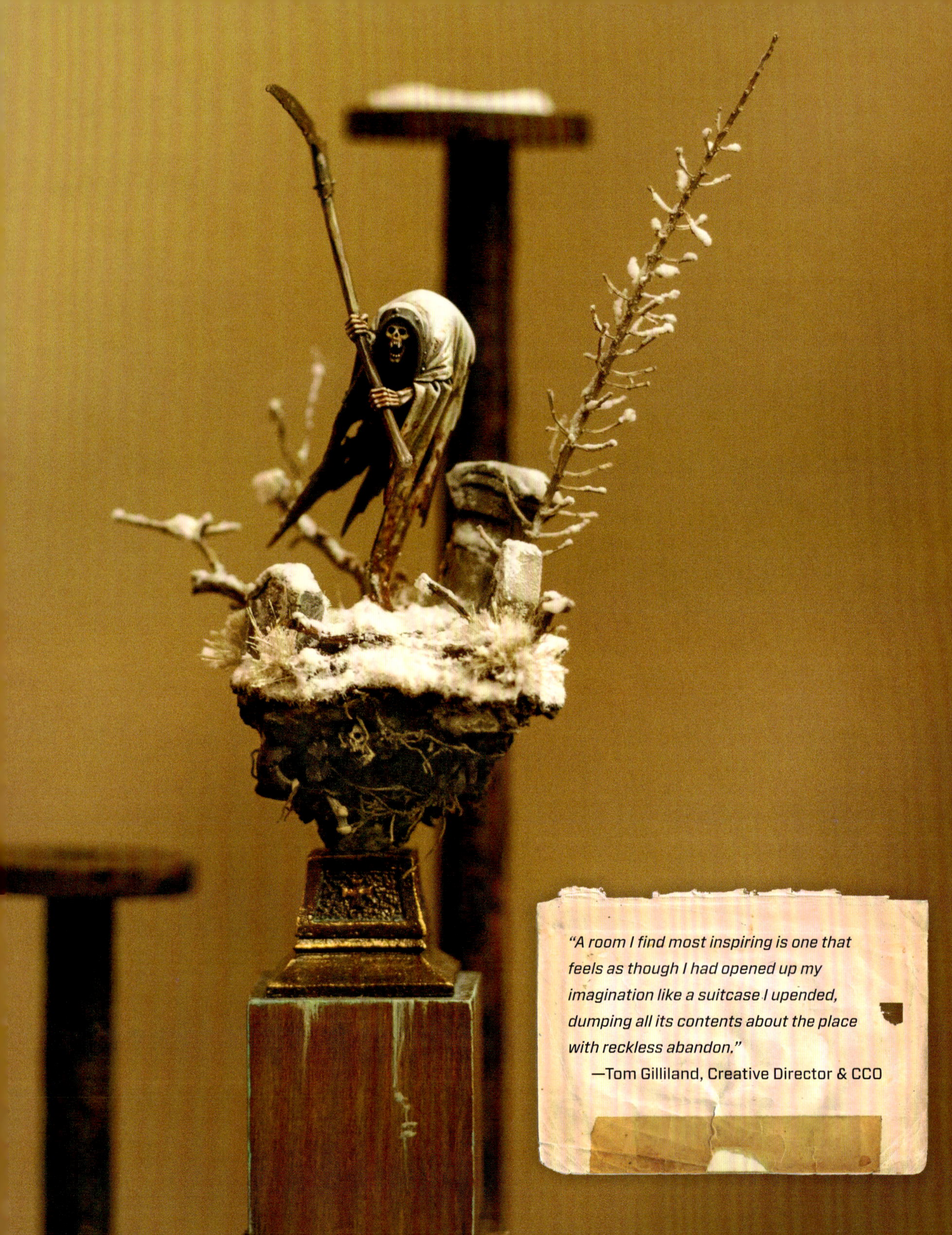
"A room I find most inspiring is one that feels as though I had opened up my imagination like a suitcase I upended, dumping all its contents about the place with reckless abandon."
—Tom Gilliland, Creative Director & CCO

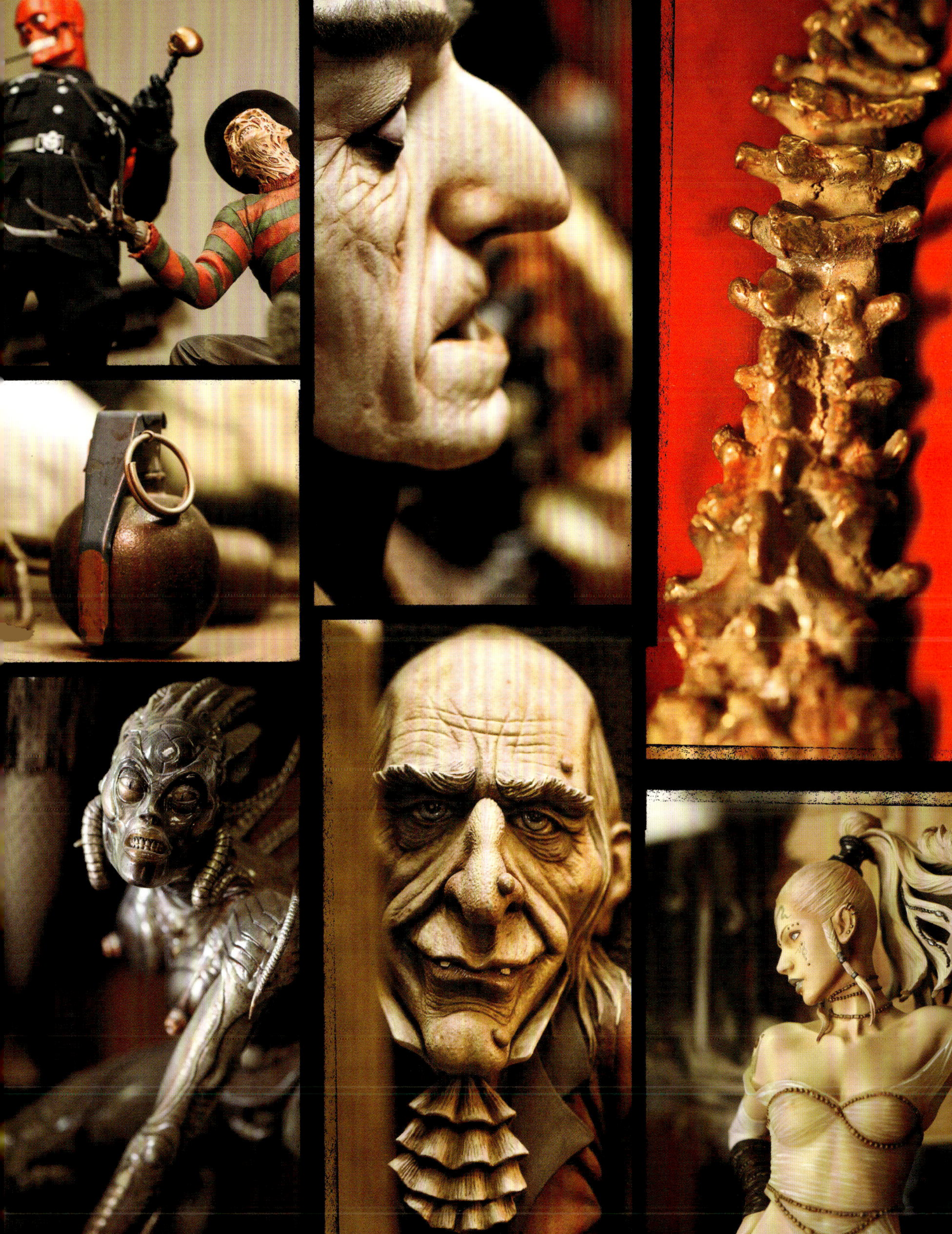

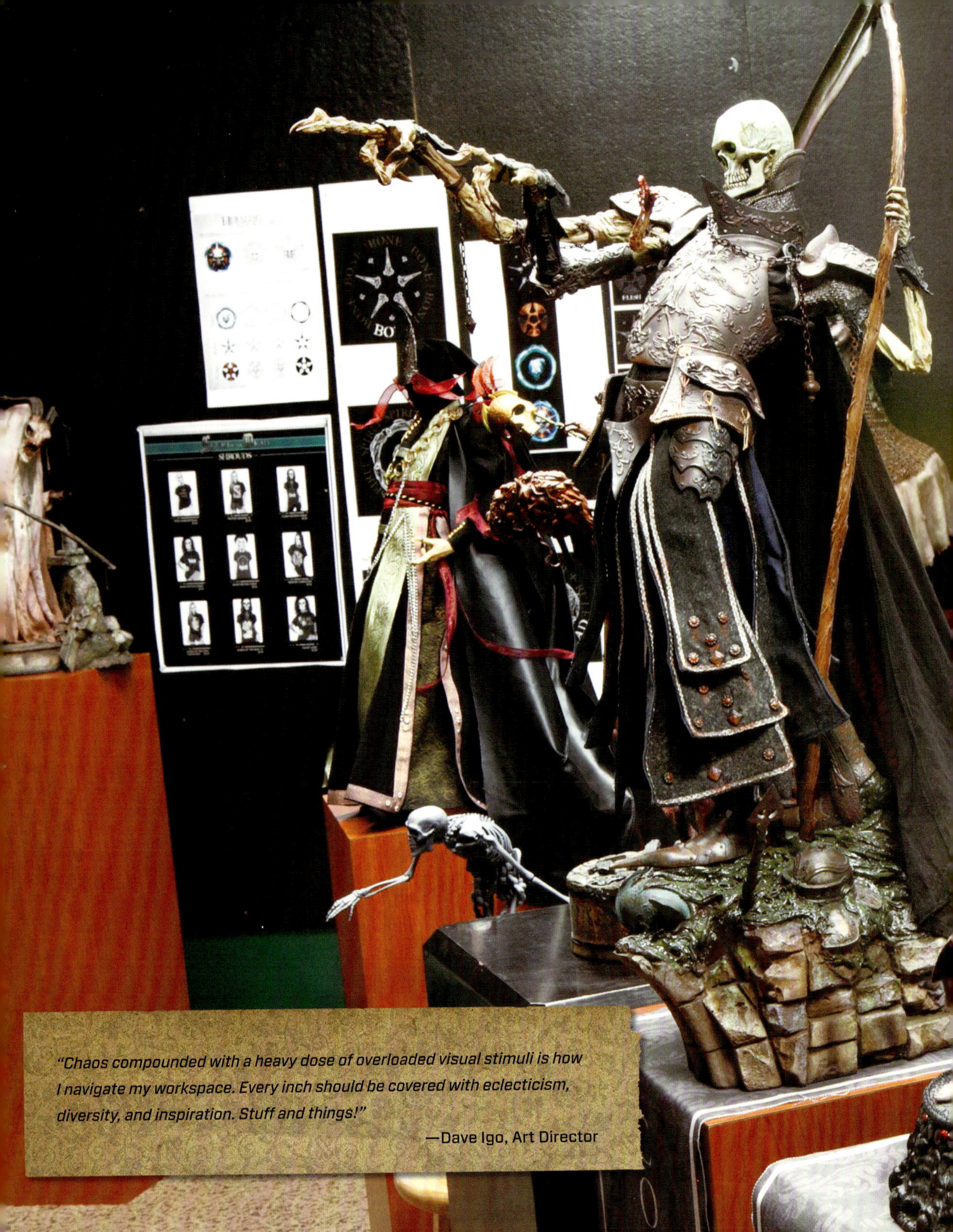

"Chaos compounded with a heavy dose of overloaded visual stimuli is how I navigate my workspace. Every inch should be covered with eclecticism, diversity, and inspiration. Stuff and things!"
—Dave Igo, Art Director

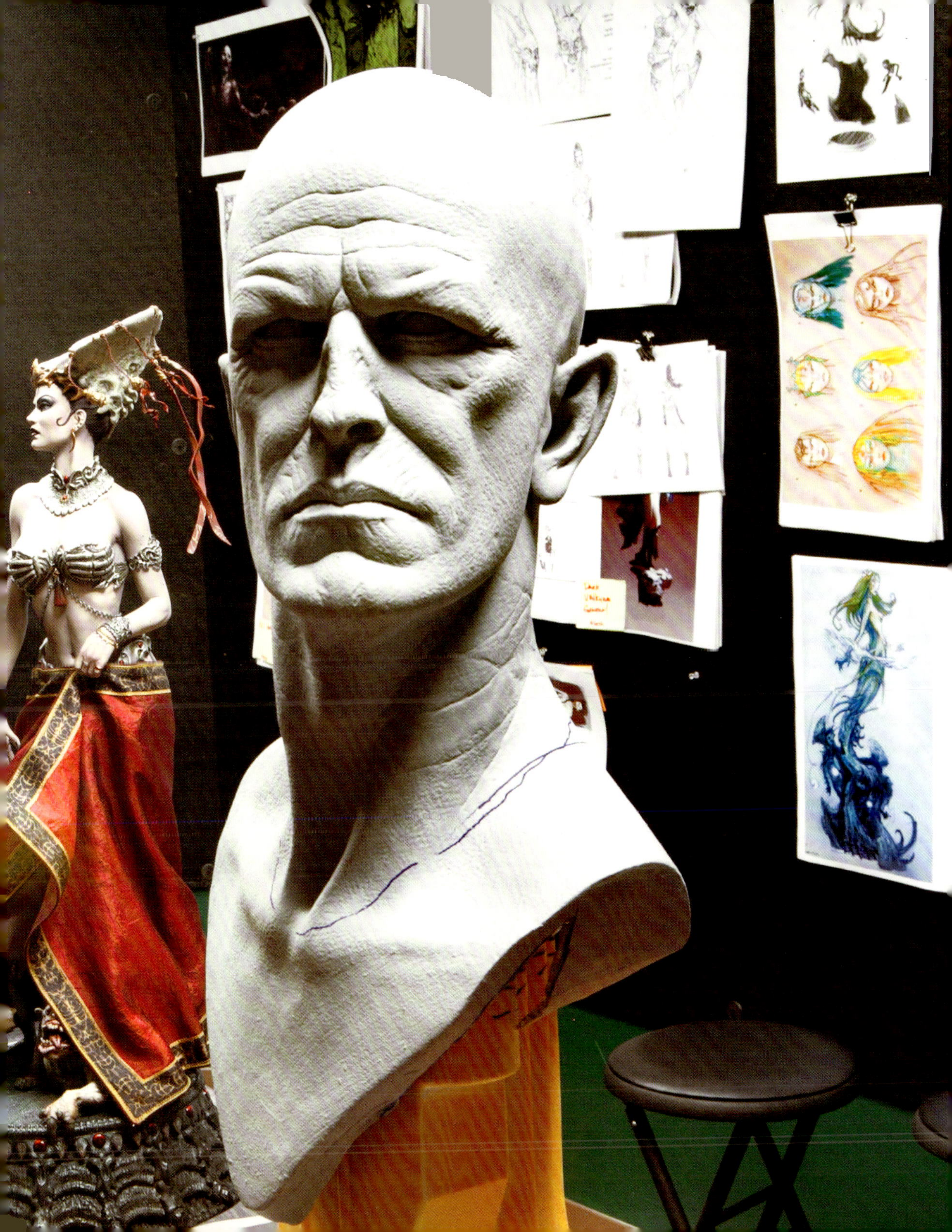

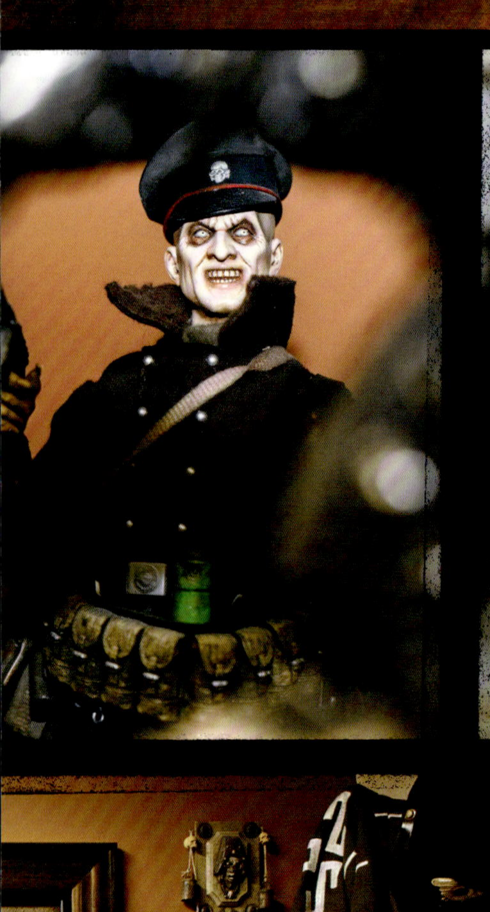
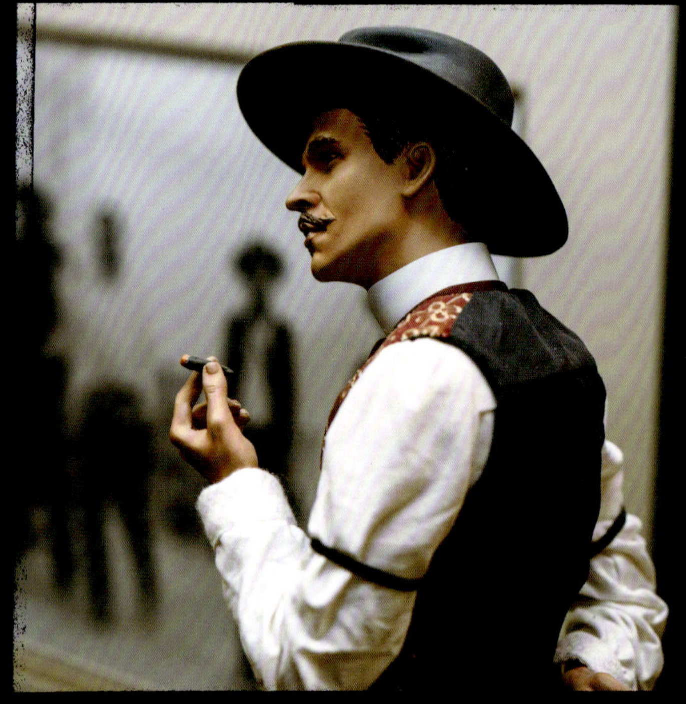
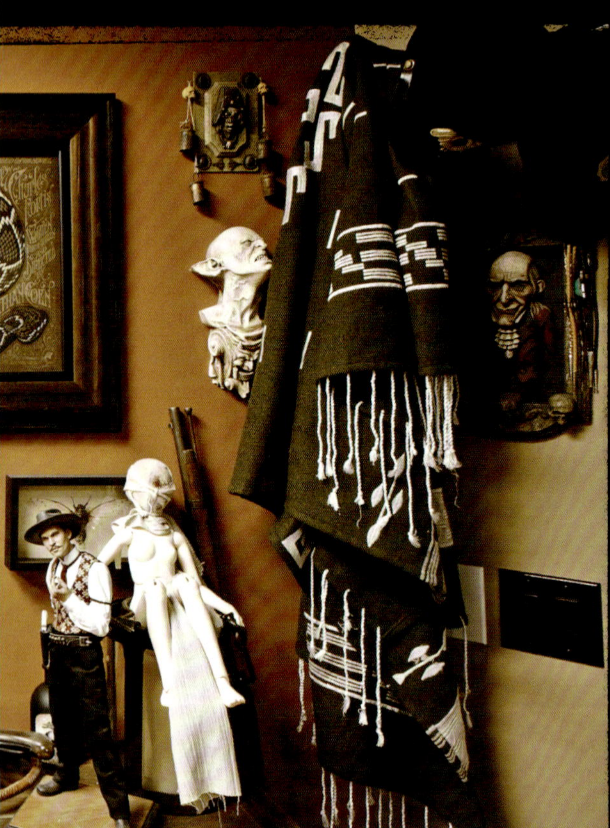
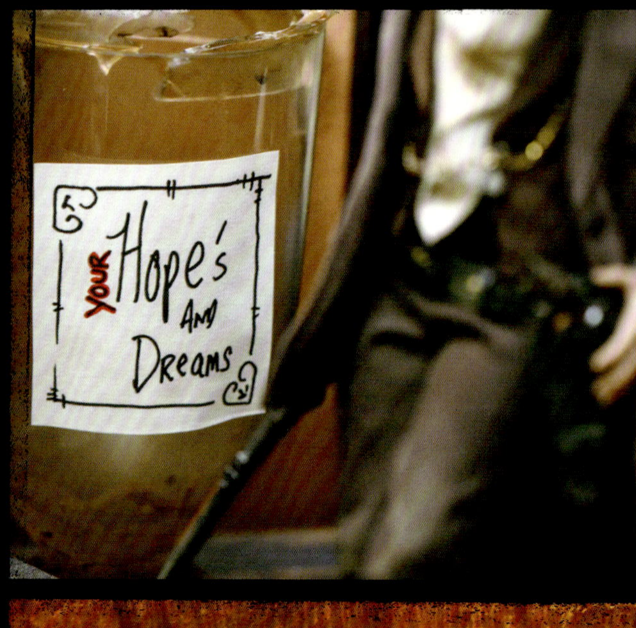
YOUR
Hope's
AND
Dreams

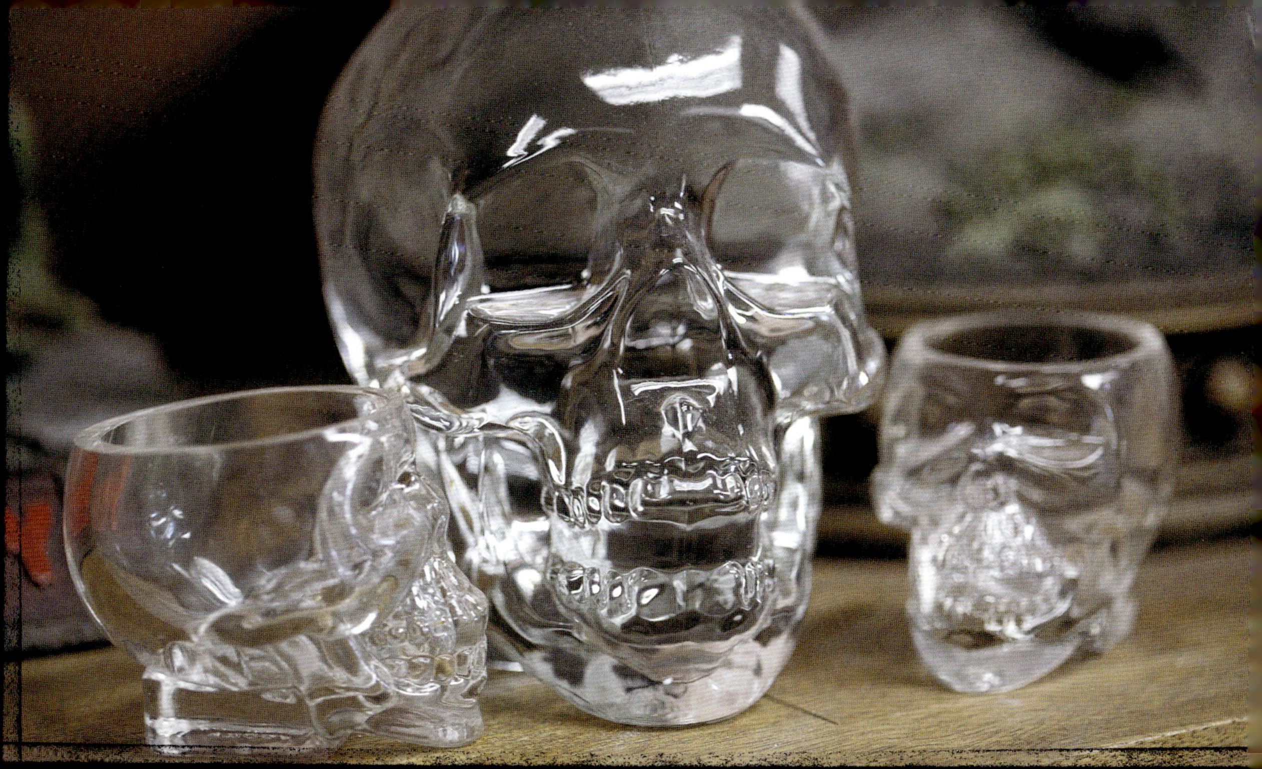

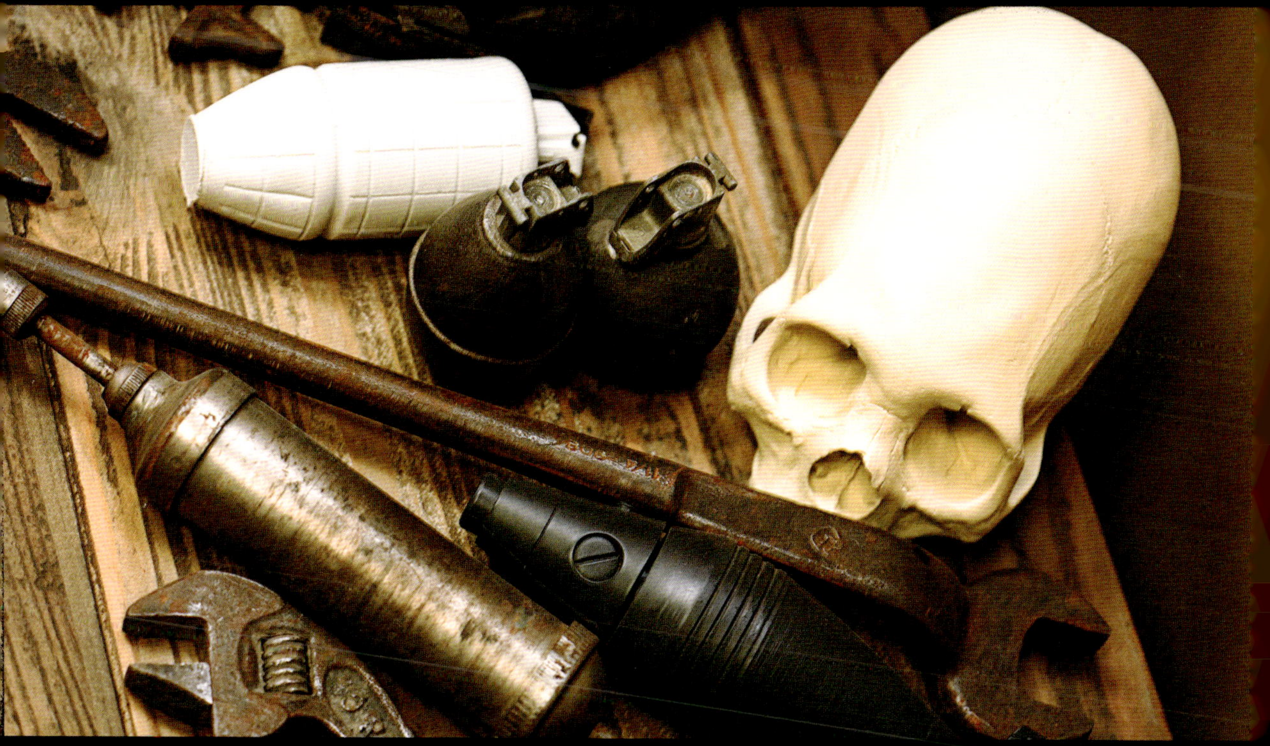

AFTERWORD

It may be obvious to say that our environment influences us, but I never wanted to leave that to chance. From the beginning of our enterprise, the artists were given liberty—and were even encouraged—to let loose and spill themselves onto the space and not solely into the art pieces they make. What I believed was that such liberty would affect us all, artists and non-artists alike. I wanted a creative environment that we could work in but also one that would help shape our view and, in ways both subtle and not, continually inspire us.

Sideshow began in a cramped pool house on the outskirts of the San Fernando Valley. That studio reeked of the disparate elements of chlorine and promise. One was unmistakable, the other a bit less so, but even then in what must have been 200 square feet I recognized how the creative space positively affected me.

After several moves and many years we finally had the opportunity to build something for ourselves, a sort of modern-day renaissance art studio, replete with all the practical trappings one might expect of a proper business: copiers and kitchen, file room and fire extinguishers, emergency exit signs and time clocks. But there was never any chance that those (and many other) practical and formal markings of an established business would be anything other than the necessary adornments of a space with an overriding creative personality.

Here, the practical makes way for or blends into the creative design, subservient to the thoughtful brushstrokes of one artist or another. What I've witnessed over the years is how the artists consume their environment, unwilling to allow it to stand separate from themselves. It's a sort of magical process of consumption, as if one were to watch a time-lapse video of an artist at work—in the end, the art and the artist are indistinguishable from one another.

Everywhere I turn in our studio I find the creative expression that sharpens my view of the space. I've witnessed over the years an evolution of my own sight that is the direct result of living and working in proximity to the artists who inhabit the studio.

They have coaxed me into seeing what I'd been missing, showed me what it means to have sight with both my eyes and my heart, and helped me understand the sometimes subtle (sometimes not) power of the creative touch.